Legacy of Minneapolis
Preservation amid Change

Legacy of Minneapolis
Preservation amid Change

John R. Borchert   David Gebhard
David Lanegran   Judith A. Martin

VOYAGEUR • 1983

First published by Voyageur Press
9337 Nesbitt Road, Bloomington, MN 55437

First Edition
5 4 3 2 1

Contents

Photo credits: David Gebhard; Burt Levy/Graphic Images; Matt Michaud; the Minneapolis History Collection, Minneapolis Public Library. Photographs on p. 7 (top), p. 12 (top), p. 24, and p. 39 (left) are from the Minnesota Historical Society.

Acknowledgments

Gratitude is expressed to the individuals and organizations that have contributed to and supported this project.

For their preeminent knowledge and dedication applied to the project: The authors—John Borchert, David Gebhard, David Lanegran, and Judith Martin

For their periodic review of research methodology and product: The project steering committee—Dennis Gimmestad, Richard Heath, Alan Lathrop, Charles Liddy, Thomas Martinson, William Scott, and Charles Skrief

For their systematic survey of every block of the City: The field survey team—Mark Bouman, Paula Brookins, Don Castleman, Tina Clarke, Steve Jordan, Mary Jane Keitel, Camille Kudzia, and Jordan Tatar

For contributions in research: Gail Bronner, Dorothy Burke, Hildegard Johnson, Stephen Murray, Muriel Nord, and Jon Walstrom

For preparation of graphics: Daniel Jones

For their review and advice: The Heritage Preservation Commission—Beth Farrell, Frances Graham, Blaine Harstad, Katherine Johnson, Camille Kudzia, Charles Liddy, John Mulligan, Robert Roscoe, Robert Samples, and William Scott

For administration: The Center for Urban and Regional Affairs of the University of Minnesota

For their support of the project: Mayor Donald M. Fraser; the City Council—Alice M. Rainville, president, Walter Dziedzic, Kathy O'Brien, Patrick M. Daugherty, Van F. White, Jacqueline Slater, Barbara Carlson, Mark Kaplan, Sally E. Howard, Walter H. Rockenstein, Dennis W. Schulstad, and Charlee V. Hoyt; the Minnesota Historical Society; the City Planning Commission; Oliver Byrum, Janet Hively, and Harold Kittleson

John Burg
Project Director

Introduction

WHEN I BECAME MAYOR of Minneapolis in July 1961, the struggle to save the Metropolitan building was in its closing moments. The Gateway redevelopment, after years of planning and negotiating, was finally under way; and among the buildings scheduled for demolition was the venerable Metropolitan, situated at Second Avenue South and Third Street, the present site of the Galaxy building. It had been an architectural wonder of its day—the tallest structure west of Chicago, with ornamentation and amenities that made it the object of enormous public interest. When completed in 1890 as the Guaranty Loan building, it was an instant tourist attraction, and for many years it provided Minneapolis's most fashionable business address. By 1961 it had become badly deteriorated, costly to operate, and something of a safety hazard. But its ornate features made it a striking landmark.

The threatened demolition stirred to action a small band of citizens who made passionate appeals to city and federal officials to spare the structure, but to no avail. Redevelopment, they discovered, was driven more by concern for the bottom line than by sentimental feeling.

The arrival of a new mayor gave the preservationists a moment of fresh hope. On my first day in office, they descended on me with a last-minute appeal, and I prevailed on the housing authority for yet another review. It was granted, mostly as a courtesy to the new mayor, with members of the authority making little effort to conceal their impatience. To them, another review meant only further delay. They were certain that it would not yield testimony any more convincing than had the earlier hearings. Once again the preservationists confronted the harsh questions. Was the structure really architecturally distinctive? By whose standards and by what criteria? Who would pay for its costly rehabilitation? Would preservation impede the development of the overall renewal program? Would the preserved building be a thing of beauty or an eyesore among the sleekly modern structures soon to rise as the Metropolitan's neighbors? The answers, as expected, were not convincing. The Metropolitan would come down the following December.

On reading the chapters that make up this volume, I was often reminded of that failed effort at preservation. In July 1961, my own consciousness—like that of most public officials and community leaders—had not been fully awakened. I participated in the final review more as a sympathetic mediator than as a champion of the cause. Since that time, having come to deeply regret the loss of the Metropolitan, I have often wondered, had I been better informed and had I taken a resolute stand against demolition, could the execution have been stayed? Most likely not; the matter had no doubt gone beyond the point of no return. But had the campaign to save the Metropolitan been better buttressed with knowledge about the building's place in the city's history and had the community been more fully sensitized to the values of preservation, the struggle, I now believe, would have been won. ·

Today, fortunately, the community's consciousness is more awakened, thanks to the sustained effort of many committed citizens. This volume is a measure of how strong that consciousness has grown during the two decades since the Metropolitan demolition. It provides a preservation framework, a comprehensive guide with which the city can evaluate the historic and architectural worth of its aging structures and districts. And it facilitates the process through which Minneapolis can make full use of the federal Economic Recovery Tax Act of 1981, which provides substantial tax credits to facilitate the preservation of buildings listed on the National Register of Historic Places. Today there would be no doubt about the preservation of the Metropolitan. And now, with studies such as the one reported in this volume, there is every assurance that the movement will continue to grow as communities across the nation acquire the knowledge they need to protect their links with their past.

There are now many preservationists at work in Minneapolis. The Committee on Urban Environment, the Minneapolis Heritage Preservation Commission, historical societies, neighborhood groups, journalists, architects, and history buffs—all have contributed to the movement's progress. One who deserves special recognition is John Burg, the urban design manager for the Minneapolis planning department. He has been the main liaison for a comprehensive study of the city's architectural resources, designed to identify landmarks worthy of preservation. With the sponsorship and financing of the city planning commission, the city council, the Heritage Preservation Commission, and the Minnesota Historical Society, in February 1980, the city contracted with the Center for Urban and Regional Affairs (CURA) at the University of Minnesota; and with Burg as project director, CURA engaged a team of four authoritative consultants—John R. Borchert, David Gebhard, David Lanegran, and Judith A. Martin—and charged them with (1) identifying structures worthy of preservation and (2) identifying for each city district a "modal" or typical block or building. Beginning with a list of 3,200 structures, the team made a series of analyses and evaluations, and in the end, they recommended 185 buildings and 9 districts as candidates for preservation. They are listed in the study's technical report, presented as an appendix to this volume. The consultants also completed the necessary work for nominating 45 Minneapolis buildings for inclusion on the National Register, and they produced a vast file of field notes, maps, and related materials that will be invaluable in future preservationist activity.

But the study does more than identify landmarks. It provides an extremely valuable framework for understanding the city's history. In the course of developing a process for assigning historical value to particular structures, the consultants painstakingly examined the stages of the city's growth, probing the complex anatomy that lies beneath its evolving institutions, analyzing the limits of climate and geography and relating them to the potentials and opportunities of a changing technology, and tracing the city's growth from a simple frontier trading society through the more complex stages of agriculture, milling, lumbering, and manufacturing to the present-day challenges of information services and electronics.

Each stage left a characteristic set of artifacts, and these are the central focus of the study. It evaluates and classifies them as it builds a rationale and a strategy for their preservation. In the process we learn again of the effect that being situated off the nation's main line had on Minneapolis: how the city's isolation compelled a tradition of self-reliance and independence, how successive generations of leaders responded with entrepreneurial zeal and inventiveness to the opportunities of their day, and how each generation left its unique architectural legacy.

We are reminded, too, of the city's natural endowments, of how the Mississippi River and the lakes, the parks, and the gently rolling terrain, the harsh winters and the changing seasons have sometimes widened and sometimes constrained our architectural responses. We are also reminded of our continuing failure, especially in the case of the river, to fully utilize and nurture these natural amenities.

The study is both a guide for constructive action and an appeal for greater diligence in protecting our physical environment. It provides an indispensable foundation for informed actions in an area of increasing importance and sensitivity.

Arthur Naftalin

Legacy of Minneapolis
Preservation amid Change

PART 1

The Face of the City

Preservation in Its Larger Setting

THIS BOOK IS ABOUT buildings and districts in
Minneapolis that merit preservation, and why. But we
want to examine preservation in the larger context of
the building, maintenance, and recycling of the city and
the continuing stream of individuals and organizations
who have passed across the stage. The face of the city
keeps changing, accompanied by a continuous process of
selective remembering and forgetting. Preservation occurs
within a dynamic, chaotic, evolving system. The
buildings that have survived are samples of what might
have survived, and the same will be true of those that survive in the future. Hence, the problem is to understand
the selection process and to improve it if possible.

The city today is partly a collection of business and
public buildings. They record a succession of memorable events and historical epochs in the development of
the core around the Falls of St. Anthony and the spokes
of railroad-industrial development that radiate from
there. The street pattern still recalls the frontier city
President U. S. Grant viewed in 1865. A few of the
buildings can remind us of the city's anticipation of its
great boom when the Northern Pacific's golden spike
was driven in 1883 and of the view from here across the
Northwest Empire in the 1890s. More buildings reflect
the economic transition of the 1910s and 1920s, the
exodus from the aging core in the 1950s, and the
massive new investments since the 1960s.

Today's Minneapolis is also a vast array of homes
assembled in a mosaic of neighborhoods. A few houses
still record the stream of immigrants who came to build
the pioneer city and the 'empire.' But most of the
homes that stand today reflect the spawning of second-
and third-generation households and their further
enlargement of the city in the building booms of this
century. Today's housing also reflects gradual aging,
obsolescence, and neighborhood turnover. The residential buildings and landscapes are powerful
expressions of both individuality and community, of
continuity and inexorable change. Thus each building is
important in part because it helps to characterize a
geographical region and historical epoch important in
the city's development.

But each building also represents a style, a culture,
and a purpose. It reflects the ideals of a specific person
or organization, the reality of a given moment when it
was built. It is an integral part of its immediate
surroundings and landscape. Each structure was created
and has survived as a result of some unique combination
of private ideals and efforts. In a multitude of ways,
those efforts have coalesced into neighborhoods, organizations, and images of the city.

The buildings and districts of the city to be selected
for historical preservation, then, should be special
samples of the works and ideals of the people who
created the city. And they should also be representative
of the different parts of the regional mosaic that has
evolved. We have surveyed the city in search of
buildings and public open spaces that best meet those
requirements. In the following pages we enlarge on the
evolution of the mosaic, on the character of individual
buildings and districts that especially merit preservation,
and on our understanding—at this point—of the place of
preservation amidst the continuing massive process of
urban change and recycling.

PART 2

Legacy of the Working City

**The Establishment of the
City Commercial Center
and Milling Industry**

IN THE AUTUMN OF 1865, the victorious General
U. S. Grant visited the frontier settlements of Minneapolis and St. Anthony and enjoyed a hero's welcome.
The residents of the villages were ardent supporters of
the Union cause. Although the total population of the
communities averaged seven thousand people during the
war years, fourteen hundred men enlisted in the Union
army. Grant's major victories during the war had come
in large measure as a result of his grasp of the
importance of transportation, especially railroads.
The future president and others of his generation knew
that they were destined to be responsible for the
opening of the mid-continent's resources, and they
understood that settlements like Minneapolis would
become the centers of decision making, manufacturing,
and transportation. Thus it was a vision of future
greatness that provided the context for Grant's remarks.
Not a great speaker by the standards of the day, Grant
gave a speech that contained little but optimistic
statements about the future of the newly reunited nation
and the important role the cities of Minneapolis and
St. Anthony would play in the opening of the northwest
frontier. His visit was important in the history of the
young cities because it established in the minds of the
residents that they were indeed a part of the nation and
worthy of notice.

As he toured the communities and crossed the river
just above the falls on the first bridge over the Mississippi, Grant saw a sprawling settlement containing as

many farm animals as people. The buildings were
largely frame houses, a few to a block. There were a
few large churches with tall steeples and bell towers. In
St. Anthony, the great Winslow House hotel dominated
all the area away from the main street, where a cluster
of larger frame and brick or stone structures for commercial uses were located. From the bridge Grant could
see the heart of the city—the mills located on both sides
of the river at the falls. They were an eclectic set of
structures and ranged greatly in size.

Minneapolis, the west bank settlement, was of
course much larger. As soon as Grant descended from
the bridge, he entered Bridge Square, the main commercial district of the area where Hennepin and Nicollet
joined. The city lots and streets were laid out in the
familiar grid pattern, using square blocks without alleys.
The grids were oriented toward the river; but the
various developers had not bothered to match the street
patterns with their neighbors', and so the settlement's
street pattern contained several irregular blocks and a
few angular streets. Grant had seen scores of towns like
this along the rivers of the Midwest. As in the others,
the residential districts of Minneapolis gradually faded
out on the edge of the city into a mixture of large
houses and farms. The principal residential districts lay
to the north along Washington, to the southwest from
Nicollet and Hennepin toward Ninth and Tenth Streets,
and to the southeast toward areas known today as Elliot
Park and Cedar-Riverside. Although there was no exclusive concentration, the wealthy residents tended to live
to the south and west in the direction of Morrison's
house on the low ridge to the south of the present
location of Franklin Avenue. The town's central block

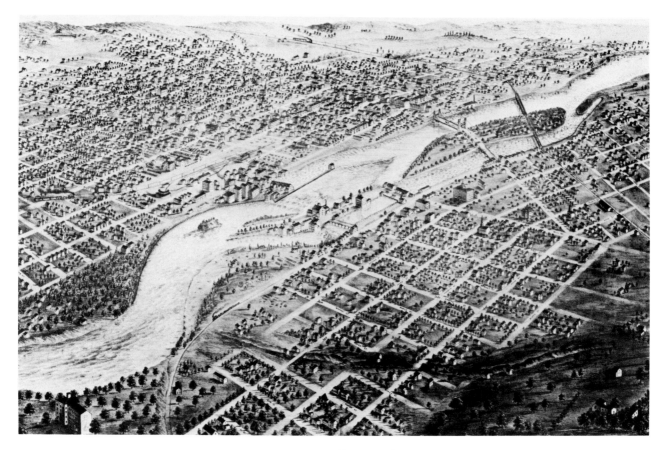

Panorama, Minneapolis and St. Anthony, 1867.

held Hale and Company, Mills Grocers, and Wakefield and Plant Dry Goods. The corner of Nicollet and Washington was occupied by the Harrison building, the largest structure in that section of town. To Grant's eyes the settlements must have presented the heterogeneous appearance of the average small towns of the time, which were hastily constructed without much regard to architectural appearance and organized around the commercial functions found along the main street.

Stores in Minneapolis were concentrated on two main streets, Washington and lower Nicollet. Both were lined with larger frame buildings of two or three stories of usable space. These buildings were all built by individual contractors and bore little relationship to each other's design. Because most of the population walked whenever they conducted business, the residential areas were all quite close to the commercial district. Inside the commercial district, the business places tried to be as close as possible so as to minimize their customers' inconvenience when shopping. Although no form of land-use regulation existed in this early city, the popu-

lation had a general notion that commercial, residential, and industrial land uses should be separated to some degree. Then as now, commercial areas were perceived as noisy and dirty; because of the large horse population in those years, they were quite smelly.

The people General Grant encountered during his brief stay must have impressed on him their determination to overcome the effects of the three major setbacks their young community had experienced. It seemed as though the towns had just been platted when the great financial panic of 1858 ended the flow of migrants, scared away nearly forty percent of the population, and forced most businesses into bankruptcy. Many of the adventurers who had stopped off here on their way to the gold and silver camps in the western mountains complained bitterly. Then just when it appeared that the economy was back on an even keel, the Civil War broke out, drawing away most of the able-bodied men as well as ending the migration of farm families. The third factor was the Sioux uprising in 1863, which reinforced the notion that the frontier was still unsafe. The major set-

MINNEAPOLIS, MINN.

Panorama from Winslow House,
late 1850s.

Nicollet Avenue, 1873.

Government Mill (built 1840s), west side of river.

tlements were not attacked by the Indians; so as soon as the Dakota were relocated, business returned to normal.

Dramatic as these events were, they could not blunt the enthusiasm of the cities' leadership for the future of this area. The rationale for a city at this location was obvious to all. The Falls of St. Anthony were the largest waterpower site between Niagara and the California mountains. The shoals and low banks above the cataract afforded an easy crossing of the river.

The Beginnings — 1847–1867

In 1847 and 1848 the first true urban functions were established at the falls: a general store operated by R. P. Russell and the sawmill owned by Franklin Steele and operated by Ard Godfrey were opened on the east bank in St. Anthony. Merchandising and manufacturing were to become the primary factors in the continued growth of Minneapolis.[1]

In the fall of 1849, John Stevens received permission to live on the river's west bank and operate a ferry if he provided free passage for those on government business. Before any permanent settlement could take place on the west bank of the Mississippi, however, the land had to be cleared of Indian title. Only the federal government could negotiate the treaties and remove the Indians. Because there were other pressing issues in Washington during those years, nearly seven years passed before the land on the west bank was purchased from the Indians. The vague legal status of the land did not stop men from squatting in the nascent city, however. During that time the illegal squatters had trouble with the army, and so they formed an association that provided some form of government and enabled them to deal with the commander of the fort as well as with the occasional claim jumper. The association of squatters recognized the original claim of Stevens, and the squatters located themselves according to Stevens's plat of the settlement. He is reputed to have patterned his new town after the English portion of New Orleans. This meant that the streets and blocks of property were set out in a grid pattern that was aligned with the Mississippi and a main street focused on the river crossing.

The land east of the Mississippi had been opened for white settlement in 1837, so no government restrictions hindered the growth of St. Anthony. When Minnesota was granted the status of a territory in 1848, St. Anthony underwent a mini-boom. By the time winter set in that year, some three hundred people lived in the community. They were housed in a mixture of log cabins and white-painted cottages patterned after those in New England.[2]

The participants in the first land boom well understood that the profitability of the settlement would be in large measure determined by their ability to attract immigrants both to the immediate vicinity of the falls and to the unsettled lands beyond. As a result, they actively lobbied the federal government for liberal immigration policies, for improved transportation, for greater security from the Indians, and for laws that would make it easy to buy land from the government. Because people of every sort were needed in this community—skilled laborers, merchants, mechanics, lawyers, farmers, and clergy—the area was viewed by outsiders as a land of opportunity, a place where an ambitious man could earn his fortune. Thus all levels of society migrated to the city.

The site of Minneapolis was particularly attractive to people from New England for several reasons. First, the economy of the eastern seaboard was well established and near the point of stagnation. Therefore, the opportunities for advancement were limited. Because the economies of New Hampshire and Vermont were based on lumbering, migrants from those states found ready employment in the Upper Mississippi Valley. During the years following 1847, many other New England millers and lumbermen followed Ard Godfrey to the new settlement. In addition to the millers came merchants, lawyers, clerks, and teachers. Many brought the capital so desperately needed on the frontier. It appears that nearly the entire leadership group of nineteenth-century Minneapolis arrived between 1855 and 1870. These people as a group had been well educated in the grammar schools, colleges, and universities of New England. After the Civil War, they were joined by Ohioans and New Yorkers who came from similar stock. The presence of this educated elite made the transition from frontier village to city quite rapid and complete. These people knew what cities were supposed to be like; they understood both the problems of government and the needs of industry, and they possessed a sense of charity and duty. On arrival they immediately set out to make the falls community reflect the cities they knew in the East. These people had a sense of destiny. They believed the region would be developed for agriculture, and they knew that one who wanted to profit from the area's growth had to be a part of the very first phases.

Aerial view, St. Anthony, 1857.

*First suspension bridge
(completed 1855).*

The First Period of Rapid Growth

In 1855 the first boom in urban growth began. At the beginning of that year, Steele, Stevens, and Isaac Atwater formed a bridge company. As soon as their toll bridge was finished, a totally unwarranted boom in the sale of town lots occurred. To be sure, there was a great deal of economic growth occurring and a diversified manufacturing strip was developed near the falls, but the expectation for increased growth was totally out of proportion. The panic of 1857 nipped that boom, and the town grew slowly until 1865.

During the war years the city was beyond the areas served by rapid transportation. Because it was difficult to get manufactured goods from the East, most politicians and businessmen believed that the Minneapolis manufacturing base would contain a wide variety of activities that would duplicate the towns of the Connecticut Valley. They envisioned a self-sufficient center, making nearly everything farmers would need, from blankets to plows.

As we have seen, the first commercial sawmill was built in 1847. Several years later, in 1854, the first merchant grain mill was in operation. This event did not seal the city's future as the grain-milling center of the world, however. The lack of consistent supply, competition from other mill towns, and the high cost of getting the flour to eastern markets combined to dampen investors' enthusiasm for grain milling. Instead they put their money in other ventures that produced goods for the local market or into sawmills. Orin Rogers opened the first furniture factory in 1854. In 1855 the first of many sash-and-door factories opened upstream from the falls. Brickyards were built from 1854 onward. E. Broad of St. Anthony began making edged tools in 1855, but a foundry was not constructed until 1859. That same year saw the Island Paper Mill built.

In 1860 Minneapolis boasted 562 manufacturers. Included in the list was the Fergason Plow Manufacturing Company, which later became Monitor Plow. In 1868 the Minneapolis Plow Works was established, and in 1873 Minneapolis Harvester began operations. By 1870 the linseed oil industry was going strong, a boot-and-shoe factory was in operation, and on Washington and First Avenue South crackers and confections were being produced. The manufacturing operations tended to cluster near the falls, but the less profitable ventures were soon pushed toward the edges of the mill district.

The state agricultural fair held in Minneapolis in the fall of 1865 was a festive affair. The chief orator of the event was the famous booster of the West and editor of the *New York Tribune*, Horace Greeley. His editorial described the attitudes he heard expressed during his visit. He said that the population of Minneapolis would quadruple in ten years (in fact, it grew from eight hundred in 1865 to thirty-two hundred in 1875). Greeley thought that the city would be developed as a diversified manufacturing town with a paper mill, a woolen mill, and perhaps eventually a cotton factory, just like the towns of New England. He was excited over the potential of the railroads and said the growth of the railroads would erase the difference between St. Paul and Minneapolis. He was also enthusiastic about the national politics of the time and endorsed protective tariffs, saying, "No where on Earth are the beneficent influences of our protective tariff estimated to be more signally, more promptly realized than throughout the great West."[3] These benefits were protection from foreign competition and thereby, the possibility of a market for local goods. In Greeley's view, Minneapolis and other small centers would be able to capitalize on the local demand. The small diversified manufacturing town predicted by Greeley and others did not materialize, however; although enthusiastic about the railroads, the early boosters underestimated their ability to tie the entire nation into one large trade area for a few gigantic manufacturing concerns and specialized industrial cities. The future of Minneapolis lay not in diversification but in specialization.

The Late Sixties and Seventies: The Era of Consolidation

During the decade and a half that followed Greeley's speech and prediction, the city underwent a gradual consolidation. The railroad companies' routes reached out to the surrounding agricultural areas and established the basic trade area for the city's merchants and manufacturers. In addition to these rather local connections, the rail lines were extended toward the south and east to make connections with the rail lines radiating from Chicago.[4] During the first seven years in this period, the basic pattern was established. In 1865 the Minnesota Central reached Faribault; two years later it was connected with the Milwaukee Road at Austin, which gave Minneapolis its first connection to Chicago. In 1870 the St. Paul and Pacific (later the Great Northern) reached the Red River Valley and opened that great agricultural region, and in the same year the Lake Superior and Mississippi reached Duluth. Two years later the so-called short line down the Mississippi to LaCrosse was completed and the travel time to Chicago was greatly reduced.

These railroad lines divided the city into several large sectors as they radiated out from the falls district. Furthermore, they provided and attracted new industrial and warehouse development to the land adjacent to the tracks. This meant that aside from the flour milling, all new development occurred away from the falls; developers were generally attracted to the fringe of the city, where large parcels of land were available at low cost. There were three rail corridors that determined the direction of industrial growth during these years. The old Minnesota Central, known as the Chicago, Milwaukee and St. Paul, ran southeast from the west bank district. This line became the focus of the farm implement industry and grain storage in the 1890s. The second major corridor on the west bank followed the course of Bassett's Creek westerly from the northern edge of the central commercial district. This line crossed the river on Nicollet Island and produced the transportation artery for the east side mills. The Bassett's Creek portion of this line would later become the focus for the warehouse district and effectively demarcate the north side of Minneapolis from the rest of the city. It connected with the St. Paul and Pacific in the eastern section of old St. Anthony, at Minneapolis Junction. The Minneapolis and Duluth line followed the same general route along Second Avenue northeast.

Throughout this period, national and local forces threatened to wipe out the struggling city. The danger of financial panics in the uncontrolled and overextended national economy was always present. Capital-intensive industries like milling and railroading were more vulnerable. The panic of 1873 was especially hard on the railroads serving Minneapolis because none of the companies were old enough to have a secure traffic base. Just when the effects of the panic had subsided,

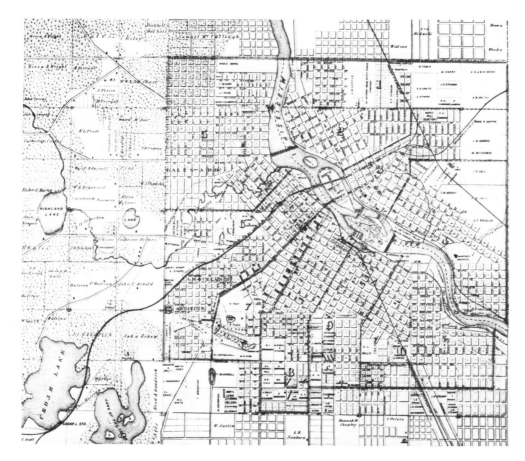

Minneapolis, 1874.

the locust plagues engulfed the new farm lands in western Minnesota and the Dakotas. From 1875 to 1878, the grasshoppers ate the new immigrant farmers out of house and home. And if these problems were not enough, conditions within the city threatened to destroy the falls, the economic base of the city. The limestone ledge over which the water fell was constantly eroding. To make matters worse, one adventurous man, W. W. Eastman, nearly wiped out the falls in an effort to beat the power company's monopoly. He wanted his own source of power, and so he instructed workmen to dig a tunnel from his land on Nicollet Island under the river to disgorge downstream from the falls. The river broke into the tunnel and the resulting maelstrom threatened the limestone ledge. Frantic efforts to plug the tunnel with timbers, boulders, and everything that could be thrown into the gaping hole eventually were successful. This event prompted the construction of an apron over the ledge to protect the falls and thereby preserve the manufacturing district.[5]

Devastation caused to mills on Hennepin Island by break in Nicollet Island tunnel, October 1869.

Lumber mills (1878–88), Minneapolis.

The final calamity of the decade was the great mill explosion that destroyed six of fifteen mills in the west bank milling complex in 1878.[6] By then the value of the location was proven, and so the mills were immediately rebuilt. Having survived this decade of testing, the city was to enter its period of greatest relative growth—the booming eighties.

The Boom Years and Golden Era

The atmosphere of the city was electric as the decade of the 1880s began. Residents had a feeling that the city's future was going to be both profitable and exciting. Three separate events epitomize the new decade. The first was a grand parade and civic festival known as the Villard Reception, which celebrated the completion of the Northern Pacific's transcontinental route. Villard's line did not give Minneapolis a direct connection to the coast, but trains could come into the city over the tracks of other companies. Local manufacturers and wholesalers were ecstatic over the prospects of the greatly increased market. Some even dreamed of entering the Orient trade. The city's celebration was widely acclaimed, and according to local boosters it "overwhelmed with shame her defeated rival," St. Paul.[7]

The second event occurred in 1884, when the

Lumber mill, west side of river, and falls, 1865.

Grand Army of the Republic held its national encampment in Minneapolis. This was the city's first major convention, and for a brief time the nation's press focused on Minneapolis. For most citizens the encampment signaled the attainment of real urban status.

Veterans encampment, Nicollet Avenue, Minneapolis.

Critics could still write, "Minneapolis is a beautiful place, but it looks like an overgrown village"; but the residents and visitors all knew that the boom was on and the little New England–like settlement hugging the falls was never going to be the same.

The third event was the construction of an enormous exhibition hall overlooking the river on the east bank just upstream from the mills.[8] The hall was located just south of the crossing, on the former site of the Winslow House, St. Anthony's resort hotel. The disappearance of the hotel and the construction of the exhibition hall illustrate the dramatic change in the interpretation of the falls. Once an object of beauty and natural wonder attracting visitors from the East and South, the falls had now become an engine of industry. The exhibition hall was built to provide the city's industrialists a forum in which to boast. The hall was in

large measure built as a reaction to the moving of the state agricultural fair from Minneapolis to a site adjacent to St. Paul. If that other city was going to have an annual celebration of rural culture, then Minneapolis would have an annual celebration of urban and industrial culture. So the grandiose structure with its tower, fountains, and landscaping was built; and for several years the expositions of manufacturing were held in it. Through the building, the citizens of Minneapolis were telling the world that the city was ready to take its rightful place among the centers of civilization.

The Expansion Process

The residents of the city had already seen their community change during the 1870s and early 1880s.

The falls had been tamed and the milling district solidly built up. On the west bank, the ranks of mills stretched southward from approximately Third Avenue to Eighth Avenue. These mills all made use of a power canal that brought water under South First Street. One set of buildings faced the siding near the Milwaukee Depot; the ones toward the river made use of new tracks built on viaducts over the river. On the east bank some of the older manufacturers held on, although the area was dominated by the huge Pillsbury Mill, which in 1881 replaced a sash-and-door factory. Lumber mills remained on the islands and over the easternmost channel of the river. The industrial districts enlarged, with two areas upstream from the falls on both sides of the river being developed for lumber-related activities and the brick-yards being moved farther north toward Camden. The expansive industrial area associated with the rail yard just north of present-day Lake and Hiawatha was begun in the 1870s, but it would not be fully developed until the turn of the century. The east bank commercial core remained localized on Main Street, while the west bank district, by now the central business district for the entire city, grew to Seventh. The northern edge was given over to warehouses, Nicollet was the shopping street, and the remainder was changing into an office service center.

As the decade passed and the population boom continued, hundreds of buildings were added to the

landscape. Seemingly everyone was a real estate speculator during the period. The level of activity can best be seen in the increase in the number of dealers in residential lots. There were 50 agents in 1870, but by 1883 the city directory listed 213. The real estate industry is just one example of the service activities that created a demand for office buildings. The more profitable ventures sought out comfortable quarters in large stone and brick buildings that were under construction in the downtown. Others located in more modest quarters or even in the houses in outlying areas.

The Rise of Flour Milling: Destiny Assured

The growth in the service industry was made possible by the burgeoning employment opportunities in the flour-milling industry and related activities. To some degree the phenomenal growth of the milling industry had not been foreseen. While Greeley and other pundits of the time predicted that the railroad would connect Minneapolis industrialists to a large region in which to sell the products, they forgot that the railroads would also make the Minneapolis market accessible to eastern producers. The large eastern manufacturers were able to sell their goods in Minneapolis at the same prices as locally produced goods. As a result, many factories in Minneapolis were forced out of business. The early ironworks, woolen mills, and paper mills were replaced by flour mills. For example, the large ironworks on South First Street, established by Lee and Hardenburgh in 1865, was torn down in 1879 to make room for the Crown Roller Mill.

In a sense, the agriculture of the upper Midwest that supported Minneapolis was created by the railroad and milling companies of the two cities. The railroads opened the land for settlement by providing easy access and selling much of the land grants they had been awarded by the national government to finance the construction of the rights-of-way. In addition, they actually promoted settlement by advertising the region's virtues in the eastern states and Europe. Naturally the railroad companies argued that these virtues were concentrated along the railroad tracks. The role of the railroads was especially important in the development of the Red River Valley of the north. The railroad companies owned vast tracts of land in the valley that they were unable to sell to small farmers. Instead, for a brief period the so-called bonanza farms existed. These were huge farms operated by corporations composed largely of eastern investors. The farms used large numbers of migrant workers during the growing season; the workers

Exposition building (built 1886), above Main Street Southeast, west of Central Avenue.

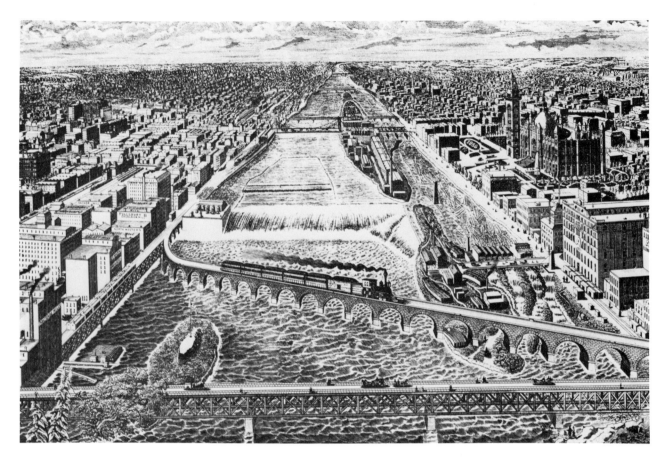

Panorama, looking up
Mississippi River, 1886.

frequently spent their winters working as lumberjacks. The flat valley and large fields were ideally suited to the use of farm machinery; as a result, grain growing became one of the nation's most mechanized forms of agriculture. This period did not last long, and the eastern farmer-speculators soon sold off their fields. Nonetheless, it demonstrated the practicality of growing wheat at those northern latitudes.

Thus the railroads spurred the settlement of the region and helped to establish the basic agricultural practices. However, one huge problem remained: the wheat. Only hard spring wheat can be grown successfully in the valley; and that grain, as its name implies, was difficult to grind into flour.

Because the kernels of wheat planted in the spring are hard, the millstones had to be run at high speed and pressure in order to crack and grind the kernels. The result was a second-rate flour that was discolored by the presence of bits of the hull. Frequently the friction set up by the millstones actually scorched the flour; to make matters worse, the flour tended to spoil easily. In

the early 1870s, Minneapolis millers adopted a technique, developed in Dundas, Minnesota, that made drastic improvements in the quality of the flour. This process involved separating the husk and bran from the flour with a series of sieves and blowers called a middlings purifier. They then substituted rollers for millstones. The iron rollers used less energy and produced excellent flour. Soon the new practices were used by every mill in the city, and Minneapolis was on its way to being the "Budapest of North America," the nation's leading milling center. That could be accomplished only if a market was created for the flour. Therefore, in 1877, William Dunwoody was sent to London to create a demand for Minneapolis flour. After nearly a year of lobbying, he returned with a sizable contract for the millers, and the profitable export trade was begun. The natural resource of the falls was not in itself enough to generate a thriving urban economy; so the entrepreneurs of Minneapolis essentially invented a new resource in the form of hard spring wheat and created a demand for their product as well.

Pillsbury A Mill.

During the previous decade, the companies controlling the waterpower rights of the falls gradually worked out their affairs with the sawmillers, flour millers and railroaders. Perhaps the most humorous and yet telling episode in this process was the newspaper coverage of James J. Hill's purchase of the St. Anthony Power Company in 1880. The St. Paul papers printed a jibe about St. Paul buying up Minneapolis, while the Minneapolis papers retorted that eventually all sharp and intelligent businessmen would come to their senses and immigrate to Minneapolis.

Thousands of workers were employed in the mill district during the seventies and early eighties. The daily traffic jams were horrendous as a wide array of horse-drawn vehicles and pedestrians moved through the narrow streets and waited for trains to pass. The men who controlled the mills were the leaders of the entire community because a large segment of the entire city labor force was directly or indirectly dependent on the activities in the milling district.

The millers were aggressively exploring ways to

Pillsbury A Mill (LeRoy S. Buffington, 1881), Main Street Southeast and 3rd Avenue Southeast.

Washburn A Mill, just before explosion, 1878.

increase production and cut costs. Although they were in general at the mercy of the railroad companies, in 1883 the millers attempted to achieve some degree of independence by building their own railroad, the Minneapolis, Sault Ste. Marie and Atlantic, or the Soo Line. This railroad was intended to carry flour from Minneapolis to a port on the Great Lakes just downstream from the locks at Sault Ste. Marie. Between 1885 and 1887, 436 miles of track were laid. The plan was only modestly successful, however, because the line ran through the cutover region of Wisconsin and Michigan, an area unable to generate much cargo on its own. Even after the Soo Line was connected to the Canadian Transcontinental at Regina, it was not dramatically profitable.

The milling industry attracted to Minneapolis several supportive enterprises. Several flour-milling-machine companies were established, as were bag factories. Bags quickly replaced barrels as containers for flour and other grain products. Because of the great demand for bags, the industry became the fourth largest in Minneapolis.

The Emergence of Downtown

Away from the riverfront, the commercial sections of the city underwent a similar transformation. The downtown areas contained several new large retail stores. In 1854 St. Anthony was the center of retail trade, with thirty-one small stores. By 1874 a new and larger retail area was established on Washington Avenue. In the early 1880s, the district was concentrated on lower Nicollet, Hennepin, and Washington Avenues. Most operations were housed in one- or two-story frame buildings; but on Nicollet and Third, Hale and Company's three-story brick building dominated the scene. In 1884 the first modern department store, the Glass Block building, was built on Sixth and Nicollet. Sea's Store, further up Nicollet at Ninth, had to provide a free bus to entice shoppers away from lower Nicollet stores. This area was soon filled in by larger office structures, such as the Syndicate Block built in 1882.

During these years the railroad lines that focused on the milling district built depots and switch yards between the west bank mills and the new downtown. The Chicago, Milwaukee and St. Paul was located at Washington and Fourth Avenue South, and the St. Paul and Pacific at Washington and Fourth Avenue North. The Union Depot was finally constructed, and the stone arch bridge was constructed across the river below the falls. A variety of industrial activity was localized along the rail corridors during the decade. Although casket makers, knitting mills, and fancy-glass makers all estab-

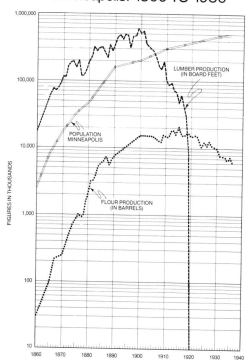

Growth and Decline of Lumbering and Flour Milling Minneapolis: 1860 TO 1936

lished themselves in the city during the eighties, most new or growing industries in some way serviced the agricultural market. The animal food and medicine industries were quite important, as was the making of farm implements. The latter industry actually outgrew Minneapolis, and in 1887 the Minneapolis Threshing Machine Company (successor to Monitor Plow) moved to Hopkins. In the early 1890s, the lumber industry on the west bank stretched as far out as Camden—well beyond other urban development.

1892—The Year of Civic Celebration

What better way to celebrate a city's position as the financial capital of a prosperous agricultural hinterland than to host the national convention for the Republican Party? That is exactly what Minneapolis did in 1892. It was a golden opportunity for verbose orations on the American dream and the success of business. After all, Minneapolis was positive proof that the system worked. The city leaped up from the ground in a phenomenal building boom during the 1880s. Its population nearly tripled in the five years between 1880 and 1885, when it increased from about 50,000 to 129,000. It reached 164,738 in 1890. These rates established the city as one of the fastest growing communities in North America.

Among the larger cities, only the expansion of Chicago was greater.

The optimistic community leaders of 1882 had been correct. Many people would make their fortune, especially those in real estate sales and in the building trades, because the central area of Minneapolis had to be rebuilt and expanded to accommodate all the new forms of commercial activity. Despite the glow of success that surrounded the Republican convention, the first signs of weakness in the city's financial base were visible. The talk of a canal across Central America, growing more serious each year, signaled the potential loss of the city's West Coast market and the transcontinental railroad freight business. Secondly, the rapid growth had been financed in large measure by outside capital. Financiers in New York, Boston, Philadelphia, and London had invested heavily in the city's railroads, streetcar system, flour mills, and sundry other activities. Therefore, the city was dependent on the national business cycle. The panic of 1893 brought to a close the city's era of rapid growth. The remainder of the decade and the first years of the twentieth century would be characterized by alternating booms and busts that made life on the agricultural frontier difficult and uncertain.

Residents of Minneapolis knew full well that their prosperity depended entirely on the success of the region's agricultural communities. After several years

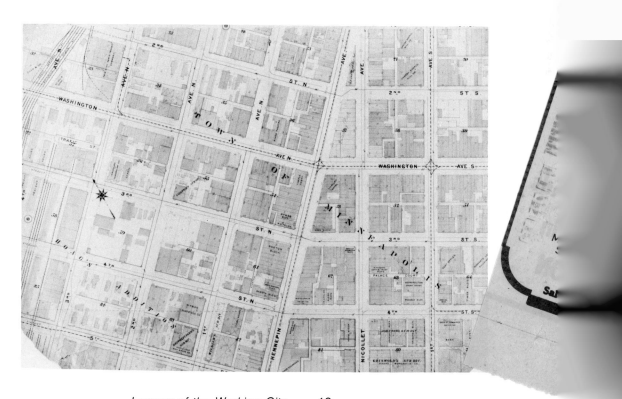

Commercial expansion—west bank (from 1903 atlas of Minneapolis, plate A).

Commercial expansion—east bank (from 1903 atlas of Minneapolis, plate 3).

of bad weather and locust plagues, the upper Midwest enjoyed nearly a perfect growing season in 1891. The frost left early and was followed by a warm spring. The sunshine was broken intermittently by gentle rains that seemed to arrive just when the crops were in need of water. The autumn was mild and dry, so every farmer was able to harvest a bumper crop. When the news of the great harvest reached all the residents of Minneapolis, this city so close to the soil, they staged a mammoth and nearly spontaneous Grand Harvest Festival of 1891 on September 23.[9] Merchants, citizens, and farmers decorated wagons and carriages with the symbols of fall, harvest, and the commerce of the city. The marchers and onlookers turned out in such large numbers that the event is thought to be the largest public gathering that the city had experienced up to that time. According to the newspaper account, three hundred thousand watched the parade. According to W. S. King, everyone was deeply moved by the religious ceremonies and glorious spectacle of people and machines. That gentle and happy celebration clearly indicates the city's role as both master and servant of the agricultural region. Its mills processed the region's grain, its factories produced farm implements, and the growing number of wholesalers provided farmers and residents of small towns with all the necessities and luxuries they could afford.

The Movement of Sawmilling Away from the Falls and the Consolidation of the Flour Industry

The lumber industry was the chief factor in the prosperity of both the city and the surrounding region. After steam saws were perfected, the sawmill industry based on logs floated downstream was quick to move away from the falls and upstream. The move upstream was hastened by the sawmillers' need for larger yards in which to stack boards for seasoning. One writer described them as "huge, unpainted pine rookeries from which high smoke stacks pierce the sky; countless piles of lumber, freshly sawed and now spread out for seasoning by wind and sunshine."[10] The steam saws were fired by sawdust. The pungent smell of burning pine combined with the sticky sweet smell of the sap in the fresh cut lumber gave the banks of the Mississippi north of downtown a decidedly nonurban atmosphere.

The northern migration of sawmills was hurried along by the fire that swept the east side row of mills and by the removal of those on the west side in 1887. By 1890 only two sawmills still used waterpower. By the turn of the century, the dozen or so steam sawmills in Minneapolis would make the city the nation's center of the lumber industry and make the industry an important source of employment. The smaller manu-

Northstar Woolen Mill.

Mill district, west side of river, 1867–69. Northstar Woolen Mill is building with cupola.

facturers of other products also left the falls in search of cheaper land in the suburbs, and so by 1892 the flour millers essentially had the waterpower of the falls to themselves—and they needed it![11] As we have seen, the millers were able to develop a process that allowed them to grind the hard spring wheat into a popular flour. Now their task was to find ways to effectively increase the power of the falls.

Syndicate Block (completed 1883), Nicollet Avenue between 5th and 6th Streets.

Flour production tripled during the eighties, going from two million to six million barrels per year. The city produced more flour than the next three largest production centers combined! The flour industry was far and away the most important aspect of the economy of Minneapolis, earning about $83 million in 1890. The increase in production was made possible by improving existing mills rather than increasing their number. Although there were three fewer mills in 1889 than in 1890, the group's average daily production increased from twenty-five thousand barrels to thirty-six thousand. The largest of the mills, Pillsbury A, alone produced seven thousand barrels a day. Along with the technical improvements came the inevitable consolidation of ownership. By 1890 only fifteen companies were involved in milling, and three of those owned sixty percent of the district's capacity.

The Minneapolis Mill Company, which controlled the waterpower rights on the west bank, and James Hill's firm, which controlled St. Anthony's, were hard pressed to provide enough power to keep up with the growing demand. Although the extraordinary Hill was always closely involved in the company, the technology of waterpower demanded an engineer as chief operating officer; during the eighties, the affairs of both power companies were managed by professional engineers. William de la Barre, an Austrian engineer, controlled

the fate of the Minneapolis Mill Company after C. G. Washburn, its long time president, died in 1892. De la Barre served as treasurer of the firm as well as manager and engineer.

De la Barre more than any other individual was responsible for keeping the waterpower of the falls a vital force in the city's economy.[12] His first problem was to secure a steady supply of water. Not only was the flow of the river unreliable due to floods and droughts, but the company had essentially oversold its supply of power. That problem was exacerbated by the practice of the flour mill operators of using more than their allocated flow of water. Four courses of action were necessary. First, the system of mill runs, wheels, and chases was improved so that more power could be extracted from the falls. Second, management procedures were revised so that the millers got the power that they paid for and not that belonging to someone else. Third, a system of reservoirs on the upper Mississippi was established by the federal government. Finally, a short-lived plan to draw off water from the Mississippi via a canal to the St. Louis River, so that Duluth could build a competing milling center, was thwarted. In the 1880s the millers soon began to install auxiliary steam engines to make up for the loss of waterpower. The power situation on the east bank was so tight that the Pillsbury A mill ran its steam engine and sold its waterpower rights to the sawmills located there from 1886 to 1887. That shortage was alleviated when all the sawmills burned down.

De la Barre was the first to keep careful records of the Mississippi's flow. It was his measurements and understanding of the river system's dynamics that provided the underpinning for the industry's lobbying efforts on behalf of the reservoir system using the northern lakes. The concept was to convert the lakes on the river between Brainerd and Bemidji—Cass, Winnibigoshish, Mud, Leech, Pokegama, and Gull—to reservoirs. This amounted to about a quarter of the river's drainage basin and was thought to contain enough runoff to stabilize the river's volume at the falls. Various surveyors were sent northward to investigate the possibilities, and land was purchased in anticipation of the scheme's success. Fortunately for the milling interests, their man in Washington, Congressman William D. Washburn (a member of the milling community), was an ardent supporter of the plan. He moved the necessary legislation through government procedures and later was known as "the father of the reservoir system." In 1905 he wrote, "I am almost entirely responsible for the conception and building of this system of reservoirs, as all the early appropriations were secured by me when in the House of Representatives in the early 80's."[13]

The system of reservoirs is yet another example of how the business leadership of the city was able to modify its hinterland in ways that would ensure the continued prosperity of Minneapolis. They continued to "create resources." People on the St. Paul Board of Trade were not pleased with these efforts to improve

Harvest Festival.

*Electric lighting standard,
Bridge Square, c. 1883.*

the economy of Minneapolis and attempted to curtail government spending to improve the project. Their attitude was lambasted by the impartial editors of the *Minneapolis Tribune,* who wrote calling the board "a collection of pecunious peddlers" willing to deprive their own city of potential gain to keep Minneapolis from benefiting from the reservoir system.

Decline of Waterpower

Despite all the efforts to improve the efficiency of the falls, all those involved understood that its potential was limited. Steam engines soon were elevated from auxiliary sources of power during periods of low water to primary sources of the mills' energy. By 1892 the industries of the city were no longer dependent on the power of the falls. New manufacturers were in a sense emancipated from the riverfront location, and they selected sites along railroad lines away from the old core.[14]

During the 1800s, experiments with hydroelectricity began at the falls and promised to solve many of the problems associated with the use of waterpower. Electricity can be transported cheaply from the generator to a large number of users. With electricity available, an operation could use the power of the falls indirectly and locate anywhere in a wide radius of the generating plant. At first the electricity generated was used to light the houses and streets on each side of the river. A company comprising men from the city's business leadership corps was first incorporated in 1881. They built their first operation in an abandoned cotton mill on Upton Island. They turned on the current on September 5, 1882, making Minneapolis the nation's first city with a hydroelectric plant. Through the eighties, the company's agent sought to convince the city's government and residents to convert their lights from gas to electricity. Eventually it received permission to string wires above city streets, and the electrification of the city got underway. The company, frustrated by low water and threatened with the cancellation of its lease, decided to abandon waterpower and followed the sawmills up river. It located in a building on Third Avenue North and fired its steam generators with sawdust.

The refinements of the waterpower technology of the eighties were accompanied by drastic changes in the transportation system. James J. Hill determined that he should bring his tracks across the Mississippi just below the falls and run them upstream between the mills and the river on a trestle system over the canals. The stone arch bridge, essentially a monument to the man and his company, was completed in 1883 at a cost of approximately half a million dollars. His depot was also built near the falls two years later. The terminal was rebuilt in 1912.

Horsecars, Streetcars, and Changing Patterns of Growth in the Central Business Area

Although the laying of new tracks in the mill district and the construction of new terminals were important events in the development of the city, the electrification of the street railways, or streetcar system, between 1890 and 1891 speeded the development process that had begun during the horsecar era. In the 1870s various corporations were formed to operate a system of horse-drawn trolleys on the streets. The first was established in 1875 and ran from the depot through downtown to the University of Minnesota. In 1877 Thomas Lowry gained control of the transit company. Lowry's brother-in-law, Calvin Goodrich, became the

Stone arch bridge, modern view. Two of the original supports were replaced during construction of the locks in 1960s.

Hennepin Avenue and Bridge Square, 1869.

company's bookkeeper in 1878 and soon was promoted to general manager. Together these two men directed the growth of the Twin Cities transit system for the next thirty-five years. Lowry and Goodrich began electrification of the horsecar lines in downtown late in 1889, with the Fourth Avenue South line. The experiment was so successful that in September of 1890 the city council ordered all horsecar lines electrified.

This focus of horsecar tracks had great impact on the growth and character of downtown Minneapolis because it made it possible to deliver large numbers of workers or shoppers to a single point without needing

Guaranty Loan building (Metropolitan building) (E. Townsend Mix, 1890), just before it was razed, 1950s.

any ancillary storage space for carriages. It also reduced the cost of commuting to work, so the downtown could attract people from greater distances than at any previous time. The development of electric streetcars coincided with elevator technology to move people within buildings. Together these advancements made practical large office buildings.

As the economy of the city began to diversify, employment in the office and service sectors of the labor force increased. This trend created a demand for larger office blocks than the buildings constructed during the 1870s in the lower loop. In addition, the prosperity of the 1880s encouraged builders and developers to construct ornate structures. After all, Minneapolis was such a successful up-and-coming town that it was alleged that here dogs never stopped to scratch themselves, because they were just too busy.[15]

The building boom of the eighties gave the downtown its initial form. Speculators controlled this growth spurt, and as a result the land area in the central district was used to its fullest. Hotels were concentrated along Hennepin, retail stores on Nicollet, corporate offices along Second Avenue, and the commodity exchanges on Third Street and Fourth Avenue. There were no attempts made to provide park land or public amenities like squares or fountains. The office buildings clustered in the vicinity of Hennepin, Marquette, and Second. Each of the office buildings built during this period was designed to express the style and individuality of its owner and architect. The most spectacular of them was the Guaranty Loan Company's building at Third Street and Second Avenue South. According to one writer of the time, "A more imposing building, or one more convenient and appropriate for the purposes for which it was designed is not to be found in the United States."[16] Begun in 1888 and completed in 1890, it was twelve stories high, built of granite and sandstone. Its interior was supposedly finished in antique oak. The most prestigious business address in the city, it housed the office of the Security and Northwestern Bank, several general business offices, and insurance companies, as well as the headquarters of the Soo Line Railroad. However, most of the space was occupied by lawyers. Best of all was the sumptuous twelfth floor, with its ladies' and gentlemen's cafe, large public dining room, and private dining rooms, as well as billiards and smoking rooms. To top it off was a roof garden, where in fine weather Minneapolitans could relax to concerts by a string orchestra and gaze out over their growing metropolis.

The most elegant and largest office in the building was occupied by the financier and real estate promoter Louis Menage. One of the many fortune seekers who came west after the Civil War and began to sell real

Lumber Exchange (Long and Kees, 1885)), 425 Hennepin Avenue.

estate, Menage probably created more housing districts than any other nineteenth-century developer. The corporation he headed was organized in 1889 as the Northwest Guaranty Loan Company, and its board included some of the city's most influential men. Menage was not allowed to enjoy his lavish seat of power for long, however. In 1893 he was forced to leave the country to avoid prosecution for fraud over a sale of certain grain elevators. Although his rise and fall were dramatic, it is safe to assume that many other speculators and investors rode a similar financial roller coaster in those wide open years of the Minneapolis boom.

Other commercial buildings that resulted from the profitable resource economy were the Lumber Exchange at 425 Hennepin, which was built in 1885, and the Flour Exchange at 310 4th Avenue South, which was built in 1892–93 and which when remodeled in 1909 was increased from four to twelve stories. The years between the construction dates of these buildings resulted in quite different stylistic treatment of the facades. Their construction gives evidence of the importance and profitability of both activities.

West Hotel, 5th Street and Hennepin Avenue.

Near the Lumber Exchange, on Sixth Street, the Masonic Temple was built in 1888–1889. This was the most monumental of all the fraternal lodges built in the Twin Cities. In a sense it was a symbol of the middle class's pride in its accomplishments. Its prominent position in downtown attests to the fact that in those years the central city was the center of the social, business, and government activities in Minneapolis.

The growing population and wealth of the city caused the struggling boards of the library and the Athenaeum to combine and raise money for a new large structure to house the city's intellectual life. In December of 1889 the building, occupying the corner of Hennepin and Tenth, was opened. The public excitement over the building and its fifty thousand books was strong enough to cause the factions within the boards of the library and the Athenaeum to forget their differences and hurt feelings. By 1892 the demand for books outside downtown had caused the opening of the first branch in Northside. As might be expected, the downtown library building had several functions. It

Minneapolis City Hall and Hennepin County Old Court House (Long and Kees, 1888–1905).

housed an art gallery, lecture halls, and the museum of the Academy of Science. Nearly all the city's cultural organizations were under one roof.

The center of the city's social life was the West Hotel (1884) at the corner of Hennepin Avenue and Fifth Street. Built by the aging investor Charles West as a monument to him and his vision of the city, it was a marble-and-brick structure with an elaborate lobby and public rooms on the ground floor. Best of all, it had central heating!

The old city hall on Bridge Square was outgrown, and work on the new city hall–courthouse commenced in 1888. The immense structure was not completed until 1905. Its presence served to establish the administrative center of the city until the present day.

To the north of downtown, the mixed commercial district of the early 1880s was slowly transformed into the warehouse sector. This process reached a climax when the Butler Brothers building was finished in 1906.

For the two decades following 1892, the city continued to grow but at a slower pace. The expansion of downtown and the adjacent warehouse district clearly reflected the city's emergence as the regional center for wholesale trade and financial matters. The developed industries, such as manufacturing furniture and farm implements, replaced sawmilling in the city's economy.

During these years the city's street system, railroad network, and pattern of downtown activities were established. Hennepin was the entertainment center, retailing was focused on Nicollet, office buildings were along Marquette. To the north of the loop were garment manufacturing and warehousing.

Nicollet Avenue between 4th and 5th Streets, 1903.

Butler Brothers warehouse
(Harry Jones, 1906), 1st
Avenue North and Sixth Street.

The First Attempts at Urban Renewal

After the turn of the century, the area around Bridge Square became an embarrassment to the civic leadership. As a result, a program of clearance and rebuilding was undertaken that was to be a prelude to a "city beautiful" plan for the entire city. The seat of government moved into the spacious city hall–courthouse structure that was finished in 1905, and in 1912 the old triangular city hall at the junction of Hennepin and Nicollet was torn down. The old buildings behind city hall were also razed, and the entire block was converted into a park. A fine public shelter, built in the then-popular classic style, was erected in the park to provide tourist information and public toilets. An inscription over its portico greeted all newcomers: "The Gateway—more than her gates, the city opens her heart to you." Three years later a marble-and-brass fountain joined the Gateway building in the park. The second major renewal project in the lower loop, the new post office, also was completed in 1915. Finally on July 4, 1917,

Old city hall, Bridge Square,
1888.

the George Washington Memorial Flagpole was dedicated to the city by the Daughters of the American Revolution. These activities in and of themselves were not able to change the area's general atmosphere of decay and decline. Certainly bigger plans were needed.

Growth along the Rail Corridors

The general process of city expansion will be described in subsequent chapters. It is, however, important to note that at the turn of the century several cores of employment had been established along the railroad corridor leading away from downtown. We have already seen how the farm-implement manufacturers moved to the southwest along the present-day Hiawatha corridor. They were joined by grain elevators and general warehouse activity.

Northeast Minneapolis was developed as an area of manufacturing and railroad-related activities during this era as well. A stockyard was located outside the city limits in New Brighton. Like all other industrial activity, the stockyards depended on the railroad.

The Soo Line, under the direction of Thomas Lowry, who succeeded W. D. Washburn as company president when the latter was elected United States senator, established extensive rail yards in Northeast Minneapolis and in the far northern portion of the city, near Camden. Although Lowry and his associates developed quite extensive schemes for residential communities for the northeastern sector of the city, surprisingly little industry was attracted to these locations. The company's interesting Shoreham Shop was not constructed until 1912.

Brewing remained an important industry in Northeast Minneapolis. In 1880 the Minneapolis Brewing and Malting Company had superseded four older companies with more ethnic names—Germania, Heinrich, Noerenberg, and Orth.

The Minneapolis Brewing Company (later the Grain Belt Brewery) together with the Gluek Company quenched the thirsts of the working population in the city for several decades. Grain Belt's interesting cluster of buildings were begun in the 1870s, with several added during the 1890s.

In the decade and a half that followed 1892, Minneapolis experienced stable growth and prosperity. The base of the city's economy remained the agriculture of the upper Midwest. In fact, the population became more dependent on it after timber cutting ceased to be important, by 1910. Successful companies built solid limestone and brick structures along the straight streets of downtown. Meanwhile, people moved farther toward the fringes, and the public buildings followed. Two

large churches were built in the western fringe of downtown in those years. As the new century began, the various economic and cultural functions of Minneapolis would separate from one another in specialized districts. This was not the result of a plan, however.

The Early Automobile Era—1917–1947

By the start of World War I, nearly everyone was impressed by the city's history of population growth: 46,887 in 1880; 164,784 in 1890; 202,718 in 1900; 301,408 in 1910. Although many expected to see a population of 450,000 Minneapolitans in 1920, the growth rate leveled off and only some 380,000 were counted in the city in that year. The optimists of 1910 could not know that, however, and so they conceived of a city of 1.5 million by 1960. In the grandiose plan of 1917 it was written, "Thus in the growth of cities it is difficult to bring the mind to realize with adequate conviction the fact that the future is just as sure as the

Grain Belt Brewery (1870 and later), 1215 Marshall Avenue Northeast.

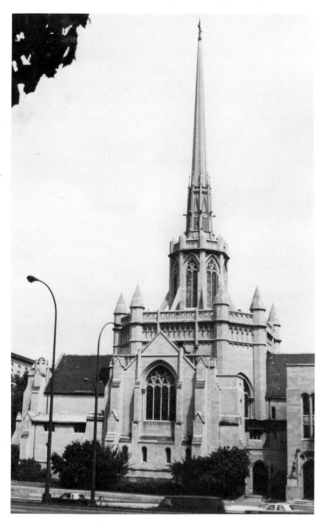

Hennepin Avenue Methodist Church (Hewitt and Brown, 1914), Hennepin Avenue and Groveland.

believed it would be an inevitable by-product of efforts to provide easier communications and access, better recreation and greater convenience. They believed a well-ordered civic life would produce a "city useful" as well as a city beautiful.

> "Make no little plans; they have no magic to stir men's blood and probably themselves will not be realized. Make big plans; aim high in hope and work remembering that a noble, logical diagram once recorded will not die, but long after we are gone will be a living thing, asserting itself with ever-growing insistency. Remember that our sons and grandsons are going to do things that would stagger us. Let your watchword be order and your beacon beauty."[18]

Daniel H. Burnham, author of this ringing call for urban planning, was until his death an advisor to the team that under the direction of Edward Bennett produced the 1917 plan for Minneapolis. Burnham and Bennett were among the nation's leading proponents of what is today known as the City Beautiful movement. Their view of the urban future was grandiose, their attitude about the human condition optimistic, and their energy unfailing as they strove to convince their contemporaries of the value of planning and rebuilding. These men and their ideas had considerable impact on the collective mind of Minneapolis, and their spirit moved a large section of the city's leadership. Therefore, it is necessary to understand what their vision of Minneapolis was if one is to comprehend the development process during the twentieth century.

A civic committee without any legal authority commissioned the Chicago architect Edward Bennett to make a plan. This team proposed to tackle several problem areas where deterioration had set in, and they recognized that traffic congestion in downtown and major arterial roads must be reduced. Their activities were based on a faith that "refuses to believe that the future will not be greater than the past, that refuses to act on the theory that the growth of ten years gone by will equal the growth of ten years to come."[19]

Their research indicated that the city was expanding rapidly toward the southwest and that if the high rates of population growth prevailed, the city would need an area of 150 square miles. In their minds, the growing use of electric streetcars and passenger cars was greatly increasing the rate of expansion. They envisioned that the residential districts would expand unimpeded over the plains south of downtown, while the industrial districts would be developed to the north and northeast. They also believed that a vast railroad transfer and switching yard would be needed in Northeast Minneapolis.

The plan of action consisted of three primary

past, that the time of doubled, tripled and quadrupled growth will come just as surely as tomorrow's sun will shine."[17] No wonder there was widespread investment in the stock market! They considered this plan to be a safe, conservative, and practical guide for the city's continual development.

Minneapolis in 1917 was clearly the financial capital of a large economic region that reached from the Rocky Mountains eastward into Wisconsin. Because the area was expected to experience a continuous increase in wealth and population, it seemed only natural that Minneapolis was going to be a very large city. According to the planners, it now needed to become great in character.

These planners considered themselves to be practical people. While they discussed a beautiful cityscape, they

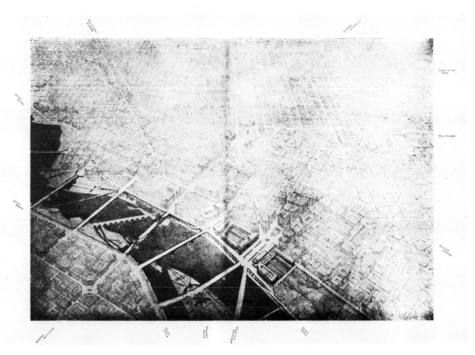

New plan of Minneapolis (from 1917 plan).

proposals: (1) to complete two great axes by lengthening and widening Sixth Avenue and Eighth Street, and to make other logical extensions of the existing street system; (2) to create a superb municipal center at the junction of these main axes, closely linked with an art and educational center at the art museum, an administration center at the city hall, and a transportation center at Gateway Park; (3) to accept and develop the unsurpassed possibilities of a neglected waterfront. In these three proposals we can glimpse what the leading citizens of Minneapolis considered to be the chief problems in the city's development to that date, so these proposals will be discussed in detail.

The Grand Boulevard

The basic concept in the new plan for Minneapolis was the construction of the great Sixth Avenue highway. It was conceived of as a response to several deep economic problems that confronted the city. It was also going to be spectacular! In essence, Sixth Avenue South (now Portland) would be extended straight southwest from its junction with Eleventh Street (where the turn in Portland occurs) all the way to the northeast shore of Lake Harriet. The course would take it through the mansion district around Fair Oaks Park and the art

museum, which gave the landscape architects great scope for designs. From Portland to the art museum it would be 160 feet wide, from the museum to Lyndale it would be 200 feet wide, and from Lyndale to Lake Harriet it would be 150 feet. In the central business district it was to be widened from 80 to 100 feet. Across the river the artery would follow the line of Second Avenue to its junction with Central Avenue. It would then split, with one leg following Central Avenue to the city limits, the other running along Division Street (now Hennepin) to the city limits. The main highway would split the angle between these two and forge out to a new garden suburb in present-day St. Anthony.

At the primary intersections along this boulevard, the designers' imagination would be given free rein. At Eighth Street would be a two-block civic plaza. The art museum and Fair Oaks Park had obvious appeal. They imagined a Minneapolis equivalent of the Place de l'Etoile and the Arc de Triomphe at a huge circular intersection at Sixth, Lyndale, and 36th Street. At the southwestern terminus would be sited a water gate leading to a picturesque embankment on Lake Harriet near the present-day rose gardens. In the other direction the bridge ends would become gates to the city, and another Place de l'Etoile would be sited in Northeast where the great intersection occurred.

Grandiose as the roadway was, it was seen as a way

Rendered by Jules Guerin

THE SIXTH AVENUE ARTERY.

Sixth Avenue Parkway.

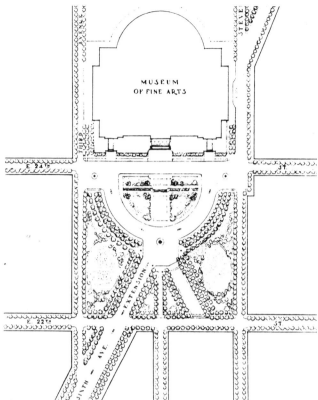

A STRATEGIC DESIGN FOR WASHBURN PARK.

Washburn Park (from 1917 plan).

neighborhoods would be privately renewed. It was noted in the plan that blight extended beyond Fair Oaks Park and, therefore, the situation warranted direct and immediate action. They wrote, "The cancer is spreading southward. . . . There is but one great remedy,—the gaining of a new artery to send life blood coursing through the decayed tissue of the city."[20]

Downtown

Clearly, the central business district was considered healthy and not in need in renewal. It was the residential fringe that was in trouble. The central district would also be restricted by the extension of Park Avenue and several new roads. One major new addition would connect the city hall block to the new civic plaza at Sixth and Eleventh. Gateway Park would be spruced up and extended, with a new street over to city hall. Furthermore, it was thought imperative to widen the streets in the central district to 125 feet immediately,

to save downtown and solve some vexing problems in the older neighborhoods. Because most of the people were expected to live to the southwest of downtown, this road would provide them with a more direct route on which to drive their cars. It would speed up the movement of business traffic, especially activities on downtown streets. But most important, the boulevard would run through a blighted area where property values had begun to decline. It was assumed that if these properties could be cleared, the adjoining

THE SIXTH AVENUE APPROACH TO THE INSTITUTE OF ARTS, THROUGH WASHBURN PARK.

*Sixth Avenue approach to
Minneapolis Institute of Arts,
through Washburn Park (from
1917 plan).*

*Lake Harriet water gate (from
1917 plan).*

Station plaza (from 1917 plan).

before the region was "infested by skyscrapers."

Among the proposals for downtown was the suggestion for a series of governmental buildings stretched from the post office to the city hall. Thus the second primary feature of the plan focused on the fringe of the central business district and called for a grand precinct of administration buildings for city, county, and federal government. The planners were convinced that existing facilities would soon be outgrown and could see no reason to delay land acquisition, only to pay high prices in the future. The designers of the new metropolis were also very concerned about the railroad depots, which they found woefully inadequate: "Dingy, cramped, inconvenient, inaccessible railway stations are stumbling blocks in the path of the city that permits them."[21] While the Gateway area and the Great Northern station were considered a fine beginning to a solution of the depot district problems in Minneapolis, the planners were concerned about the Union Depot and were fearful that Minneapolis might be put at a disadvantage when compared with St. Paul, with its

monumental new Union station.

As a final statement on downtown, the planners agreed that skyscrapers should be quarantined within the region already infested.[22] In their minds, skyscrapers were unhealthy because they could create an unventilated, sunless office condition as bad as the notorious tenement. Furthermore, skyscrapers were thought to cause great increases in traffic congestion at their base. Finally, many argued that they were incapable of paying for themselves.

The Riverfront

If the prospect of a central business area dominated by skyscrapers was abhorrent to the planners, the idea of a solidly built-up riverfront fired their imaginations with enthusiasm. In their words, the riverfront was an "untouched municipal gold mine." While Europeans developed riverfronts intensely and in return received considerable tax revenues, American cities generally

The river (from 1917 plan).

ignored their riverfronts and allowed slums to grow unhindered. Minneapolis was no exception. In order to rectify this situation, a series of two-tiered roadways was to be constructed from Riverside Park north through the falls district to a point where they would meet new parks to be developed above Broadway. Exquisite park embankments were to follow these routes as well. One major problem with the beautification of the river, in the minds of these designers, was the characteristic lack of style of the city's bridges. They asked, "If Paris were so inflicted, would any citizen of Minneapolis visit the Seine?"[23]

The second major impediment was the character of Nicollet Island. They believed that the island should be converted into a park. Its location was ideally near to the city center, but apart from it, and near to the transportation system. One innovative idea was to build a huge stadium on the island; it was also suggested that the island could double as an airport. As they pointed out, "Areas for aeroplanes to alight in must ultimately be provided." If the land were acquired immediately, Minneapolis might even host Olympic games once the European war ended and happier times returned.

A new Paris on the Mississippi may seem farfetched today, but in the first decades of the twentieth century Minneapolis was considered the real capital of the upper Midwest. After all, its businessmen dominated the economic life of the entire region, with the Iron Range the single possible exception. Because the trade area of Minneapolis was larger than northern Europe, there was no reason to believe the city should be inferior to a European capital.

While city-beautiful planners seemed to be well aware of the automobile age and sought to redesign the street system so the growing number of vehicles could be easily accommodated, they either ignored or were unaware of the cracks developing in the city's industrial foundation.

Problems in the Milling Industry

Changing technology and the rapid growth of flour mills had forced the sawmills away from the falls and the established large lumberyards on each bank of the river north of the old core. In the new locations, the sawmill industry continued to prosper as the managers substituted steam for waterpower. This technology was extremely efficient because the steam engine ran on sawdust, which eliminated the disposal problem. From 1895 to 1905, Minneapolis was the nation's leading lumber center; then it was all over. The readily available supply of logs was exhausted, and in 1919 the last sawmill closed.

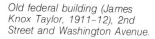

Old federal building (James Knox Taylor, 1911–12), 2nd Street and Washington Avenue.

Dahlen Printing Company building (originally Fleischmann Yeast Company building) (A. L. Dorr, 1907).

Flour milling, backbone of the city's economy, was to follow a similar but more gradual decline. The peak production level occurred in 1915 at 20 million barrels. By 1935 it had declined to 6.5 million, and by 1960 it fell further to approximately 5.5 million. Although the power capacity of the falls was not adequate to meet the millers' demands, the advent of steam technology eliminated most concerns over an eventual limitation on milling capacity. The decline in milling was the result of a shift in international trade. In the first years of the century, approximately thirty percent of flour was sold in the export markets. At the turn of the century some 5 million barrels were exported, but in the mid-twenties the amount dropped to about 75,000. The reason for the change was the emergence of Buffalo, New York, as a milling center. That city is closer to eastern markets and well situated for the export trade. Wheat from the Dakotas was loaded into lake freighters in Duluth and sent directly to Buffalo at rates considerably less than those charged by railroads. Because manufactured and packaged flour did not enjoy such an advantage in rates, nor was it easily shipped via water, Buffalo had a stranglehold on the chief industry of Minneapolis. Although the local millers complained bitterly to the Interstate Commerce Commission about the rate structure the ICC had established, nothing was done. In 1917 Buffalo wheat was fifteen cents a barrel

cheaper. By 1930 the difference had increased to thirty cents. Although this shift in activity had a great impact on the economy of Minneapolis because of decreased demand for labor and lower property taxes on mill property, the flour milling companies did not suffer. Over eighty-five percent of the milling capacity of Buffalo was owned by Minneapolis firms.

The Diversification of the Economy

In 1917 the agricultural hinterland of Minneapolis was prosperous. The demand for wheat in Europe had prompted a further westward advance of the agricultural frontier. The rapid advancements in farm machinery increased the productivity of farm families, and they were encouraged to borrow money for more improvements. It appeared that the growing farm income would spur a great boom in the Minneapolis wholesale trade, which had increased markedly after 1892. The district north of downtown was almost solidly built up with warehouses and loft buildings that held small manufacturing concerns.

The railroad corridors that had been well established during the nineteenth century began to attract more industrialization as firms continued to flee the congestion of the central district. As early as 1874, Monitor

Plow, later International Harvester, located on a large tract of land on the western edge of the central area. Farther out on the railroad tracks along the present Minnehaha corridor, a host of smaller firms settled in. Most obvious were the grain elevators and other agriculture-oriented firms. Their buildings were utilitarian, and although large, were of a plain design. They could easily be abandoned if the company ran into financial difficulties.

The railroad corridors in Northeast Minneapolis did not attract as much industry after 1917, and the community that depended on them stabilized.

The Boom Years of the 1920s

During the early 1920s, downtown Minneapolis under-went a period of rapid growth. The magnificent 1917 plan was ignored, and developers continued to build as the previous generation had and paid little attention to issues of public open space and harmony of design.

In 1929 the greatest building of the decade, the new Foshay Tower, was finished. The building, patterned after the Washington monument, was to be the center of a far-flung public utilities holding company. John Philip Sousa composed a march to commemorate the grand opening. The city's tallest skyscraper was never occupied by Foshay, because his corporation went bankrupt soon after the structure was dedicated. The less grandiose twenty-seven-story Rand Tower dates from the same year. Its lavish lobby was finished in marble and decorated with an aviation theme. Two years later the Northwestern Bell Telephone skyscraper was finished, giving Minneapolis a nice cluster of tall buildings.

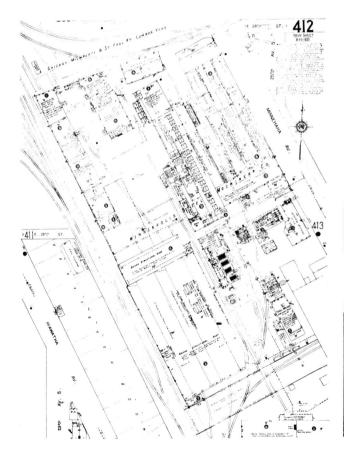

Lake and Hiawatha, 1912.

Foshay Tower (Magney and Tusler; Hooper and Janusch, 1926–29), 821 Marquette Avenue.

*Rand Tower (Holabird and
Root, 1928–29), 527 Marquette
Avenue.*

White Spot Cafe (1932), 600 block of 10th Street.

(See Part Four for further discussion of specific buildings.)

These three buildings gave evidence of the changing notions of the city's economy. As financial institutions and service organizations began to replace manufacturers as the city's source of income, a new cityscape was created. During those years, the office tower replaced the mill as the symbol of prosperity. The shape of downtown buildings was affected by the height regulation of 1916 and the zoning laws of 1929, as well as other laws intended to improve the quality of urban life. Clearly, efforts at city planning were having an impact.

The prosperity enjoyed by the upper class during the twenties prompted the construction of several large cultural institutions beyond the fringe of downtown. The most dramatic was the Basilica of St. Mary, begun in 1907 but not totally finished until 1926. A little farther out, at 1710 Lyndale, was Walker's new art gallery (1928), a gift from one of the city's most ardent supporters. The decision, after considerable debate, to locate the auditorium on the upper fringe of downtown

has had great effect on the locations of subsequent hotel development.

In 1931 construction on the new post office was begun, and the block in front of it was cleared for Pioneer Square. This project was hoped to spark a redevelopment of the Gateway area. Despite this fine building, the area remained much as it had been.

Downtown in the Midst of Depression

A research team directed by the sociologist Calvin Schmed conducted a detailed survey of the central business district in 1934–35 (see figure, page 48). As this map indicates, the area could be divided into several small specialized areas. The central business district itself was surrounded by less prosperous areas. To its northwest lay the warehouse district, which figured so prominently in the social history of the city. To the northeast lay hobohemia, or the Gateway district skid row. Light industry and weaker businesses lay to the

Flame Bar and Cafe building (1938), 1521 Nicollet Avenue South.

south, while two residential districts to the west were divided by the Hennepin Avenue automobile sales district.

In the main business district were found the large department stores that had earlier relocated from lower Nicollet, the expensive small shops, and the large office buildings of banks, railroads, insurance companies, and the various commodity exchanges. In 1927 the Young-Quinlan building was built in the 900 block on Nicollet. The main business district also contained the government buildings and the larger hotels. The downtown afforded entertainment in the large movie houses and vaudeville theaters on Hennepin. The latter were drifting toward burlesque and featured a cruder sort of entertainment than most families wished to see. By the mid-thirties, the strength of the central district had begun to wane as the population moved toward the suburban fringe. The retail stores pursued the retreating population in a constant pattern. Beginning with a few general stores along Bridge Square, the stores, as we have seen, moved up Nicollet. The movement was led by the exclusive and expensive shops. The places the stores abandoned were taken over by operations selling a cheaper and lower quality line of goods. In 1850 the center of the shopping district was Washington and Nicollet Avenues. By 1910 it had moved to the southeast corner of Fourth and Nicollet. In 1935 it was on

the northeast corner of Seventh and Nicollet.

Observers of the city in these years did not expect a continuous movement of the retail district, because many of the shoppers were people who worked in nearby offices. Because these people walked to shop and because buildings as large as the department store could not be easily built in new sites, it was assumed that only the smaller expensive shops, which catered to women who drove downtown and therefore needed parking, would continue the move to the southwest. By the mid-thirties, parking was already a main concern for the central city business community.

The retail shops and banks were originally concentrated in Bridge Square. By 1880 the center of banking was at Washington and Hennepin, where nine banks operated within one block of each other. By 1935 their center had shifted to Fourth and Fifth Streets between Marquette and Second Avenue South. The banks had to be accessible to their largest patrons—therefore the shift to locate between the retail district and the diversified industrial district to the south. Other office functions sought locations similar to the banks' because they too wished to be accessible to their primary clients. Thus a generalized office district developed to the south of the primary shopping street.

The theaters followed the general movement from the lower loop, although they remained on Hennepin.

The hotels, which were originally clustered near the bridge, spread even farther than this. Although the cheaper hotels stayed near the office district, the luxury establishments like the Sir Francis Drake and the Sheridan moved well beyond the central business district to be near the auditorium.

As we have seen, the number of permanent residents of the district was declining. Those that remained had very definite characteristics, however. In the Gateway the population was overwhelmingly male and older. In the rest of the area, low-income whites dominated.

The decade of the 1930s was in general a period when Minneapolis, like other American cities, stagnated. The Foshay Tower, which had been dedicated with such enthusiasm and fanfare, lorded over the city's dull,

drab, and troubled central business and industrial districts. The automobile technology caused great increases in the rate of suburbanization of both residences and manufacturing establishments during the 1920s. The strength of downtown shopping centers was maintained by the growing presence of office workers, but it was clear that the most stylish stores would relocate as soon as economic conditions improved. The warehouse district just north of the city center was becoming obsolete as well. As the size of trucks increased, its narrow streets became even more congested and delivery time increased. Flour milling, the city's basic industry, was in decline and its future in the city was doubtful. The Gateway district was becoming more depressing and showed no signs of ever becoming the symbol of a bright, prosperous, and welcoming

Post Office (Magney and Tusler, 1931–33), 100 South 1st Street.

Emerson-Newton Implement Company (Kees and Colburn, 1904), 708 3rd Street South.

metropolis. In retrospect, it now seems as if Minneapolis really needed the war and the increased demand for labor, agriculture, goods, and machinery it produced. While the war increased people's incomes, the shortages and rationing prevented any new construction. The old city aged, but not gracefully, during these years.[24]

The Postwar or Freeway City

Although the years after World War II have brought great changes to the city, the continued growth envisioned by the planners and boasters of earlier days has not been realized. Instead, the population of the city has decreased. Changes in technology have made several major pieces of the economic landscape obsolete, and they have been abandoned. The fate of these once-crucial places has been either clearance or some tentative efforts at revitalization and reuse.

The pent-up demand for new housing and more accessible warehouses and factories was unleashed in the

F. C. Hayer Company building (Joseph Haley, 1886), 3rd Avenue North and 3rd Street.

Minneapolis Heat Regulator Company.

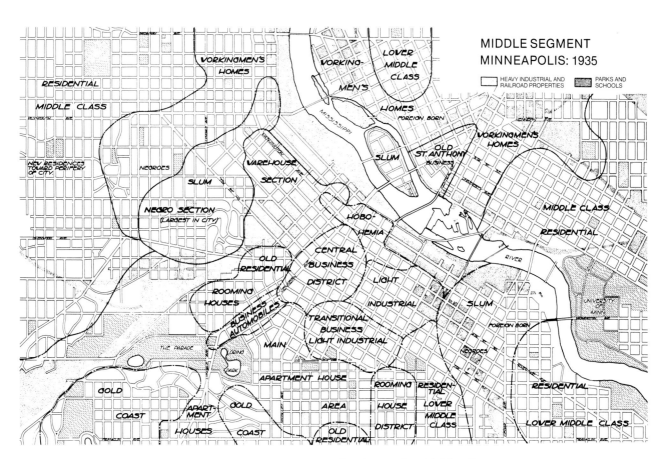

Land use and social delineation of the Minneapolis core area, 1935.

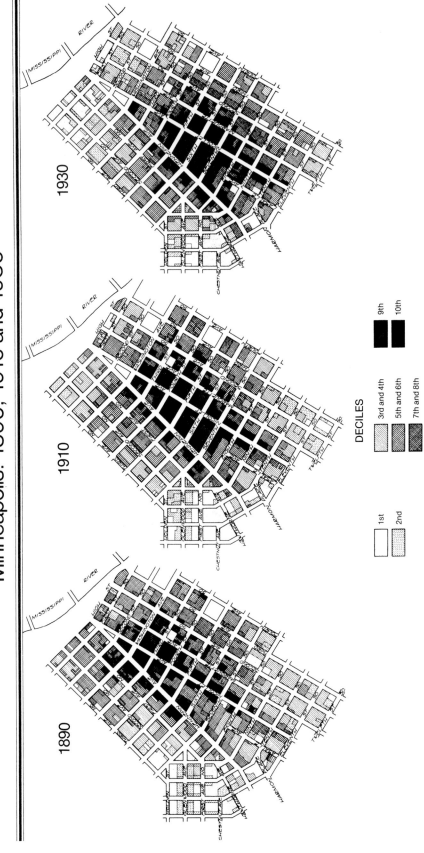

Land Values
Central Business District
Minneapolis: 1890, 1910 and 1930

1890

1910

1930

DECILES

1st

2nd

3rd and 4th

5th and 6th

7th and 8th

9th

10th

Downtown Minneapolis land values, 1890, 1910, 1930.

early 1950s. The result in Minneapolis was both start-ling and exciting. Two competing forces were at work transforming the landscape. Developers were rapidly building up the suburbs to the south of the city, where Victor Gruen's innovative enclosed shopping center, Southdale, was revolutionizing retailing. This movement was aided by the gradual construction of the freeway system. Countering this trend was the formation of a public-private partnership led by the Downtown Council, which produced a concerted effort to rebuild and revitalize the central city. The most recent event in the thirty-year struggle between downtown and the suburbs is the relocation of the metropolitan area's prime sports facility—the stadium—into the downtown.

The Contemporary City Center

The rebuilding of the central area has been guided by three major plans produced by the city planning department under the leadership of its then-director, Larry Irvine. When he was hired, Irvine brought to the city a sense of what can be accomplished when the public and private sectors collaborate, as well as an understanding of planning methodology. The plans, the Central Minneapolis Plan (1959) (never adopted), Metro Center '85 (1968), and Minneapolis Metro Center: 1990 (1978), all resulted from an extensive research effort and a program of community input. They share several common themes, which have provided the basic elements in the redevelopment program. These elements are:

1. Downtown Minneapolis should remain the most important place in the upper Midwest.
2. The city center should be compact, with related activities located close together.
3. Accessibility in the center should be improved. An important feature of improved accessibility is the separation of pedestrian and automobile traffic, with the construction of fringe parking facilities and a carefully orchestrated program of street im-provements, many of which were first set forth in the street plans of 1924 and 1940.
4. The downtown should be a place for people and should provide a range of cultural, entertainment, and residential facilities.
5. The public-private partnership should continue.

   Although the 1959 plan was not formally adopted, it had tremendous impact on the city. It set the tone for all subsequent planning and contained several key pro-posals. One of them, the Nicollet Mall, has a dramatic effect on downtown. The plan is unabashedly optimistic. It opens with the statement, "This is a plan for growth"—strong words during a time when suburbaniza-

tion was rampant, with Southdale growing, and shortly after the time when General Mills' headquarters moved out of downtown in favor of the western suburbs. These planners looked ahead "to a future containing many problems and much promise." The writers also proudly said, "Central Minneapolis is the most important area in the entire Upper Midwest."

There were several problems identified in the plan, however. First was the stagnation of office space expansion. Between 1947 and 1958, office space in the core expanded at a rate of one percent per year (for an annual average of 38,000 square feet). At the same time, office space in the outlying district expanded at a rate of one hundred percent per year (for an annual average of 75,000 square feet). During that period, two-thirds of the office space built in the Minneapolis area was in the outlying area. Furthermore, the planned clearance of the Gateway area would eventually remove about 300,000 square feet of lower-rent office space. Retailing along Nicollet had experienced gains in sales per capita of Minneapolis residents; but when the suburban centers began to open in 1954, sales slowed down. For the entire period, however, the sales in the central business district were stable. To make matters worse, the standing stock of buildings was in poor condition. Fully one-half of the buildings devoted to retail sales or to mixed retail and office use were classified as being in poor to bad condition and marked as a liability to the area. There had been no new hotel construction since the twenties, and the traditional industries no longer were important generators of employment. Most of the housing was in poor condition, and further blight was expected unless large numbers of buildings were removed. Cultural facilities were judged to be non-existent within the central area, and traffic congestion was made worse by the large number of vehicles passing through the center without stopping. In sum, the plan concluded that tremendous forces in society were working against the growth of the central area.

The planning department's responses to the goals and problems were to call for (1) a bypass or ring route—a suggestion first made in the street plan of 1924; (2) a freeway terminal—large parking facilities connected to centers of employment by an internal circulation system; (3) encouragement of high density building; (4) further efforts to renew the Gateway district; (5) development of a park on Nicollet Island; (6) a series of second-level sidewalks, skyways; and (7) promotion of the Nicollet Mall project.

The Nicollet Mall was the first of its kind estab-lished in a large American city. It was viewed as the highest priority project because it was expected to strengthen downtown retailing and make the downtown more attractive for other workers. The plan stated that

Changing Institutional Patterns
Central Business District
Minneapolis, Minnesota

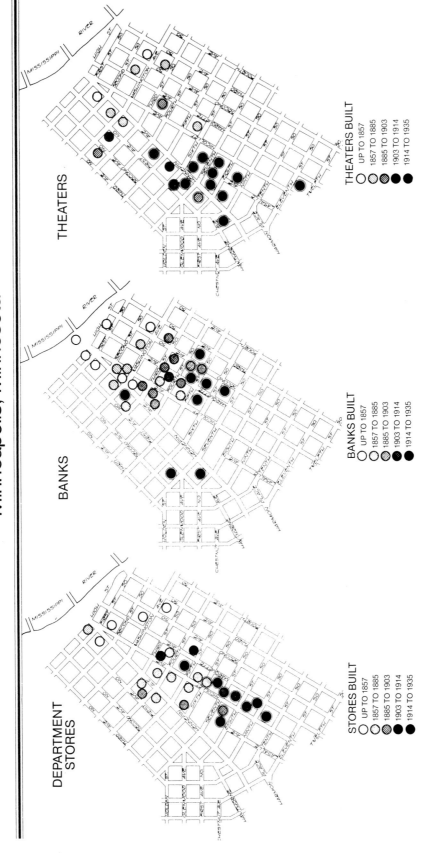

DEPARTMENT STORES

STORES BUILT
○ UP TO 1857
○ 1857 TO 1885
⊕ 1885 TO 1903
● 1903 TO 1914
● 1914 TO 1935

BANKS

BANKS BUILT
○ UP TO 1857
○ 1857 TO 1885
⊕ 1885 TO 1903
● 1903 TO 1914
● 1914 TO 1935

THEATERS

THEATERS BUILT
○ UP TO 1857
○ 1857 TO 1885
⊕ 1885 TO 1903
● 1903 TO 1914
● 1914 TO 1935

Land use changes by economic category, downtown Minneapolis.

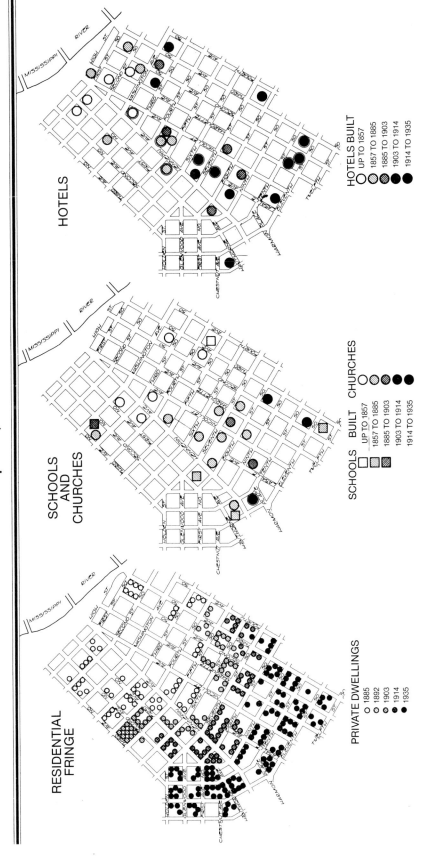

Changing Institutional Patterns
Central Business District
Minneapolis, Minnesota

HOTELS

HOTELS BUILT
- UP TO 1857
- 1857 TO 1885
- 1885 TO 1903
- 1903 TO 1914
- 1914 TO 1935

SCHOOLS AND CHURCHES

SCHOOLS BUILT   CHURCHES
- UP TO 1857
- 1857 TO 1885
- 1885 TO 1903
- 1903 TO 1914
- 1914 TO 1935

RESIDENTIAL FRINGE

PRIVATE DWELLINGS
- 1885
- 1892
- 1903
- 1914
- 1935

Land use changes by
economic category, downtown
Minneapolis.

Legacy of the Working City · 49

the future attractiveness and economic well-being of the city center depended on the mall. It was expected to be successful because the city's shopping area was already compact, containing eighty percent of all retail space, and the street had the highest volume of pedestrian traffic in the city. The mall was designed by the firm of Lawrence Halpin. Construction began in 1963, with the city as general contractor, and was completed in 1968.

Most of the suggestions made in this plan have been implemented; the mall, the skyways, the ring road, and the convention center have been built. The street improvements have been made and the clearance programs accomplished.

The eradication of old Minneapolis did evoke some resistance in 1959, when plans to tear down the old Guaranty Loan building, or as it was then named, the Metropolitan building, were announced. The Hennepin County Historical Society, journalists, and citizens interested in architecture tried to pressure the city council into reversing the decision of the city's housing and redevelopment authority (HRA), but to no avail. In an unsigned article in the *South Minneapolis Shopping Guide* of February 7, 1961, a commentator wrote, "It may be characteristic of our times to demolish and destroy, just as we exhausted our natural resources, but is it really advisable to butcher a building like this one to satisfy some commercial interests? . . . change referred to as progress seems necessary irrespective of the consequences." The writer proposed the building be converted to a historical museum to be owned and operated by the city, if indeed the structure could not be made profitable. The cause was taken up in the courts, but the Minnesota Supreme Court upheld HRA's right to condemn it. In December 1961 the demolition process began.

For the most part the new building brought about by the city's planning effort was greeted with enthusiasm. The First National Bank building (1959) was of an innovative design and in sharp contrast with the notion that a bank building must look like a pile of rock in order to inspire trust. Further evidence of the increased importance of the financial activities of the city was the construction of the Northwestern National Life Insurance building in 1963 and the Federal Reserve Bank in 1968–72.

Metro Center '85, a sumptuous plan, was published in 1970. In many respects it is a testimony to the expansive governmental programs of the 1960s. It is an exciting document, calling forth a vision of a beautiful, upbeat, and humane city center. The federal government had provided the city with the tools for redevelopment—the urban renewal act of 1949 and the interstate highway program launched in 1956. Although these programs had been used to clear the Gateway area

First National Bank (Holabird, Root, and Burgee; Thorsov and Cerny, 1959), 120 South 6th Street.

and build some public housing, the full impact of the freeway system was yet to come. This plan makes a great departure from the earlier document because it has sections devoted to social planning, the most important of which dealt with job training for the unemployed.

The writers of the plan clearly felt good about the city's recent past; but they believed that if the future revitalization of the central area was to be successful, it would require community support as well as careful planning. The planning called for was clearly underway, but community support for large government programs was hard to win in the tumultuous early 1970s.

The center's strong points continued to be its compactness and the new attitudes of the community. Government services had expanded greatly during the 1960s. New office space was being constructed at a great rate. Since 1960, 2.4 million square feet had been constructed; and by 1970, one-half of the office space in the metro area was downtown. Although retail establishments continued to leave the center area, a fourteen-percent increase was enjoyed by those that remained.

Metro Center '85: Aerial view of Minneapolis, 1970s.

This increase was largely attributed to the mall.

The effort to make the city a national convention center was bearing fruit. A total of 1240 motel and hotel rooms had been added and $16 million spent improving the convention facilities. Industry and warehousing continued to decline, however, and the downtown housing stock was in a state of flux. Perhaps one of the most important steps in the redevelopment of the city was the passage of a new zoning law in 1963, which greatly improved the existing set of rules, definitions, and processes.

The plan of 1970 set out to encourage the growth and location in the city center of administrative and financial institutions, as well as cultural and service establishments. To the basic ideas of improved transportation, clustering of functions, compactness, and diversity, this plan added concern for design and visual identity and for air quality, as well as a hope for a mass-transit system. Finally, a great cultural center on the site of the old Milwaukee Station was envisioned. This

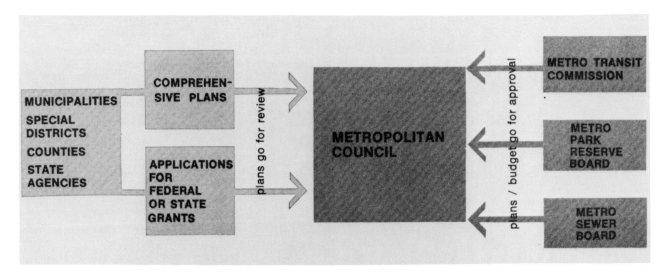

Metro Center '85:
Organizational structure for
metropolitan development.

development was to include a symphony hall, two theaters for legitimate productions, an art museum, and a large multipurpose exhibit hall for a museum of science and technology, as well as promenades and parks along the river front. It also called for the development of a bright-light entertainment district along Hennepin Avenue that would serve a varied clientele.

New housing was encouraged so as to give the downtown a nighttime population. Thus new housing was expected in the Gateway area, where the River Towers apartments were built in 1964; along the riverfront; adjacent to Loring Park; and in Elliot Park.

Industrial redevelopment was expected to occur to the north of downtown, and between downtown and the University of Minnesota campus in an area called Industry Square. These new areas were hoped to generate needed jobs for the population of the older neighborhoods ringing downtown.

Between the publication of the 1970 plan and the publication of the latest plan in 1978, some thirty major buildings were added to the city skyline.

Although the record of buildings added to the city is impressive, several events made a new plan for downtown a necessity in 1978. The now-famous energy crises and double-digit inflation, a growing interest in historical preservation, and the construction of major buildings that either were unforeseen in 1968 or were built in places other than the sites initially proposed, made new effort mandatory.

Furthermore, the IDS Center (1973) had been a tremendous success, perhaps even more successful than originally expected. It ties together the skyway system and provides both visual and behavioral focus for the city. Its construction, together with that of the Federal Reserve Bank (1970) and the Peavey building, set up a series of office relocations that lasted nearly the entire decade. In the late seventies another set of large office buildings was constructed, which has set in motion a second wave of relocations.

The recession of 1972–73 put a halt to many new projects; but when it ended, a boom of residential building around Loring Park got underway. For many years, however, housing for the elderly was all that was constructed downtown.

Unanticipated in the early plans were Orchestra Hall in its present location, the hospital complex, and of course the Hubert H. Humphrey Metrodome (1982). Although the skyways have been extremely successful, the expected mass-transit program did not materialize. The freeway terminal concept is very much alive, and the construction of the Third Avenue distributor will fulfill the very early visions of an integrated internal and external transportation network serving the city center.

The net result of the change during the 1970s was a somewhat larger and apparently economically stronger downtown. The ambience of the city had clearly been improved by the addition of open spaces, plazas, and Orchestra Hall.

The Minneapolis Metro Center plan for 1990 contains 123 general planning principles that when applied to specific areas and projects will provide for a city that will continue to make downtown the center of the upper

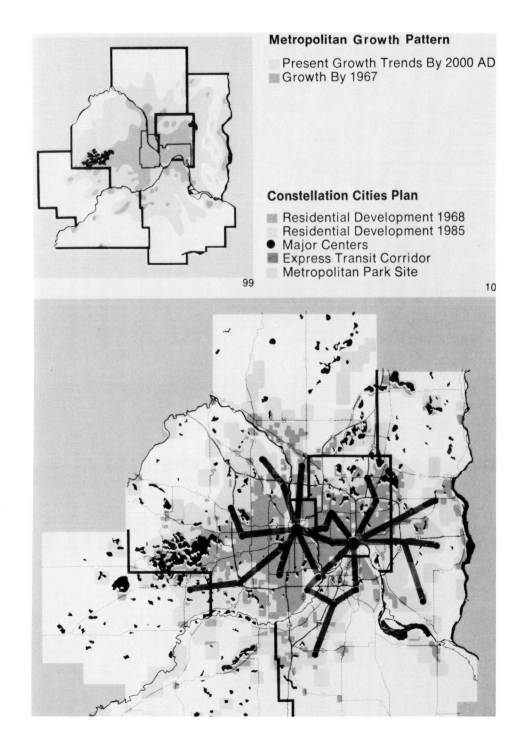

Metropolitan Growth Pattern

Present Growth Trends By 2000 AD
Growth By 1967

Constellation Cities Plan

Residential Development 1968
Residential Development 1985
● Major Centers
Express Transit Corridor
Metropolitan Park Site

99

10

Map of office, retail, and entertainment districts from Metro Center '85.

Midwest. The plan for 1990 calls for a compact downtown tied together by a series of attractive and comfortable pedestrian routes—a city designed to maximize opportunities for human interaction. Retail activity will remain concentrated along Nicollet and will be enhanced by the addition of new department stores. Along the Marquette–Second Avenue corridor, office space will be concentrated. Medical services will remain concentrated

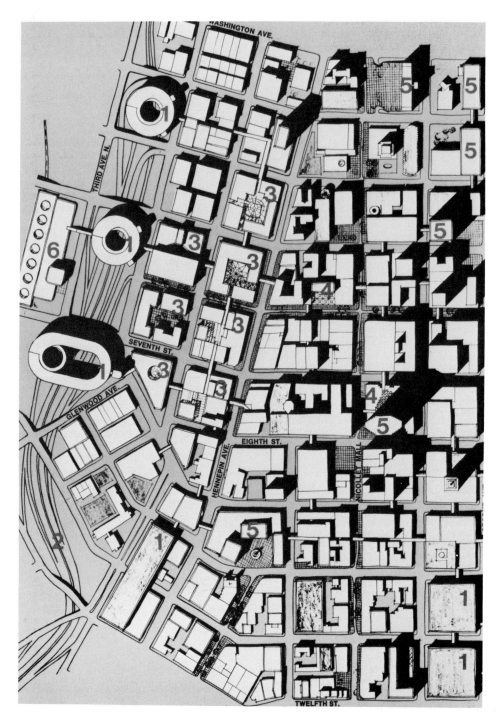

Table from 1978 plan of new buildings in downtown.

near Elliot Park. More hotel rooms are anticipated, in fact needed, if the city is to become a national convention center. The plan calls for a revitalized Hennepin Avenue, much transformed from its late-seventies character.

Planning efforts during the 1980s will be project oriented. The areas of primary concern are the riverfront and the Hennepin Avenue entertainment district. The spectacular housing developments around Loring Park are clearly a success. The Third Avenue North

Metro Center '85: Riverfront.

The Riverfront

In 1972 the new plan for the riverfront was announced. Entitled "Mississippi/Minneapolis," the plan contained several features reminiscent of the plan proposed in 1917. The river will be made accessible and a great deal of housing will be provided – some two thousand units. While the new density matches the old concept, the building styles will be extremely different. In addition, instead of the old structures being removed as was advocated in 1917, many are to be reused and reconstructed. While there will be no Olympic Stadium on Nicollet Island, it will be developed as a park. The function of this part of the river is to be redefined. Instead of being an area of heavy industry, it will become a mixed commercial-residential district focused on the amenities of the riverfront rather than the utility of the falls.

Flour production at the falls fell steadily after 1930. Mills closed down and several structures on the west bank (Anchor, Cataract, and Pillsbury B) were torn down, as was the Phoenix mill on the east side. In 1965 milling on the west bank ended entirely. Only the Pillsbury A remains in operation. The waterpower at the falls was converted to hydroelectricity by 1960.

An attempt to revitalize the commercial activities along the Mississippi was made in the fifties and earlier when local congressmen were finally successful in the efforts to convince the federal government to build locks around the falls. When the locks were completed in 1963, extravagant claims were made about the impact the so-called upper harbors project would have on the city. Representative Walter Judd went as far as to say, "I don't know of any public works appropriation that I voted for that will bring as many benefits as this one in the next 50 or 100 years."[25] clearly, we must wait a while to see if he was correct, because nearly twenty years after the completion of the locks, industry has all but vanished from the riverbanks. The primary traffic through the locks is coal for Northern States Power generation plants and scrap iron from the North Minneapolis junkyards.

The scrapyards along North Washington are the latest phase in the cycle of land use along the river above the falls. Like the brickyards and sawmills before them, these operations need large areas of land at low cost. Because their product is bulky and of relatively low value, river barges are an efficient form of transportation. However, the junkyards are there because until now the riverbanks were not highly valued.

The plans for the falls area call for developing a mixed residential and commercial area of high density but preserving vistas along the river. Building programs on the east bank are well developed and will be discussed in the subsequent chapter on neighborhoods.

Conclusion

Although the city has experienced a continuous process

Downtown Minneapolis today.

of development and change, this survey of its history has been organized around six eras of varying length, during which important changes in the pace or direction of change occurred. In the first period, the commercial function around the falls and what was to become downtown was organized. In the era of consolidation, during the late 1860s and early 1870s, the city was connected to an agricultural hinterland. Sawmilling and flour milling were established at the falls. In the era of commercial expansion (1880s and 1890s), the city entered its golden age when fortunes were made and the population boomed. This period ended at the turn of the century. After that date the city continued to prosper and grow, but at a lower rate. The first two decades of the twentieth century witnessed an expansion of downtown and the suburbanization of the industrial activity. The fifth era lasted from 1917 to 1947. It was marked by an increase in suburbanization, brought about by greater use of the automobile and the development of city planning. Finally, the city of today, dominated by freeways, new buildings downtown, and an exciting plan for a revitalized riverfront oriented around residential and recreational activities, emerged after World War II.

PART 3

Legacy of the
Neighborhoods

Creating the Mosaic

"Minneapolis has been especially blessed since the date of its first settlement, for numbering among its citizens men peculiarly gifted in organizing and bringing to fruition large enterprises."[1]

Isaac Atwater
1893

WHILE GIFTED MEN built up their large Minneapolis enterprises, many others also labored to make those efforts successful. Everyone—ordinary citizens and leaders—made decisions about where and how to live. Together they left us a residential landscape that has always spread out from the core and filled the land between the rail corridors. In the beginning, the pioneer commercial and industrial core at St. Anthony Falls occupied only a tiny part of today's central district. The surrounding houses were also scattered within what is now central Minneapolis. In that small, simple residential compound the creation of today's vast, complex mosaic of neighborhoods began.

THE EARLY SETTLERS

The pioneer settlers of St. Anthony and of Minneapolis had city-building on their minds. They came from New England, with names like Atwater, Cheever, Gale, Hoag, Northrup, and Russell. They came with backgrounds in business or training in the law, intending to prosper in their chosen careers and to create a city they could be proud of at the same time. What they found when they arrived was a small town: St. Anthony had 538 residents in 1850, while Minneapolis remained off limits to settlers. The

magnificent waterpower site at the falls inspired great confidence in many early residents, instilling in them a belief that a place with such a resource had to succeed, despite the odds. As a later observer described, the process of growth in these years was evolutionary: "Gradually the young community took on the appearance of an eastern village. From log cabins the style changed to the white painted cottages of New England, where most of the settlers began life."[2]

Memoirs of the early years underscore the difficulty of life in any pioneer settlement. One woman remembered that in the winter of 1849, milk cost 50¢ per quart (about $2.75 in 1980 currency).[3] Harlow Gale, in writing to his future wife soon after his arrival in 1857, told of financial failures brought on by the absence of any local banks. In Gale's mind, though, financial difficulties were far outbalanced by the beauty of the land and by his optimism about the future: "There are two hotels going up, one 100 by 120 feet; the other, 100 by 166 feet; three churches; schoolhouses and dwellings daily and nightly. Oh, we have a beautiful town! . . . This will surprise Millbury friends, who think I am among Indians and wolves and a fit residence only for either culprit or cannibal."[4]

Gale went on to describe the social life of this pioneer community, writing of evenings filled up with political speeches, singing, churchgoing, and partygoing. The impressions received from such descriptions are ones of hardy people determined to imprint civilization on the wilderness. As one writer quoted from an early St. Anthony newspaper, "Slowly but steadily a cosmopolitan influence and spirit is gaining ground."[5] This cosmopolitan tone was verified by the fact that through-

Bridge Square, 1870s.

out St. Anthony in the early 1850s, brick structures were already replacing the frame buildings of the frontier town.

St. Anthony had a ten-year jump on the west side of the river, which remained under military control until 1850. When the west side of the river opened for settlement, it soon generated two centers: one at Bridge Square, where the suspension bridge from St. Anthony landed on the west side, and the other below the falls, at about Tenth Avenue South. The Bridge Square site soon took precedence over the other centers, eventually becoming the core of downtown Minneapolis. Even the most optimistic of the early residents could not imagine how successful their new home would become. As the *Minneapolis Tribune* in 1911 quoted an old settler, "It was foreign to the minds of Bridge and First Street merchants that business would ever be extended as far out as Washington Avenue and never did they dream that the site of the Milwaukee railroad station and tracks would be used for such a purpose on so unsightly a marsh. . . . Even as late as 1870 a thought was

hardly given to Nicollet Avenue as a business street. Hennepin Avenue made no claim to being a business street, but predicted that it would be the fashionable residence portion of the city."[6]

Impressive levels of growth seemed to be mandated for the small settlements at the falls. Between 1850 and 1860, the two towns increased their combined populations by almost one thousand percent. The numbers were not that large—an increase of 5,344 persons was unimpressive compared to later decades—but they did indicate the future directions of both towns. Minneapolis was incorporated in 1855 and soon began drawing most newcomers across the river. "Many of the settlers recorded as coming to St. Anthony only made it a stopping place until they could secure a foothold on the west side of the river. . . . Some spent part of their time in St. Anthony and part on their potential farms."[7] When title was finally cleared to the land on the west side of the river, settlers hastily claimed land wherever they could. Some of them became rich as a result.

One of these pioneers tells of pushing through the mud

between Harriet and Calhoun, then through an almost impenetrable jungle, to reach a hundred and sixty acres for which he had paid three hundred dollars. Now he is about to plat that piece and sell it at two thousand dollars an acre he smiles to recall his early feelings. When he arrived and saw the land all covered with great trees and a jungle of brush he wept bitter tears at having been cheated. Another pioneer relates that he refused the lots near where the Nicollet House now stands in payment for a cow "because they were covered with water and cattails."[8]

It should be noted that the lots this poor fellow refused were near the intersection of Washington Avenue and Nicollet.

Among the first generation in Minneapolis, it would be unusual to find someone with one career only. Almost everyone could claim multiple interests, both financial and civic. Those who started the lumber and flour milling businesses also had money invested in railroads. Doctors, lawyers, and businessmen served as mayors and aldermen, as well as starting most of the cultural institutions (for example, the library, the art

institute, most churches). Even those who came with established careers often gave them up and started something else on arriving here. Samuel Chute did this on settling in St. Anthony in 1857. Trained as a physician, he became one of the foremost real estate brokers of Minneapolis. Indeed, nearly everyone seemed to have been buying and selling real estate during the years up to 1890. The early settlers usually acquired large tracts of land when first filing claims. Joel Bassett, for example, once controlled a chunk of land on the west bank of the Mississippi from the creek that bears his name up to West Broadway. Even small claims were impressive by our standards—Edward Murphy had only 80 acres, but it included all of the land currently occupied by Augsburg College, Fairview and St. Mary's hospitals, and Riverside Park.

Many things have been written about the first generation of settlers in St. Anthony and Minneapolis. They are generally conceded to have been hardworking, successful, and full of foresight. There is no doubt that they excelled at building institutions that would endure, along with their business enterprises. Why they so con-

Stevens house (1849); moved to Minnehaha Park, 1896.

Morrison house (1858); on site of Minneapolis Institute of Arts.

sciously created these institutions is less clear. Undoubtedly the process of creating and building churches, of starting the university, and of putting together the art resources that led to the founding of museums helped people who were living in a frontier setting to feel some connections with the towns and cities they had left. But some of the reason for the flurry of "founding" activities also had to do with *who* these people were and how they viewed themselves. Referring to the end of the first group of migrants (which included the Pillsburys and Washburns), Horace Hudson wrote in 1908, "The families who came here, from 1854 to 1860, and laid the foundations of the Minneapolis to be, were in character and culture the choicest product of the east. No new settlement ever showed a larger proportion of college men and cultivated women. Indeed, it may be doubted whether the official and intellectual status of Minneapolis has ever since averaged as high as during those six earliest years."[9]

Perhaps the greatest need in the first years of settlement, aside from food, was for shelter. The earliest migrants lived in quickly constructed frame dwellings that were notable for their simplicity. The emphasis was on shelter from cold and rain, rather than on style. Almost none of the earliest landscape remains today, except in rare photographs. The only physical remains

are the Godfrey and Stevens houses, in Chute Square and Minnehaha Park respectively. Both are small, very unpretentious clapboard structures, notable only because they have survived as long as they have. The need for shelter was dealt with simply—by building houses. There was nothing "planned" about this period of development; people built houses wherever they could get title to land. Those who came here in the 1840s and 1850s had to be prepared to be inconvenienced a bit. Some camped outside while constructing their dwellings; others boarded in lodging houses or with newfound acquaintances. Those who came with sufficient economic resources stayed in one of the early hotels, often for months at a time.

EMBRYONIC URBAN PATTERN

The pattern of land use in the early years was quite mixed. Houses, stores, and industries were all located close together. Neighborhoods, as we understand them, were nonexistent. People of all economic categories lived near one another because everyone needed to be close to the two town centers and to the industries along the river. Before the 1870s there was little or no economic segregation, partially because there were few very wealthy people. The fortunes that were to be made were just beginning to appear then; before that virtually everyone was dependent on credit from the East. There were few examples of people moving far away from the small centers on the river in the early years, unless they intended to farm. Dorilus Morrison stands out precisely because he did what few others did: In 1858 Morrison built a home, Villa Rosa, on ten acres at what became 24th Street (now the site of the Minneapolis Institute of Arts). Morrison was a businessman and civic leader, not a farmer, and it is unclear why he moved so far away from the center of activity, where he spent most of his working hours. Few others are recorded as having been so adventurous.

Improvements in building technology during the early years of settlement helped change the face of both towns. People who had committed themselves to living here wanted to make their surroundings as permanent as possible. Consequently, the frontier structures of the early years were usually replaced within a decade or two. Brick and stone were increasingly used for commercial structures and for the homes of the well-off citizens. Frame construction came to be used primarily for residences before very long. When Minneapolis and St. Anthony were incorporated into one city in 1872,

Nicollet Avenue, 1903.

most of the old town centers had been, or were being, rebuilt with two- and three-story brick or stone commercial structures. Residences were slowly being squeezed out to the periphery of the old centers. On the west side of the river, this meant that new residential construction of the 1870s was occurring on 6th and 7th Streets, rather than nearer the river.

One consequence of this rapid rebuilding process was that it wiped out much of the original towns of St. Anthony and Minneapolis. Only the most "sentimental" of this generation of buildings remains—but not even on their original sites (for example, the Stevens House, which was moved once to make way for the Union Depot,[10] and then again to ensure its salvation). In their zeal to build a city of importance, the early settlers of Minneapolis quite understandably lacked any interest in preserving much of what they first built. In many ways the generations that followed were not much better at this task. The first generation of Minneapolis buildings were disposed of, at least in part because the people who built them never thought of them as permanent. They wanted to be remembered by structures that looked more enduring than the frame houses and stores that first appeared. The two- and three-story masonry buildings constructed near Bridge Square in the 1870s and 1880s probably presented the image that the founding generation wanted to project. Unfortunately, very little of the "second generation" of Minneapolis buildings remains today either. In a continuing fit of zeal to clean up downtown, most of these structures were removed during the large Gateway clearance of the 1960s.

Throughout the 1870s, and even a bit earlier, Minneapolis began to go through a series of adjustments that signaled its transition from a small town to a growing city. The sense that lingers on about this period is one of incredible possibility, but tempered by outside events that affected residents. One series of events that the city responded to was the Indian raids of the 1860s. Though these did not actually touch Minneapolis, the city sheltered those who fled the countryside for safety. They served as a reminder that Minneapolis, though rapidly changing, was still on the frontier, and still subject to frontier experiences.

Winslow House (1856), above Main Street Southeast and west of Central Avenue.

62 · *Legacy of the Neighborhoods*

Panorama, Minneapolis, 1879.

Another event that was felt in the city even though it occurred far away was the Civil War. Hostilities between the North and the South effectively closed river commerce between these parts of the country, and so ended Minneapolis's heyday as a tourist mecca for Southerners. An early Minneapolis landmark, the Winslow House—whose primary market was tourists from the South—eventually went bankrupt due to cessation of river traffic. City residents were beginning to realize their connections to the rest of the country, even though they felt removed from it. The major transition for Minneapolis in that period was undoubtedly the appearance of the institutions that would shape the city for years to come. The banks, the railroads, and the industrial empires based on milling and processing were beginning to make their presence felt through the decisions investors made about where to locate, how much to expand, and how the companies would involve themselves in the daily workings of the city.

GROWING POPULATION

The population of Minneapolis continued to increase dramatically throughout the late nineteenth century. By 1870, slightly more than eighteen thousand people lived in the as-yet-unconsolidated two towns. For the most part, the sources of immigration continued to be the eastern United States and Canada, though some numbers of Germans also showed up in the early years. What stands out most clearly about the immigration of these years versus that of the post-1880 period was its pronounced non-Scandinavian cast. If the founding of churches is used as a guide—considering that in the nineteenth century, churches were one of the first cultural resources to appear in any community—Minneapolis stands out as an Anglo-Saxon Protestant town. The first church to appear was a Catholic one, situated on Pierre Bottineau's claim in what became Northeast Minneapolis. The only other church of an identifiably ethnic character before 1860 was a Norwegian Lutheran congregation, also located in

Northeast. Every other church at that time was Anglo-Saxon Protestant: Presbyterians (one congregation), Congregationalists (two), Episcopalians (three), Baptists (three), and Universalists (one). During the 1860s, each of these groups increased in number, as did the Catholics, and a Quaker congregation also appeared. The German Lutherans established two churches in this decade.[11] It was not until the late 1870s and the 1880s that large numbers of Lutheran churches began to appear, signaling the full-scale migration of Scandinavians to Minneapolis.

The 1870s were a time of growth, but also a time of consolidation. Minneapolis was beginning to take on the aspect of a city during this decade, as large houses were built on the southern end of what is now downtown and the business district was established. The very fact that houses were being pushed away from Bridge Square by commercial uses underscores the specialization of space that was occurring. Photographs of Minneapolis in the late 1870s depict a recognizable nineteenth-century urban landscape: three- and four-story masonry buildings next to remnants of the one- and two-story frame structures from an earlier time, and even then, a feeling of the built-up area extending far into the distance. Though sidewalks are prominent in most of these views, the streets are clearly unpaved and full of ruts.

The process of city building, particularly during the 1870s, was a very self-conscious one. Minneapolis residents demonstrated their desire to achieve a cosmopolitan feeling in many ways, but did this most clearly in their efforts to bring "city" amenities to the frontier town as quickly as possible. For example, Alexander Graham Bell invented the telephone in 1875, and Minneapolis had a working telephone exchange by 1878. It connected two hotels, the city jail, the Pillsbury mills, two livery services, a restaurant, a grocery, a meat market, and a doctor.[12] The city adopted electric lights just as rapidly. Thomas Edison's system was perfected in 1879, and by 1883 Washington Avenue was brightly lit at night.[13] Similar progressive measures were undertaken to provide a modern water system and to electrify the street railway system when that became possible. All of these efforts underscore the attitudes that Minneapolis residents displayed toward the idea of progress. They were in favor of it and of almost anything that would make their city resemble (in a good way) the cities of the East, which many of them knew well.

By the early 1880s the "boom" was on for Minneapolis. In that decade the most spectacular numerical growth occurred. Between 1880 and 1890, Minneapolis grew by more than two hundred fifty percent, an increase of about twelve thousand people per year. These were the years in which important advances in milling technology created a prominent place in the American economy for the city. These were also the years in which the dominant settlement patterns of Minneapolis's neighborhoods were established.

The rapid influx of people during the 1880s underscored dramatically the need for quickly built housing in almost every part of the city. The need for shelter was an immediate one and was most often met in an ad hoc fashion. During this decade entire neighborhoods of small frame houses were built in places like Phillips and Seward in South Minneapolis, through lower Northeast, and along the length of the river through North Minneapolis. It is remarkable that such a quantity of housing got built in such a short period of time. One historian explained the ability of the city to accomplish this task in the following way:

Lumber was at hand for a building boom in residential construction which would be unequalled for three quarters of a century. To illustrate the magnitude of this boom, consider the year 1882 when Minneapolis was one of the largest lumber producers in the world. Of the 314 million odd board feet of lumber produced that year nearly all of it went into construction of the buildings in the Twin Cities area. . . . The average three bedroom "ranch" home being constructed today requires approximately 20,000 board feet of lumber. Simple arithmetic indicates that 15,000 houses could be built with this quantity of lumber, or that in the single year of 1882 lumber from Minneapolis mills could have built the entire present day suburb of Bloomington![14]

Another method of meeting the pressing needs for

MINNEAPOLIS POPULATION

Year	Population	% Growth
1850	538	
1860	5882	933%
1870	18080	207%
1880	46887	159%
1890	164738	251%
1900	202718	23%
1910	301408	49%
1920	380582	26%
1930	464356	22%
1940	492370	6%
1950	521718	6%
1960	482872	-7%
1970	434400	-10%
1980	370951	-15%

Romanesque Revival apartment flats (T. A. Clark, 1888), corner Chicago Avenue South and 10th Street. Typical of core area development in 1880s.

shelter during the 1880s—today a fairly uncommon one—was to move structures from one place to another. Most of the pressure for rebuilding naturally occurred in the downtown area, where most existing housing was located. Instead of existing houses being torn down, often they were simply picked up and moved to new locations where the need for housing was great. As one observer noted, "In the eighties the streets were not infrequently obstructed with these traveling homes— many of them in a condition which would warrant instant demolition. But since it was a problem to house the people who wanted to live in Minneapolis, can the Minneapolitans be blamed for saving everything that offered a roof for the protection of more 'population'?"[15]

It is due to this moving phenomenon that many older structures appear in many parts of the city where they seem just a bit out of place if one looks closely. For example, there are four Italianate cottages in the Seward area, rumored to have been moved from the site of the new city hall sometime in the 1880s. These houses obviously date from the 1870s, and it is just as obvious that during that time virtually no one lived in what is now Seward. A storefront structure in that same area is said to have been moved in from the Cedar-Riverside area when brick structures replaced the frame stores of Cedar Avenue. It was not uncommon for churches to be moved as well. As downtown Protestant

congregations prospered and outgrew their old churches, these buildings were often sold to other congregations and moved to outlying parts of the city. Bethlehem Presbyterian Church, for example, owned lots near 26th Street and Pleasant Avenue; when Westminster Presbyterian Church got ready to move to a new church structure at 7th and Nicollet, the old church on 4th Street was given to the Bethlehem congregation and moved out to South Minneapolis.[16]

Perhaps the most outstanding characteristic of the boom period of settlement, to modern eyes, was its unplanned nature. No environmental impact statements were filed to determine what could be built, nor were studies carried on to recommend where people should live. There was no overall plan for sorting out and settling the immense numbers of people pouring into the city during these years. Most often people settled wherever they could find housing that they could afford, near places of work or institutions that they valued. Many newcomers, and especially the Scandinavians who spoke little or no English, used the standard immigrant method of finding shelter: They contacted someone they knew or someone whose name had been given to them, sought the person's advice, and often ended up living with that person until more adequate housing could be found. Carl Hansen described this process for his own family's arrival in Minneapolis during these years, and indicated that their experiences were quite the norm.[17] Churches that offered services in a foreign language were a strong attraction to many new residents, and often the presence of these institutions could entirely account for the ethnic makeup of an area (for instance, St. Joseph's Catholic Church in the German section of North Minneapolis and Augustana Swedish Lutheran Church in the heart of Scandinavian South Minneapolis).

The unplanned nature of Minneapolis's development during the 1880s had some unfortunate consequences in later years. Park Avenue, for example, was just being built up as a stylish, high-income boulevard at this time. As the wealthy residential areas along 7th, 8th, 9th, and 10th Streets downtown were taken over by business enterprises, some of these folks decided to move "to the country"—to Park Avenue's wide, inviting, and genteel landscape. Over the next twenty years quite large, often architect-designed, houses were spaced between Franklin Avenue and 26th Street by people who were bank officers and industry executives. But the building boom here was short-lived, and it changed character steadily after the turn of the century. The last of the great Park Avenue houses was constructed in 1921. Even by 1910, many houses in the immediate area were being converted into multifamily dwellings as more areas offering high-income housing were developed elsewhere in the city.

POPULATION EXPLOSION, AREAL EXPANSION

As the population of Minneapolis exploded during the 1880s, it was no longer possible to build most new structures near the center of the city. People began to search for housing away from downtown in all directions. This was possible because the real estate entrepreneurs had already crossed the landscape of the city and had begun to lay out subdivisions for all levels of society. One of these developers, Henry Beard, typified the activities of his contemporaries. Beard settled in Minneapolis for the second time in 1882; he had spent most of the 1870s in Minneapolis engaged in the insurance business, before returning East to become a minister. On Beard's return, real estate drew his interest. As Atwater described his career:

> He bought lands in the newer parts of the city and made improvements. He developed the property along the bluff on Lowry Hill, grading Mount Curve Avenue at his own expense. On the east side of the river he invaded the sand prairie sloping up the bluff, and laid out New Boston. Here he built one hundred houses and made the locality accessible by securing an extension of the street railway. He also graded the street and built the first houses at Lake of the Isles. On Block 111 of

Henry Beard.

the town of Minneapolis, situated on Washington Avenue, between Twelfth and Thirteenth Avenues South, he erected a fine stone block of stores and tenements to accommodate a demand for dwellings at low rental, centrally located, for the use of laboring men. It consisted of eighty-seven flats and seven stores, and was provided with gas, water, and sewerage long before any city sewer was built in that part of the city.[18]

If all this wasn't enough, Beard was also primarily responsible for the city's acquisition of Lake Harriet Boulevard. Clearly, this was a man of public spirit, but also one who knew the market and responded to it. Like many successful developers of his time, Beard built houses for every spectrum of the population, rich, poor, and in between.

DIRECTIONAL THRUSTS

Before the developers could go to work, the site of their development plans had to be considered. Minneapolis's growth was effectively constrained only by the physical limits of access to downtown and to the industrial corridors. The river was a major constraint. From the earliest point, settlement had spanned both sides, so the river needed to be bridged. It seemed that the area lying south of downtown Minneapolis would be the easiest path of expansion, since it required no bridges. But the northern sections of the city, on both

Rail Facilities

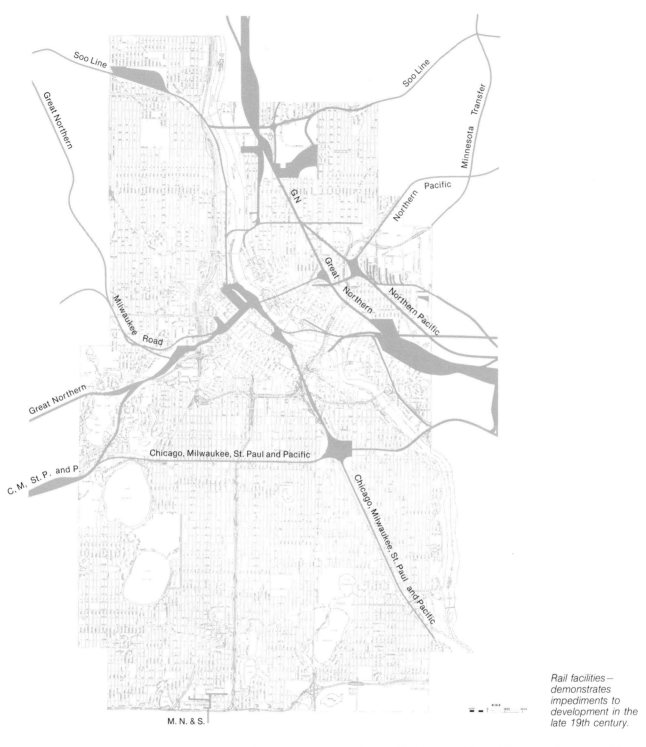

Soo Line

Great Northern

GN

Soo Line

Minnesota Transfer

Northern Pacific

Great Northern

Northern Pacific

Milwaukee Road

Great Northern

Chicago, Milwaukee, St. Paul and Pacific

C, M, St. P. and P.

Chicago, Milwaukee, St. Paul and Pacific

M. N. & S.

SCALE

*Rail facilities—
demonstrates
impediments to
development in the
late 19th century.*

sides of the river, could not be ignored, for industry was firmly entrenched in this part of the city by the 1870s. The river was not the only obstacle, however. Between downtown Minneapolis and the north side residential areas lay Bassett's Creek, which regularly flooded in the spring, making it difficult for anyone to cross. Not until after the turn of the century did a sufficient number of streets and bridges enable residents on the north side to feel connected to the rest of the city. In Northeast Minneapolis problems of a different nature constrained development. A multitude of railroad tracks cut through the area, many at grade level, making the pattern of development choppy, and unattractive for high-income housing. South Minneapolis, away from the ridge that

Development of
Street Railway and Bus Systems
in Twin Cities

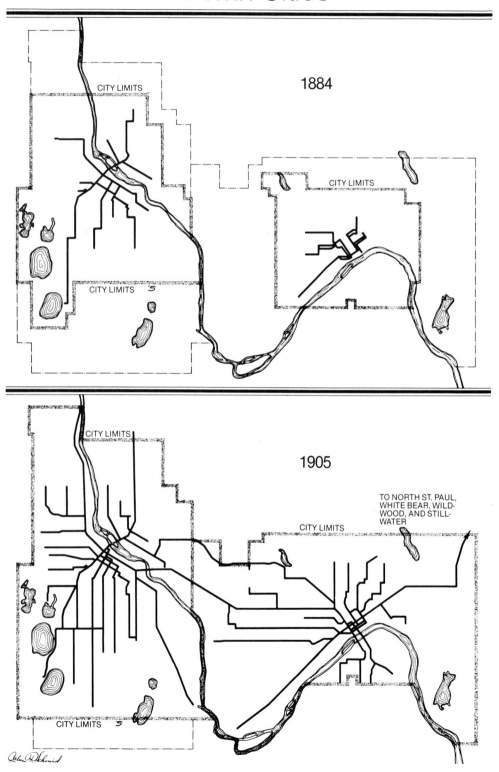

1884

1905

TO NORTH ST. PAUL,
WHITE BEAR, WILD-
WOOD, AND STILL-
WATER

extended west below Loring Park, lay on a wide belt of flat land interrupted only by a few low and swampy spots until reaching Minnehaha Creek. Once it was clear that Minneapolis would be the dominant center, the southward spread of development was inevitable.

Expansion outward from the center of Minneapolis, regardless of direction, was usually determined by the pattern of transit development. Houses were constructed in some areas before transit lines reached out—for example, along Hiawatha Avenue and near 31st and Lyndale—but that was not the norm. They were examples of housing constructed specifically for workers in nearby industries, often the railroads. The railroads that ran through Minneapolis did not engender much suburban development; they were for hauling goods from west to the east. Unlike many older cities, Minneapolis never developed many areas outside the city from which people commuted in by railroad. Downtown Minneapolis was not crowded enough to merit desertion on that scale, and the street railway system developed fast enough to make suburbanization of that type unnecessary.

The one commuter line that did develop was known as the Motor Line. Beginning in 1879, it ran from Lake Calhoun to the city limits at 24th Street and then along Nicollet and 1st Avenue to 1st Street near the river. By 1881 this steam train extended its range out to Excelsior. The effect was to support a boom in suburban real estate, but it did not last. As one contemporary observer wrote, "Along the line land values were nearly as high as they are at present [1913] and additions were platted far beyond any hope of settling them. A few people indeed moved out upon these plats but there was little real development. They soon found themselves marooned in the woods; for in 1887 the Minneapolis street railway swallowed its competitors and abandoned the Minnetonka line."[19]

The motor line had one other extension—to Minnehaha Falls—that served chiefly as a pleasure ride in the summers.

Thomas Lowry, perhaps more than any other person, could claim responsibility for the shape of the city's residential areas. By 1893, just forty years after the west side of the river was opened for settlement, Lowry was being acclaimed for his creation of a transit system that served not just Minneapolis but St. Paul and the outlying suburbs as well. The Minneapolis Street Railway Company *was* Lowry's creation, and commentators spoke of it, and of him, in glowing terms.

The streetcars, even in the primitive days of the faithful old horse and the uncertain mule, have always kept in advance of actual development, and there has been no real cause for complaint because of a lack of efficient service. It has been the effort of the company to keep the lines a little in advance of the limits of population, and thus furnish the public a certain means of intercommunication. This company has been the leading factor in building up and developing the outlying districts of the city. It has made it possible for the laboring man to purchase a home in the suburbs and yet be promptly at his work in the center of the city at any given hour. It has aided the growth of the city in innumerable ways.[20]

Lowry's interest in street railways was originally a tangent to his primary investments, which were in real estate. He soon realized that streetcars offered ample investment opportunities, and they could be paired with real estate investment as well. Lowry did not originate streetcars in Minneapolis. Some of the pioneer entrepreneurs, including men like Washburn, King, and Morrison, began the first street railway company but never actually ran a line. Lowry reorganized their company several years later and ran the first horsecar in 1875.

The first line ran from near the passenger station of the St. Paul, Minneapolis, and Manitoba Railroad at Washington and 4th Avenue North, down Washington to Hennepin, on Hennepin across the suspension bridge to Central Avenue, then on 4th Street Southeast to about 13th Avenue near the University. In the same year another line was constructed down Washington Avenue to 19th Avenue South; this was extended the next year to Riverside Avenue and down Riverside a few blocks. A third line, begun in 1876, ran down Hennepin Avenue to 12th Street and then to Portland Avenue.[21] During the next decade lines were extended in all parts of the city. Before 1890, horse-drawn streetcars were operating on Hennepin, Hawthorne, Western (Glenwood), Washington, and Riverside Avenues, 1st, 4th, and 8th Avenues South, and Central and Monroe Streets Northeast.[22] By 1890 the system began to be converted to electrical power and merged with the St. Paul system, which Lowry also controlled. When Atwater wrote of the Minneapolis streetcars in the early 1890s, he described a system with 115 miles of track and its own powerhouse, calling it the "most complete and best managed street railway system in the world."[23]

There is little direct evidence that Lowry and his company predetermined the social composition of different parts of the city depending on where streetcar lines were extended. Lowry, like Beard, had an interest in developing all of the city, and for all classes. However, there are some clues to a belief that all those engaged in real estate development at this time seemed to share: that homes should be provided for all classes, but not necessarily in the same parts of the city. Lowry was involved in one effort to build homes for the working class in Columbia Heights, near a large industrial area being developed in the far Northeast section of Minneapolis. W. D. Washburn and others took care to identify their market as "men of business" who needed to "get away from the noise of the city."[24] Though possibly not intended, the pattern of platting and improving land in the city did effectively separate different social groups.

Another factor in the spread of the city in these years, though not felt in full force until the twentieth century, was the park system. Most of the current parks did not attract residents in the early years because their sites either were too far away or were simply not considered attractive. Lake of the Isles, for example, was primarily a swampy marsh; the high bluff north of the lake was considered prime real estate, but the lake shore itself did not impress anyone as a place to live. People travelled to Lake Harriet to picnic in the 1880s, but few wanted to live so far away from the city. The vaunted Minneapolis park system had a humble beginning. Murphy Square was for a long time the only designated park space in the city. Not until 1880, when Charles Loring got a city forester appointed, did most people realize that park land should be acquired well in advance of the obvious need for it. In 1882, Hawthorne Park (on the north side of downtown) was purchased, and Franklin Steele Square was donated to the city. By 1883 a board of park commissioners had been created, against much opposition. Supporters claimed that public parks were, as Colonel William King said, "a scheme which will bring more capital, more population and add more to the city's renown than any other scheme that could be devised." Opponents of the park board, including the city council and the Knights of Labor, protested that "the door is left open to rob the working classes of their homes and make driveways for the rich at the expense of the poor."[25]

Despite protests, the park board was created and quickly set about its task of acquiring park land for Minneapolis. The board hired H. W. S. Cleveland, a well-known landscape architect, to help turn the few existing parks into a coordinated system. Cleveland, still harboring memories of the Chicago fire, suggested an extended series of boulevards planted with trees that could serve as a firebreak. The Mississippi was to be the backbone of the system, and a wide boulevard was to be created at Lake Street, in Cleveland's words, "south of the present thickly populated portions of the city, but destined to be densely occupied by buildings of every description."[26] Lyndale Avenue to the north of Central (Loring) Park would also become a boulevard, with a park to be created around 26th Avenue North

(Farview Park), behind the pesthouse or city hospital. Cleveland proposed to make almost no use of the lakes in his plan, failing, as one observer noted, "to grasp the key to the ultimate creation of a grand and elastic system of parks and boulevards."[27] Throughout the 1880s the park board far surpassed Cleveland's recommendations, acquiring Loring, Farview, Riverside, Minnehaha, Powderhorn, and Glenwood (Wirth) Parks, as well as much of the land for parkways around the lakes and along Minnehaha Creek. As Parsons wrote some years later, "That less than ten years in a wild time of money-making could bring about this accomplishment is another proof of the solidity of Minneapolis, as well as a monument to the men who fostered the park idea."[28] A good deal of foresight was required in the nineteenth century to reserve land for public use while much of the city was still unsettled. Due to the foresight of Charles Loring and others, Minneapolis today has more land around amenities like the river than most other American cities.[29]

THE TIMING OF NEW ADDITIONS

The political boundaries of Minneapolis were being steadily expanded throughout the last quarter of the nineteenth century. The original town of Minneapolis hugged the west bank of the river, while St. Anthony stayed close to the east bank. In 1872, when the two towns incorporated, the northern boundary reached about six blocks north of Broadway and the southern boundary was at Franklin Avenue; the western edge varied from Lyndale to Irving and the eastern edge was approximately at what is now Stinson Blvd. By 1883, the northern boundary stood about five blocks above Lowry Avenue and the southern edge had reached 46th Street. Four years later the political boundaries attained approximately their current shape: 54th Street on the south; the river and the county line to the east; and the existing northern and western city limits. The only annexations after this would be to the south.[30] What this pattern of annexation indicates is that well over two-thirds of the entire city was added within only five years. This fact underscores the magnitude of population growth and residential construction that occurred in the decade of the 1880s.

It was in the 1880s too that Minneapolis first surpassed St. Paul in population and established itself as the dominant center of the upper Midwest. It is easy to underestimate the strength of the rivalry between Minneapolis and St. Paul in those years. Those who have written about it describe a pitched battle when the time came for each census. St. Paul accused Minneapolis of returning fraudulent population counts in 1885; in 1890 several Minneapolis enumerators went to

Minneapolis Parks 1880-89

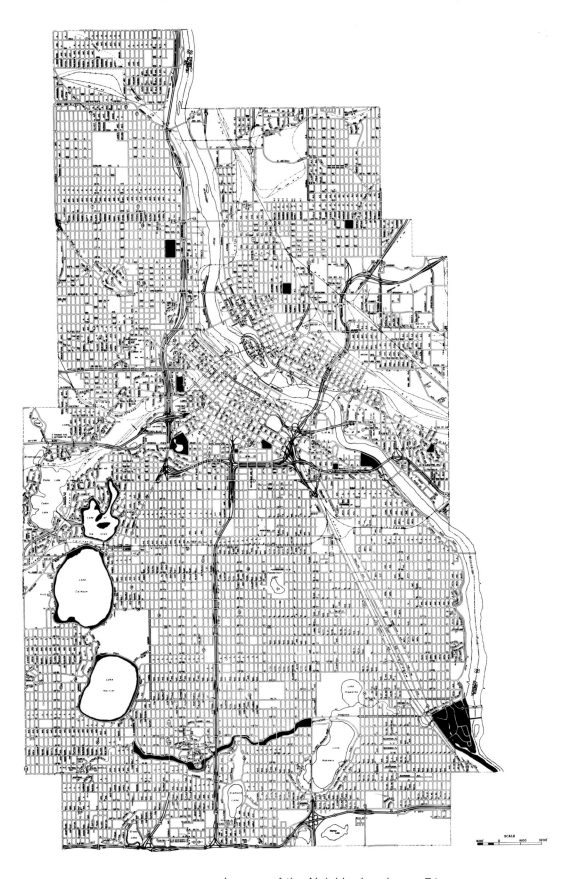

Minneapolis Parks and Parkway Systems- 1980

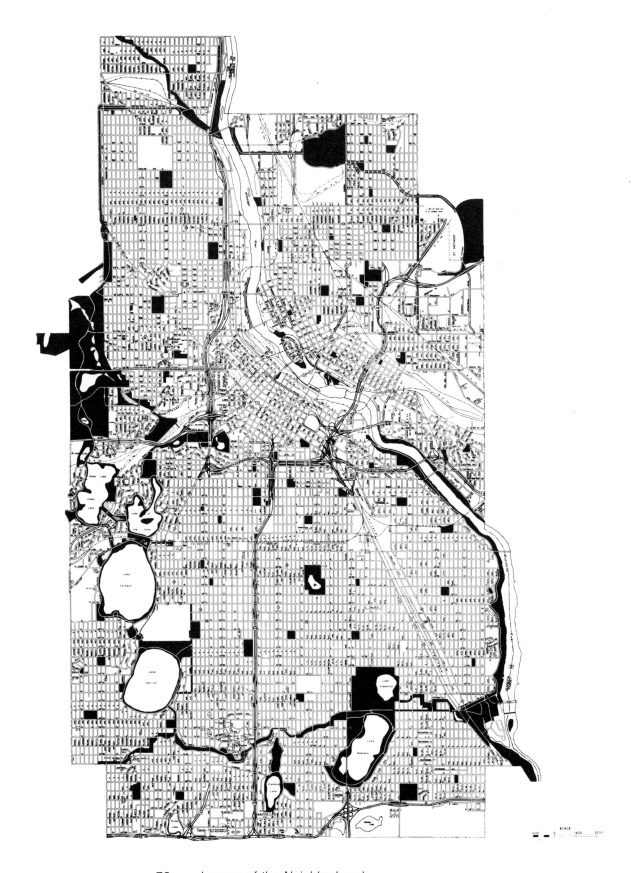

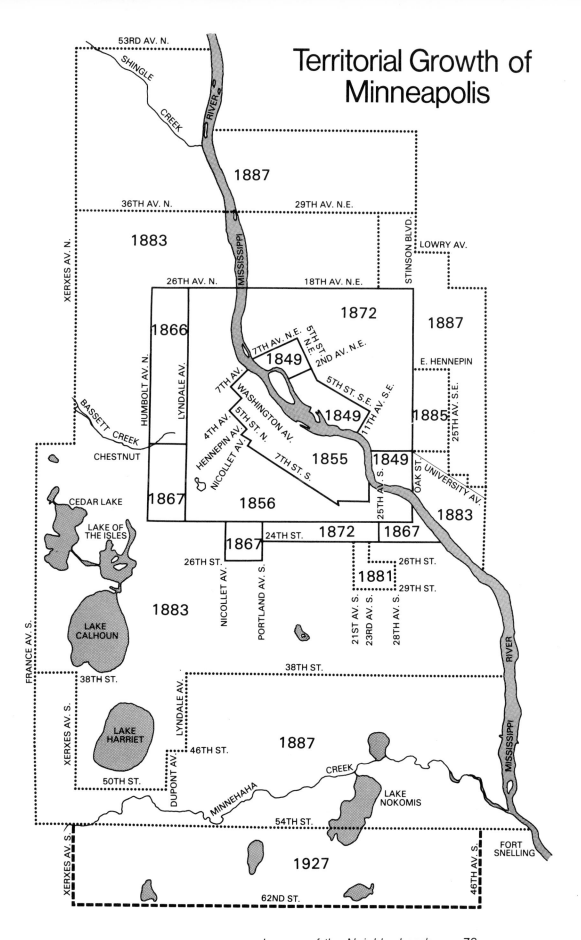

Territorial Growth of Minneapolis

53RD AV. N.

SHINGLE CREEK

RIVER

1887

36TH AV. N.

29TH AV. N.E.

1883

XERXES AV. N.

MISSISSIPPI

LOWRY AV.

STINSON BLVD.

26TH AV. N.

18TH AV. N.E.

1872

1887

1866

HUMBOLT AV. N.

LYNDALE AV.

7TH AV. N.E.

5TH ST. N.E.

2ND AV. N.E.

1849

E. HENNEPIN

7TH AV.

WASHINGTON AV.

5TH ST. S.E.

5TH AV. S.E.

11TH AV. S.E.

25TH AV. S.E.

1885

BASSETT CREEK

4TH AV.

5TH ST. N.

HENNEPIN AV.

1849

CHESTNUT

NICOLLET AV.

7TH ST. S.

1855

25TH AV. S.

1849

OAK ST.

UNIVERSITY AV.

CEDAR LAKE

1867

1856

1883

LAKE OF THE ISLES

24TH ST.

1872

1867

1867

26TH ST.

26TH ST.

1881

29TH ST.

FRANCE AV. S.

NICOLLET AV.

PORTLAND AV. S.

21ST AV. S.

23RD AV. S.

28TH AV. S.

1883

LAKE CALHOUN

XERXES AV. S.

38TH ST.

38TH ST.

LYNDALE AV.

LAKE HARRIET

46TH ST.

1887

MISSISSIPPI

50TH ST.

DUPONT AV.

CREEK

RIVER

MINNEHAHA

LAKE NOKOMIS

54TH ST.

FORT SNELLING

XERXES AV. S.

46TH AV. S.

1927

62ND ST.

Concrete block house, 2729 3rd Street North. The outer edge of growth in 1890s.

activity was an overextension of both credit and land development, which caught many investors short during the panic of 1893. But while it lasted, the boom in land values was a wonderful thing. Several contemporary observers described the scene.

> Lots were eagerly bought on speculation, and anything went. The platted area of the city was rapidly enlarged. Suburban farms were abandoned and turned into city plats, and additions extended from Shingle Creek to Minnehaha, and from the Ramsey County line to Minnetonka. Real estate offices multiplied, agents swarmed everywhere, and the fever pervaded the whole population.[33]

> A few figures which the "hustlers" placed upon property, seem, when considered in this day of sane development, beyond belief. The newspapers in 1883 advertised lots at Lake Calhoun at from $650 to $1000 each and acres beyond that lake at $500 each. We know that twenty years later they could have been purchased at half those prices. . . . Men attended sales of lots, purchased without proving the property, then went home boasting of the fact, only to discover later that their land was a foot under water or otherwise inaccessible. . . . Money in this was passed from buyer to buyer with such surprising swiftness that Minneapolis was credited with thirty-eight millionaires—a number sadly decreased in the time of trouble that followed this wild expansion. . . .[34]

trial for fraudulently entering names on the records. Parsons writes of this time that "a committee of business men scurried about to find every inhabitant whose name could be added to the roll. Some visited factories to secure the names of operators who lived in cheap lodging houses and had perhaps been missed; others stood on the street corners interviewing pedestrians; still others went gleaning information through the offices and stores."[31]

Finally the report of the census superintendent arrived, saying of Minneapolis, "Families have been swollen to enormous size; the capacity of boarding houses has been taxed beyond their limits. St. Paul is as bad."[32] Minneapolis had padded its rolls by twenty thousand, while St. Paul had added almost ten thousand fictitious residents; but Minneapolis was ahead, and would stay that way.

One element that stood out about the boom period of the 1880s was its extensive nature. Land was sold off, subdivided, and platted far beyond where most people were willing to live. The result of this rampant

Despite the extension of platted land and the construction of new houses far out into the countryside, and despite the large influx of new residents into the city, not every effort of this sort was successful. Some developers' names appear all over the plat maps—Philo Remington and Louis Menage fall into this category—while others concentrated on a small part of the city. But both large and small developers, and even some of the most important people in the city, were caught when the spiraling inflation of land prices finally slowed down. Henry Beard's New Boston development in Northeast Minneapolis was not the success he intended it to be; the middle class was not attracted to that part of the city in the same way that they flocked to the area south of downtown. Nor was W. D. Washburn's development for businessmen in far south Minneapolis an immediate success. It remained sparsely settled for almost thirty years after the original plat was filed. Though the boom period was not a success for everyone, some observers did find that good things resulted. One noted that working men had been able to buy and build their own homes and that the residential portions of the city had been solidified. The same observer added that there had been a marked tendency toward better quality architecture and that this had improved the city greatly.[35]

By the early 1890s the frantic real estate boom had ended, and development efforts were scaled down to more manageable proportions. The new methods of development were described in the following way:

The development of "additions" along rational and logical business lines has become common and profitable. It is now the reasonable theory that any given section of the city must take on something of a uniform character. The real estate agent nowadays plats his addition, and determines from general location and surroundings what class of residences and occupants it should appeal to. He then advertises for that class and fixes his prices at a suitable figure. In this way Lowry Hill was offered to the public after the panic of 1893, at prices and on terms that would appeal only to the best class of home builders. A little further out a notable example was Sunnyside and Linden Hills and Lynnhurst at Lake Harriet, Kenwood and other additions in the vicinity of Lake of the Isles were developed on this plan. The name of each soon meant something to the public; property was given a definite place and value. In the same way additions particularly designed for the occupation of artisans and the industrial classes were

platted and presented to those who would find the prices and localities suited to their needs.[36]

It is clear from this observation that, unlike in the earlier years of the city's development, a pattern of class segregation was developing in the 1890s and was accepted. Elite residential areas were beginning to be spatially distinguished from other parts of the city, at least in part because some formerly inaccessible areas were finally being made accessible and only the wealthy could afford to live in these places (for example, Lowry Hill). The middle class too was beginning to set itself apart geographically from other city residents. This was evident in the buildup of areas like the Wedge and Whittier. Some mansions were built in these parts of the city; but most of the houses were large, comfortable structures meant for middle-class residents. Their communities were located near the areas where the elite settled, but were clearly separated from them. In the examples of the Wedge and Whittier, the bulk of the middle-class houses constructed in the 1890s were located between the mansions of Lowry Hill and

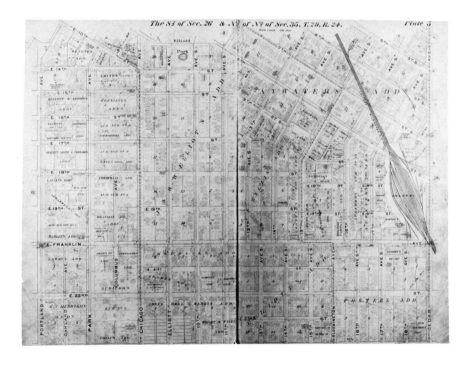

Inner area, Park Avenue and
Phillips, c. 1900.

617 19th Avenue South.
Typical of inner city density in
1880s.

Washburn–Fair Oaks, away from the high bluff line.
The working classes and the many foreign immigrants
were being left the parts of the city that no one else
wanted anymore. Most of the new construction at this
time was explicitly *not* for poor people, so those groups
inherited the older sections of the city and most of the
areas located near industries.

Viewed closely, Minneapolis readily discloses where
construction occurred before the advent of the auto age.
The period between about 1875 and 1910 is marked on
the landscape by certain styles and types of structures.
Residences dating from this period generally encompass
Italianate, Eastlake, Queen Anne, and Colonial Revival
styles of construction. The oldest structures are located
in a vaguely circular pattern around downtown, though
in places this pattern doesn't hold tightly. For example,

Three apartment buildings on
First Avenue South: 1900–02
(1919), 1904–06 (1919),
1908–10 (1922). The first
generation of redevelopment in
residential areas.

76 · *Legacy of the Neighborhoods*

Kortgaard house, 3rd Street and 29th Avenue North, c. 1885.

on the north side of the city, close to the river, are many pre-1900 houses—located much further away from downtown than are similarly aged houses on the south side. It would be easy to assume that these were all workingmen's houses, built for laborers of the lumber mills along the river. But many of the structures were quite substantial. Norwegian immigrant Kristian Kortgaard was president of a downtown bank but lived in a large concrete block house at 3rd Street North and 29th Avenue, on a block with many other large houses.[37] On the far reaches of Northeast is another grouping of older houses; these are two-story brick structures and may have been some of the homes constructed for managers of Lowry's Columbia Heights industrial suburb. In South Minneapolis most of the pre-1900 houses are above or just below Lake Street. The only real exception is a group of older houses in Linden Hills, west of Lake Harriet. With the exception of the Northeast grouping of houses, all of these were on or very close to a horsecar or streetcar line.

Transit development brought another kind of landscape along with it. As houses were constructed along the lines throughout the city, stores cropped up at the intersections of car lines to serve nearby residents. On some of the major car lines across the city, large commercial nodes developed at certain intersections. The grandest of these tended to be along the Lake Street line, though West Broadway and Central Avenue Northeast had their share as well; the corner of Hennepin and Lake, or of Chicago and Lake, became the epitome of this sort of commercial development, with its large stores, restaurants, and theaters. Enough large commercial nodes developed along those lines to create substantial storefront landscapes along much of the length of the streets. Even more common, perhaps, were the smaller commercial intersections away from the major car lines. Remnants of these can still be found at Glenwood and Penn Avenue North, at East 38th Street and 23rd Avenue, and in many other locations across the city. Though these corners and others like them no longer serve intersecting transit lines, they have usually retained some semblance of their commercial functions.

St. Mary's Russian Orthodox
Church (1905), 1629 5th Street
Northeast.

St. Joseph's Church (Carl
Struck, 1885–86), 1127 4th
Street North; now razed.

The old-fashioned groceries, meat markets, and bakeries
have disappeared, to be replaced by small chain stores
like 7–11; but the old streetcar corners still serve their
original purpose to some degree.

CHANGING CHARACTER OF THE NEWCOMERS

As Minneapolis gained population and spread out,
the characteristics of newcomers to the city began to
change somewhat. The swelling numbers of migrants in
the 1880s and 1890s reflected the vastly increased
number of foreign-born persons arriving in the United
States during these years. In the late nineteenth century,
the sources of immigration changed dramatically. England, Germany, and Ireland were no longer providing
the bulk of newcomers to the United States; now people
were pouring in from places like Sweden and Norway,
Italy, Russia, and Poland. Minneapolis was most
affected by the first two groups, though the others
appeared here as well. The newcomers did not
automatically blend into the American, Protestant
culture that the earliest Minneapolis residents had

established. Necessarily, institutions had to change or
grow in response to the shifting immigration patterns.
The foreign-born migrants to Minneapolis brought some
institutions with them and adapted others from what
they found here. Churches and societies are the most
obvious examples of both processes. The decade of the
1880s was a boom period for the founding and construction of churches. Almost every religion established and
built a number of new churches in these years; the
Catholics alone added nine new congregations in that
decade. Established congregations often went on a
building spree too, enlarging older structures and
building new ones for growing congregations – nearly all
of the major downtown congregations put up new
structures in the 1880s. This was the decade, too, in
which the Lutheran Church established itself as a force
in the religious life of Minneapolis – at least sixteen
Lutheran churches were built or expanded during the
period. The social life of the city also began to change.
The clubs and societies founded by the first settlers
(including various Masonic orders, the Minneapolis Art

League, and the Minneapolis Club) were joined by organizations like the Dania Society and the Swedish Benevolent Association. The appearance of groups like these reflected both the established groups' inability to meet the needs of the newcomers and the new migrants' need to establish an identity for themselves in the social life of the city.

Sometime between 1895 and 1915, Minneapolis experienced a full-blown Colonial Revival architectural experience. In many parts of the city variations on this theme are the dominant style even today, and structures of this kind can be found in all but the very newest areas. Whether large and detailed, with prominent front porches, like the examples found throughout the northern section of the Wedge, or small and unpretentious, as in the cottage variations near Lake Harriet, these houses sheltered the full range of middle-class Minneapolis residents in the late nineteenth and early twentieth centuries. By the end of the period, Colonial Revival houses were being joined by examples of another very common Minneapolis style—Craftsman houses, usually in a vague bungalow shape. Like the Colonial Revival surge, this mode of construction spread over most of the city. The two housing types are often mixed on the same blocks; but where they are geographically separate, the Colonial Revival structures tend to be close to transit lines and the Craftsman structures tend to be a bit farther away. The two types of construction were so widespread, and so popular, that all but the very edges of the city were at least touched by them.

Before Minneapolis began to call itself "the city of lakes," it was widely known as a "city of homes." People who touted the image meant to convey by it the image of a city of "individual homes, detached houses, dwellings which belong to the occupants."[38] The founding fathers of the city were credited with having laid out a generous townsite, where the lots were large and the streets were wide. The real estate men who pushed the borders of settlement outward were viewed as having given the city "elbow room." Horace Hudson delineated the residential landscape of Minneapolis just before the automobile began to make its presence felt (1908), and summarized the city this way:

> Built on this plan [the one described above] there was no excuse for crowded tenements or unsanitary piling up of buildings in narrow limits. Even the very poor have been generously housed in detached, if not comfortable houses. In the grade above the lower level there have been some houses built in rows after the eastern fashion but they have never been very popular. . . . A marked peculiarity of the Minneapolis residence districts is the absence of show streets or exclusive districts devoted to the homes of the wealthy. There is a decidedly demo-

Two "spec" bungalows in typical Craftsman and Colonial Revival (Budgman and Rayan, 1914), 4725 and 4729 Bryant Avenue South.

Three "spec" houses (c. 1890),
1914, 1916, 1918 13th Avenue
South.

cratic lack of exclusiveness. And, while there are
hundreds of costly and most beautiful homes, there are
few which show extravagance. The city has no palaces.
The great preponderance of residences in the city are
those of the middle class; although it is a fact that
within a few years there has been a very large number
of houses built and paid for by the so-called working
class. Whole additions have been built upon by laborers
and artisans. Among the better class of homes there has
been a decided tendency within the past decade towards
the planting of trees, vines and shrubbery, the beautification of grounds by gardening, the planting of hedges
and the building of walls—all tending to give the city an
air of permanence and solidity. Added to this is the
constantly increasing attention to architecture and
evident appreciation of the advantages of the beautiful
building locations on the lakes and parkways of the city.
. . . The apartment house came in with the great
growth of Minneapolis in the eighties but has never
been as popular as in some other cities. Flats are used
largely because detached houses at moderate rentals are
scarce, landlords finding the apartment houses the most
profitable investments.[39]

This analysis makes the process of developing
Minneapolis sound much more logical and placid than it
probably was. It glosses over the problems and the
chaos inherent in building up and filling out a city, but
accurately states some of the social and visual effects of
the first stages of the building process.

TRANSITIONS IN THE AUTO AGE

After 1910, and certainly by the end of World War
I, Minneapolis began to fill in some of the open spaces
between blocks built up during the heyday of the
streetcars. The streetcar system was, of course, still in
full operation and heavily used during the 1920s; but as
automobiles appeared, its influence diminished. The
signature residential style of the 1920s was the Revival
style, in its Tudor, Mediterranean, and Classical
permutations. Period Revival structures were built in
the newer areas untouched by earlier development—for
example, south of Minnehaha Creek near Lake Nokomis
and along the eastern shore of Lake Harriet—or between
large areas of Craftsman houses dating from about 1910.

Typical Period Revival house.

Because of their appeal to middle-class and upper-middle-class buyers, these structures tend to be concentrated in the southern half of the city rather than to the north or northeast. Builders of this type of housing looked for a location with water, hills, and trees; and most of these locations were to the south or southwest of downtown Minneapolis. For those who were less well off, or less style conscious, variations on the bungalow theme continued to be built in great numbers. Bungalows are found all over the city, beyond the old city limits of the early 1880s; but they tend to dominate certain areas, notably some of the neighborhoods to the north and to the southwest of Minnehaha Park. In some parts of the city, it is possible to find whole blocks of nothing but Craftsman bungalows dating from the teens or early twenties—good examples are Portland Avenue between 46th and 47th Streets or Park Avenue between 43rd and 44th Streets.

During this period, some shifts in the pattern of development occurred. Since land subdivision and housing construction were no longer tied to the

extension of streetcar lines, the movers and shakers of the city no longer seemed to have a strong hand in determining the dimensions of future construction. Of course, the original generation of Minneapolis city-builders had died off by this time, and their descendants seemed more interested in suburban real estate. For the most part, this phase of the city's growth was carried out by small developers and contractors, working with relatively small plots of land.

Another shift occurred that would have profound consequences for the future of the city. It was the attraction of the suburbs—and particularly of the Lake Minnetonka area—for the very wealthy and for those who aspired to wealth. Most of the city's elite had maintained summer homes on Minnetonka for decades; but beginning in the teens and twenties, more of these families began to choose the more rustic setting as their primary residence. It was the heyday of private clubs—like the Minneapolis Athletic Club with its sleeping rooms, dining room, and recreational facilities—which made being unable to get back and forth between the city and the suburbs in inclement weather quite tolerable, and so made it possible for even the busiest businessmen to have homes far from town. As the lake area became more and more popular, the descendants of the first settlers deserted Minneapolis. This meant that older houses, including many "family homes," were left behind to be destroyed and replaced by something else or to be subdivided for decidedly less affluent residents. Thus began the process of decline for many of the older parts of the city that had been rather substantial and impressive when first built (for example, Park Avenue).

The process of upper-middle-class, or elite, abandonment of the city had several different consequences, depending on the location of the formerly high-valued housing. Houses located in the downtown area that were no longer wanted by the elite families were usually torn down and replaced by business buildings or were donated to a worthy cause or favorite group. For example, the Women's Christian Association, a group that tried to provide "proper" housing for single young women who came to Minneapolis, was given John Pillsbury's house at 819 2nd Avenue South in 1900 and the William Dunwoody home at 52 South 10th Street in 1905. Both of these houses were eventually replaced by newer structures, which serve similar purposes even today.[40] When the prestigious Minneapolis Club was formed in 1886, it purchased the residence of former mayor Alonzo Rand at 7th Street and 6th Avenue South.[41] If formerly elite houses were located in areas that were popular, but for a less wealthy portion of the population, they could be cut up into apartment units (a favorite mechanism in Lowry Hill East and West during the thirties and forties), or they could be replaced by more profitable apartment structures (as was the case in the Loring Park area during the teens and twenties). If the houses in question were in a rapidly declining area, they were cut into rooming units and allowed to deteriorate until there was no option but to destroy them (this was true of many large houses in the Oak Lake area during the 1930s and many formerly elite houses on Nicollet Island).

As people spread further throughout Minneapolis in the teens and twenties, the institutions of daily life went along with them; churches, schools, fire stations, and libraries spread throughout the city as well. Often we tend to think that people are settled in the newer parts of a city for a long time before such institutions begin to appear. It seems that in Minneapolis, during the late nineteenth and early twentieth centuries, a different sequence of events sometimes took place. In response to political pressure for services, the appearance of some institutions might predate the heaviest period of settlement in an area or happen just at the start of the process. For example, Frederika Bremer School was

Fire Station #13 (Collins and Kennison, 1923), 4201 Cedar Avenue South.

opened at Lowry and North Emerson in 1887. There were some houses already constructed a couple of blocks to the north, several blocks to the south, and farther east along the river, but most of the houses immediately surrounding the school were not built until around the turn of the century or later. Similarly, the fire station at 42nd Street and Cedar in south Minneapolis was opened in 1923, when most existing houses in the area were well to the north or west of it; most of the houses nearer the station itself were not built until the 1930s, and many lots remained empty until after World War II.

During the period of auto-related buildup of Minneapolis the composition of the population continued to change. During the teens and twenties the city went on increasing in population, but at slightly lower rates than in some earlier decades. Foreign-born migrants still came to Minneapolis—now primarily from Poland and Russia. But more and more migrants seemed to be coming from the rural hinterland surrounding the Twin Cities. Young men and women poured into the city from the Dakotas looking for jobs and adventure. At the same time, some of the earlier European migrant groups were maturing—that is, the first generation migrants were aging and beginning to die, and their children were fast becoming Americanized. This was reflected in shifts of population around the city. For example, the children of Scandinavian migrants were pushing farther and farther out through south Minneapolis, away from the historical core of Scandinavian settlement near Seven Corners. And the largest concentration of Jewish settlement moved continually westward, across Near Northside, in these same years. The dominant Minneapolis residential landscape came about during this time, as the children of the immigrants assimilated the common housing aspirations of most Americans. Single-family houses of modest scale were built in all sections of the city to accommodate the housing needs of this group.

The aging and assimilation of the older immigrant groups was accompanied by other social changes that were reflected on the landscape. Levels of education, income, and consumption were increasing throughout American society during the teens and twenties. The enlarging yearbooks of the university tell part of the story: More and more people were getting more and more education, and simultaneously improving their position in society. As people's positions improved, they had more money to spend on necessities like housing

and to put into community institutions like churches and schools. Multiple Minneapolis monuments appeared to reflect this fact—the standard English Gothic school building, built throughout the teens and twenties in all parts of the city. Some of these have been closed or replaced, but many are still standing (for example, Central High, which is no longer in use). As more people moved into white-collar jobs and into middle-class society, they tended to have fewer children; and the smaller households required less space. On the landscape, this phenomenon accounts for the prevalence of smaller single-family homes at all edges of the city. In the older close-in neighborhoods, space was at a premium; houses were squeezed together and relatively fewer single-family dwellings could be found. In the parts of the city developed at this time, there was more space between dwellings and many fewer multiple units

Central High School (W. B. Ittner, 1912–13; later additions 1964), 3416 4th Avenue South; now closed.

*El Lago Theatre (1927), 3500
East Lake Street.*

were constructed. The landscape was also studded with
structures that reflected the growing reliance on
automobiles and the ability of residents to spend money
on things other than necessities. Garages and movie
theaters—like the former El Lago theater on Lake Street
or the Granada (now the Suburban World) on
Hennepin—dot the parts of Minneapolis built up just
before and during the 1920s.

The Residential Regions of the City

As each phase of development spread throughout
Minneapolis, the characteristics of age of construction
and direction of growth combined to create somewhat
unique landscapes in each major section of the city. The
differences are not glaring—they are fairly subtle and are
easily missed. Because each part of the city experienced a
slightly different pattern of population succession and
each was affected somewhat differently by the adaptation
of prevailing architectural styles and new technology,
each has a feeling or tone that is particularly its own.

NORTHEAST

The part of Minneapolis called Northeast extends
north of Hennepin Avenue on the east side of the
Mississippi River. It contains some of the land first
settled by white people in the entire city, but also
contains some of the newest housing built in Minneapolis. Interestingly, the newest houses sit on the pieces
of land that have been settled the longest, their aging
predecessors having been removed in the interest of
improvement. Most of this section of the city was built
up by the turn of the century. As one moves northeast,
houses dating from the 1920s and 1930s, and even some
postwar houses, are prominent, but all of these compose
a smaller proportion of the total housing picture than
does the older housing stock. Perhaps because the
industrial character of Northeast was well established by
1900, developers may have been less attracted to this
area. The pattern of development after 1920 seems to
have been slow enough to have been fed almost entirely
by internal growth. Like many other communities whose
desirability is questioned by outsiders, Northeast has

Divisions of Minneapolis Residential Areas

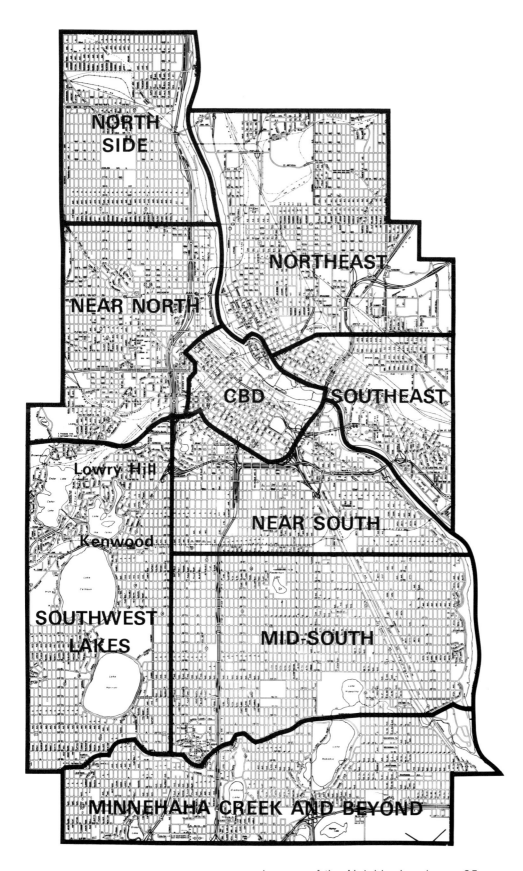

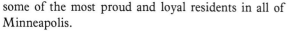
531 8th Street Northeast, 509 8th Street Northeast. Home improvements cover historic details in houses from 1880s.

some of the most proud and loyal residents in all of Minneapolis.

The earliest houses that remain in Northeast are two-story frame structures. Usually whatever details might have identified these structures stylistically have been obliterated by home improvements like stucco or asphalt re-siding. Consequently, although many houses are as old as, or older than, those in other parts of the city, they are not as immediately appealing to the eye. The bric-a-brac that usually distinguishes houses of the 1880s is almost completely lacking here. Eastlake and Queen Anne styles can be identified by roof lines and house sizes and shapes, but most other clues are missing. Most of the styles that can be easily identified include Colonial Revival structures, small Craftsman houses, Cape Cod and Period Revival houses. One of the more interesting details of Northeast's development involves the large proportion of duplexes found in this part of the city. The reasons for so many duplexes are unclear, but may have something to do with the ethnic variety of the area and the large number of extended families found in ethnic communities. The group of duplexes between 2533 and 2539 Monroe Northeast are good examples of this phenomenon.

Northeast is recognized throughout the rest of Minneapolis as being more "ethnic" than the rest of the city. The names on stores and mailboxes confirm the

general validity of this belief: Eastern European surnames are prominent here (Kramarczuk's deli and Surdyk's liquor store in lower Northeast are just the beginning). Several Eastern Orthodox churches, St. Maron's Catholic Church, and the Slavic Evangelical Baptist church, all located in Northeast, underscore the ethnicity of the area. The Scandinavians who long dominated the population of Minneapolis are here too—especially in the "hill" area west of Central and north of Lowry.

SOUTHEAST

Southeast Minneapolis lies on the east side of the Mississippi, south of Hennepin Avenue. Like Northeast, just to the north, Southeast has some of the oldest housing in Minneapolis—the major difference between the two areas in this regard is that in Southeast, most of the antique structures have been preserved to some degree. All of the area west of Union Street and south of 8th Street Southeast was developed by 1885 and everything over to Oak Street was built up by 1892, so many of the remaining houses date from those decades.

632 Erie Southeast (fraternity house), 518 Ontario Southeast. Older and newer housing in Prospect Park.

Italianate and Victorian structures dominate the oldest group (for example, the Fisk house at 424 5th Street Southeast and a large Queen Anne house at 159 Arthur). The next largest period of construction was between 1892 and 1914: It saw the buildup of the area between 8th Street and Hennepin and between University and River Road, primarily in late Victorian, Colonial Revival, and Craftsman structures. There was a small amount of postwar development on the fringes of the Como area, but it was minuscule compared to the earlier periods of construction. Until the decade of the 1960s and the appearance of redevelopment, very little "new" housing was built in Southeast.

The pattern of housing development is very mixed throughout Southeast. That is, very few blocks (except in Prospect Park) demonstrate a uniform development facade. Houses dating from the 1870s and 1880s can be found next to houses dating from 1900 or 1910, and now all of these are mixed in with apartment buildings dating from the 1960s and 1970s. Only Prospect Park has a cohesive feeling to it—almost everything in this neighborhood reads as late nineteenth- or early twentieth-century construction. Other parts of Southeast used to have the same feeling before direct and indirect intrusions from the university began to alter them. An example of direct intrusion can be seen in the western portion of Prospect Park (west of the freeway interchange). This used to be a less fancy version of the housing on Tower Hill; but as university dormitory and parking needs grew, structures to accommodate the needs were built into this area. Indirect intrusion is more visible in the Dinkytown area, where the pressing

need for off-campus housing was met by developers who tore down old houses and built large numbers of walk-up apartment buildings.

The population of Southeast has always been a mix of working-class and middle-class people (the latter being prominently represented by university professors and staff). In the years since 1960, students have come to exert a stronger influence on the area as their numbers have increased. The transformation of former single family homes to fraternities and sororities is only the most telling indicator of this shift. There has never been a pronounced ethnic cast to the population of Southeast. Native-born Americans were dominant in the early years, and third- to sixth-generation Americans are still dominant today.

NORTHSIDE

The Northside of Minneapolis lies on the west side of the Mississippi and extends from Lowry Avenue north to the city limits. This part of the city was relatively unsettled before the 1890s, except for a few blocks near the river at Lowry. In the 1890s and just after the turn of the century, settlement began to spread west along Lowry to about Humboldt, and another node of settlement developed in Camden at 42nd and Lyndale. Houses built at that time included small Eastlake cottages such as 3501 North Humboldt and

1700 block of Morgan North, 2831 3rd Street North. Late 19th and early 20th century Northside houses.

larger Queen Anne structures such as 713 North 46th Avenue. By 1914 the area between 34th and 40th Avenues near the river began filling in with Colonial Revival houses and Craftsman bungalows. During the 1920s and late 1930s, the area west of Humboldt filled in up to the Soo Line tracks and the area above Camden was settled as far north as 49th Avenue. This was the single largest period of development in Northside, and bungalows and Cape Cod houses are far more numerous than any other kind. Northside also experienced a substantial development spurt after World War II, when the northern edges of the area were filled up with postwar ramblers and bungalows. The areas developed from the 1920s on are fairly homogeneous in style and type of architecture. Except for one or two senior citizen high-rises, this part of the city has experienced almost no redevelopment to cause the original structures to disappear.

Like other areas of Minneapolis that are relatively removed from downtown both in distance and in function, Northside has no very pronounced ethnic

*Boardwalk condominiums
(1982), near Broadway and I94.*

character. It largely served as a stepping stone away from the ethnic clusters to the south, particularly for the Scandinavians and Germans who first dominated the Near North portion of Minneapolis. As the area to the south declined in public estimation beginning in the 1920s, Northside became the place where migrants from below Lowry could move to demonstrate their social and economic mobility. There are few monumental structures on the Northside (except for churches and schools), but neither are there the density and crowding that were common to the south. People moved here to attain the American dream of a single-family house with a yard, surrounded by neighbors who shared common interests and beliefs.

NEAR NORTH

This area encompasses all of the land on the west side of the Mississippi between Lowry Avenue, Highway 12, and the western city limits. It is a part of the city that is associated in the public mind with "project architecture," though it is much more diverse than that general label would indicate. Near North is one of the older areas of Minneapolis, though the large amount of redevelopment in the last twenty-five years hides this fact well. All of Near North between the river and Girard Avenue was developed by 1885.

The general mix of housing ranged from workers' cottages near the river (of which almost none are left) to the substantial Victorian houses of Oak Lake (all now obliterated); the area to the north of Plymouth Avenue is a better guide to what Near North used to look like—most of the older structures south of Plymouth have been replaced. By 1892 the Forest Heights addition at Broadway and Irving had been developed with large Queen Anne and Colonial Revival houses. Between 1892 and 1914, Near North filled up incrementally, so that by the latter date the area was fully developed north to Lowry and west to about Penn Avenue. Craftsman bungalows and Colonial Revival houses dominated this period of development. The latter structures are especially notable in the area surrounding North Commons park. The remaining section of Near North, between Penn and Xerxes, was filled in by 1940 with bungalows and some Period Revival structures.

The large amount of newer construction that now marks the part of Near North east of Penn Avenue is entirely a result of recent replacement construction. In the process, the density of this area greatly increased, as single-family houses and duplexes were replaced by apartment buildings and high-rises. An unusually large amount of subsidized and public housing has been built in concentrations around this part of the city. This has given Near North an unwarranted image as a "project" area. Indeed, there are public housing projects here, but they are not the large and ominous structures that populate common images of public housing. Sumner-Field, the first public housing in Minneapolis, has ably sheltered Near North families for almost fifty years.

Near North Minneapolis is one of the few parts of the city that has clearly experienced a distinct succession of population groups moving through the area over the years. Not surprisingly, this succession of people has been marked on the landscape in various ways. Perhaps the most obvious mark can be seen in the use of certain religious structures. Buildings that were obviously constructed as synagogues for Jewish congregations are now being used as black churches (for example, the former Mihro Kodesh Synagogue at Oliver and Oak Park Avenues). This process aptly describes the second major transformation in the population of Near North—

the shift from being a predominantly Jewish community to becoming a predominantly black community. But before this shift, which occurred in the 1950s and 1960s, there was an earlier shift from American, French, German, and Finnish residents to predominantly Jewish residents. This earlier shift began around the turn of the century in the part of Near North that was closest to downtown and the river, and proceeded through the 1930s, when the Homewood addition west of Penn Avenue finally became part of the growing Jewish Northside community.

One part of Near North stands out fairly dramatically from the rest. Bryn Mawr, between Highway 12 and the Bassett's Creek spur of the Great Northern, is an islandlike area that is now formally part of the Calhoun-Isles community, though for years it was

Mihro Kodesh Synagogue (S. J. Bowler, 1926), 1000 Oliver North; now a Baptist church.

Three Colonial Revival houses on Bryant Avenue South: 2432 (1899), 2436 (1899), 2440 (1898).

considered part of Near North. This area developed very slowly over a number of years, and has about it almost the feeling of a small town. The first houses in Bryn Mawr were Craftsman and Queen Annes built after the turn of the century. Throughout the teens and twenties, bungalows were mixed in; and in the postwar period, many ramblers and Cape Cods were added. Because it is isolated from the rest of Near North — separated by the railroad tracks and the Meadows — this area has been far more stable than most of the Near North community.

LOWRY HILL-KENWOOD-SOUTHWEST LAKES

This hill-and-lake-filled part of Minneapolis occupies a large area extending from Highway 12 to Minnehaha Creek. It reaches from Lyndale Avenue to the city limits on the west. It was not one of the first parts of the city to be settled, though even in the 1850s and 1860s early residents made use of the lakeshores for recreational pursuits. Much of this area was not even officially added to the city until the mid-to-late 1880s.

Some blocks were developed by 1892, particularly in the immediate vicinity of Lyndale and Lake, the major streetcar transfer point between downtown and Lake Calhoun. Smaller Eastlake and Queen Anne houses dominated this period of construction.

The portions of this area closest to downtown or to one of the lakes developed first. For example, the sections that were developed by 1903 included the northern half of the Wedge, most of Lowry Hill and the east side of Lake of the Isles, most of the eastern side of Lake Calhoun, and the Linden Hills area on the western shore of Lake Harriet. All of these areas have some structures, usually large Queen Anne houses, dating from the 1890s and an abundance of Colonial Revival homes from around the turn of the century. The predominant characteristic of these houses is that they are spacious and numerous. It is not uncommon to find almost entire block faces of Colonial Revivals — the 2400 block of Bryant is an excellent example, with its uniform roof lines and ubiquitous colonnaded front porches. Most of these houses quickly betray their

Two former lake cottages combined to form one residence (1902), 2617 40th Street West.

upper-middle-class origins; they were built for people who were well-off, and the attention to detail is still evident on their facades. Another important component of construction in these areas at this time was the lake cottage. Today these have disappeared in large numbers, or have been altered extensively, but many can still be seen in the area south of Lake Calhoun and west of Lake Harriet (for example, 2521 and 2617 W. 40th Street). There was some development in these areas during the first decade of the twentieth century. Large pockets of Colonial Revival houses and smaller Craftsman and Prairie School houses were constructed in the southern part of the Wedge, at the northwest and southeast corners of Lake of the Isles, near 36th and Dupont, and in scattered locations west of Lake Harriet. Again, these were houses meant for the prosperous middle classes who were flocking to lakeside residential property during these years.

During the teens, twenties, and thirties, the largest amount of land in this part of Minneapolis was developed. Most of the land west of Lake of the Isles, south of Lake Calhoun, and all around Lake Harriet (except to the north, where Lakewood Cemetery is located) was built up during these years. The dominant form that this construction took was the Period Revival house, in all of its Tudor, Mediterranean, and Gothic permutations. It is a measure of how difficult some of

this land was to develop that many houses from this period are right on lakeshore property, while houses from an earlier period are several blocks from a nearby lake. Most often the reason for this pattern is that property on the lake was either very high or very low and had to be improved at great expense in order to develop it. Another sort of building style from the twenties that appeared sporadically throughout these areas was a variety of apartment buildings. Usually these were built close together, as in the Mall area near Lake of the Isles. In the postwar years some new construction occurred, notably on the hilly ground just northwest of Lake Calhoun and on scattered parcels west and south of Lake Harriet. The most frequent form of construction in these places was large and expansive ramblers. This type comprised most of the newest structures until very recently, when high-rise condominiums began to appear west of Lake Calhoun and between Calhoun and Isles. As has been the case throughout the history of the area, development in the later phases continues to be directed at upper-middle-class residents who can afford the expensive houses and condominiums.

NEAR SOUTH

This term is being used to refer to that broad section of Minneapolis that lies between downtown and

Granada Apartments (C. J.
Bard, 1929), 1456 Lagoon
Avenue.

Post–World War II houses,
3600 block of Zenith Avenue
South.

Dania Hall (Carl Struck, 1886),
Cedar Avenue and 5th Street
South. Typical of late 19th
century commercial structures.

Lake Street and reaches from Lyndale Avenue to the Mississippi. Like similar parts of Near North and Northeast, this is among the oldest areas in the city. The central portion, approximately between Blaisdell and 27th Avenue South, was fully developed by 1892; closer-in sections like Cedar-Riverside were fully built up even before 1885. Houses dating from these periods most often are small Eastlake and Queen Anne structures, many of which have fallen into substantial states of disrepair. These structures not only are small but are usually sited on small lots, and they have the effect of creating a dense streetscape where clearance has not yet intervened. One senses from the sizes and siting of these houses that they were built for working-class people who needed good basic shelter but who could not afford much space or many amenities. Along with the houses came commercial structures that were built along the streetcar lines. This part of the city is particularly rich in still possessing remnants of nineteenth-century commercial strips that are fairly intact; Cedar Avenue near the university, Franklin Avenue near Bloomington, and Nicollet Avenue near 26th Street are all good examples of this period and style of development. What one finds is a mixture of two- and three-story masonry commercial buildings that usually had apartments above the first-floor stores.

During the mid-to-late 1890s, only one major section of the Near South went through an intense period of development—the northern part of the Whittier neighborhood. In many ways this area has been and still is distinct from other parts of the Near South area. It was developed very differently: larger lots, much larger and more elaborate houses, all intended for prosperous upper-middle-class residents. It is not uncommon to find houses here that had maid's quarters and that still have enormous carriage houses. Much of the housing in the Near South area was built for

decidedly less ostentatious purposes, and the speculative quality of most of the housing still reads as such today.

The southern and eastern parts of the Near South tended to develop a bit later than the northern portion. The only other sections built up during the 1890s and around the turn of the century included a few blocks around the 29th Street rail corridor at Portland and near 30th Avenue South. The next substantial areas of development came during the first decade of the twentieth century and focused on blocks around 27th and Garfield, and even more importantly, in the eastern part of the Seward neighborhood. The dominant styles in both places tended to be small Colonial Revival houses and Craftsman bungalows. Duplexes appeared in substantial numbers throughout these areas as well. Only one very small section of Near South developed after 1914, the area near the Mississippi just above Lake

Row of Craftsman bungalows (early 1920s), 3700 block of 21st Avenue South.

Street. Bungalows and Period Revivals dominated in this small enclave. Residents of the areas developed in the twentieth century tended to be a mixture of skilled workers and professionals, and even today these remain the most stable and best maintained sections of the entire Near South area.

There is one type of residential use that has been and continues to be quite important for the Near South area: multifamily, or apartment, buildings. Though we associate buildings of this type with the twentieth century, they were being built in parts of Near South in great numbers from the 1890s on. Fourplexes were probably the earliest variety and can be found throughout this part of the city. But they were soon joined by buildings designed for twelve or more families (such as the recently razed Red Flats at 13th Avenue and 21st Street). By the time that older parts of Near South were ready to be redeveloped—such as the land around Park and Franklin in the teens—apartment construction had become an accepted mode for this area. Though there has been virtually no construction of single-family homes in this area in the postwar years, many apartment buildings of recent vintage have been built. In most places they take the form of two-and-a-half-story walk-up buildings, which fit jarringly into their surroundings. They have been supplemented in the multifamily category by numerous high-rises for the elderly, which dot the landscape of Near South but are particularly concentrated along the eastern half of Franklin Avenue.

The population of the Near South area, like that of Near North, has fluctuated greatly in recent years. From an early population base of native-born Americans on the west and foreign-born Scandinavians on the east, the population base has shifted to encompass today whites, blacks, and the largest Indian community in the Twin Cities. What they all have in common, whether young or old (and there are few who are in between), is their relative poverty. This part of the city still retains many former mansions of the rich and powerful. These are now cut up into smaller units or have become offices and institutions.

MID-SOUTH

Lying just below the Near South region, this very large part of the city reaches from Lake Street to Minnehaha Creek and from Lyndale Avenue to the Mississippi. To a great extent, this area is a product of the early twentieth century. Only a very small section around 32nd and Nicollet was built up by 1892. Most of the blocks just south of Lake Street had been developed by 1903, except in the area lying east of Minnehaha Avenue. For the most part structures built

in these places were Colonial Revival houses and duplexes, though some individualized Queen Annes can also be found (for example, the Healy houses near 31st Street and 3rd Avenue). Nearly half of this entire region was developed in the years between 1903 and 1914. Generally this phase of construction took place north of 40th Street, except in the corridor between Nicollet and Lyndale, where expensive, custom-built houses drew people almost all the way to the creek. The hallmark modes of construction through most of the area developed by 1914 were small Colonial Revival houses and duplexes and Craftsman bungalows.

During the late teens, the twenties, and the thirties, almost another half of the Mid-South region was built up, encompassing the area between 40th Street and the creek, but extending well up toward Lake Street on the eastern end near the river. Craftsman bungalows of every size typify the housing stock of this developmental period and are perhaps *the* identifying house type for all of south Minneapolis—they are that common here. But throughout this area there are also large numbers of Period Revival structures, particularly as one moves closer to either the creek or the river. By 1940 most of the Mid-South region had been developed, except for scattered low-lying blocks that were too difficult to build on at an earlier time. During the postwar period even those places were finally marketed. They tend to stand out as aberrations in the building pattern, since the housing stock is identifiably newer than anything around it. These spots also are noticeable for the distinct terrain differences that they exhibit. For example, when driving into the largest of these tracts at 42nd and Bloomington, one goes rather precipitously downhill into a former swamp (which still fills with water at every heavy rainfall).

The population base of the Mid-South region is almost uniformly middle class, and always has been. This part of the city, like its counterparts on the Northside and in Northeast, attracted upwardly-bound residents of both American and foreign-born stock, though usually not first-generation immigrants. Moving to this region was, for those who had grown up in the close immigrant quarters of Cedar-Riverside, a sign that they had "made it." The small bungalows that fill the landscape represented the attainment of the American dream to many who moved here. Only in the part of the region very near Minnehaha Creek and in the large section that encompasses Washburn Park were the circumstances somewhat different. Those areas attracted people in the upper reaches of the middle class just as this social group was increasing dramatically in the teens and twenties. The larger houses, larger lots, and sometimes winding streets tell of aspirations that went

Wakefield House (Purcell, Feick, and Elmslie, 1912), 4700 Fremont South.

beyond simply a house and a yard. The presence of many Purcell, Feick, and Elmslie houses–in the most up-to-date Prairie School style of these years–indicates the presence of an above-average level of sophistication and income for some parts of the Mid-South region.

MINNEHAHA CREEK AND BEYOND

This region extends across the entire width of Minneapolis and reaches from Minnehaha Creek to the southern city limits. It is another fairly uniform area. Single-family houses of the twenties, thirties, and fifties are the dominant mode of construction. Period Revival structures line the southern bank of the creek just as they do the northern one, and they nearly surround Lake Nokomis as well. A small amount of earlier development occurred close to Minnehaha Park, at the end of the Hiawatha streetcar line. Houses were built here around the turn of the century in the usual Colonial Revival and Queen Anne boxy styles and were for many years the only construction in the entire region. Development occurred first in the northeastern

corner, then moved to the southwest. The northern and eastern stretches of the area beyond the creek were mostly built up by 1940. The southern and western reaches, and especially those areas south of Diamond Lake and around Grass Lake, were all developed in the postwar period. Though ramblers and Cape Cods are found here, as in every postwar area of development, the houses here tend to be larger and a bit more elaborate than the norm for the styles. One can occasionally find here remnants of the past, too. For example, a well-preserved turn-of-the-century farmhouse on 60th Street near Thomas Avenue remains a clear indicator of the truck-farming past of this former part of Richfield township.

In every way the region beyond Minnehaha Creek is an extension of the Mid-South area on the other side of the creek. It too is middle class, and its landscape betrays this fact convincingly. Houses and yards are well maintained by residents, and there is a large amount of open space due to the presence of three lakes, the creek, and the nearby falls area. Unlike the southwest lakes

Legacy of the Neighborhoods · 97

4140 and 4150 Edmund Boulevard.

region, this area does not attract large numbers of outsiders to its lakeshores. The water bodies are used largely by residents, and families with children are more visible than on the lakes that attract numbers of young joggers and roller skaters.

Variety within the Regions

Though the regions summarized may appear at first blush to be quite homogeneous, there are some important and consistent variations within each region. Each contains some common and some uncommon expressions both of individuality and of community. Places that have remained fairly stable—that have served similar cultural and economic groups over time—express notions of community simply through being what they always have been. Places that have experienced great changes in the ethnic background and economic circumstances of residents over time tend to display elements of individuality, sometimes in the buildings

themselves, or in how residents transform the landscape.

There seems to be no sure way to predict what pattern a given area will follow; there are too many variables that have to do with people and their individual preferences. However, there are some tendencies that are rather noticeable. Just looking at Minneapolis's history and observing the changes that have occurred leads one to conclude that the rate of alteration of the landscape has something to do with income, but the correlations are not exactly clear. The greatest amount of alteration to structures has occurred in what used to be the richest and the poorest areas of the city, regardless of what region they are located in. Those areas that were built for the middle class and that have remained middle class have experienced little or no change, although the houses themselves may be almost seventy-five years old.

EFFECTS OF THE LAY OF THE LAND
In certain parts of the city, variation in the landscape occurs because of differences in terrain that

could not be ignored or eliminated by developers. Either high ground or very low ground can lead to such alterations because either can be expensive to build houses on. The most obvious case of landscape alteration due to terrain happens in Minneapolis whenever the grid pattern of streets hits a breaking point, whether a lake, the creek, or the river. Most sites of this kind enticed developers into building something a little bit bigger and a bit more expensive than most other structures in the area. The shoreline of Lake of the Isles is the best example of this tendency. Though the surrounding area is filled with large, expensive homes, those built on the lake itself seem even bigger and more elaborate—for example, the picture-perfect Colonial Revival at 2350 Lake of the Isles Boulevard, which is about twice the average size for houses of this type. Slightly less elaborate houses line the shores of the other lakes, but a similar effect can be observed. Walking a block or two away from any of the lakes usually puts one in a decidedly less ostentatious atmosphere. So, with few exceptions, the river bluff, lakeshores, and creek frontage are where one looks to find the most tasteful,

most expensive, and best-designed landscapes in Minneapolis.

Though Minneapolis is a relatively flat city, it does have some hilly spots; and it would be reasonable to assume that developers would use high land in a way similar to the use of the lakeshores. To some degree this assumption is valid. Lowry Hill and Washburn Park—both of which rise well above the surrounding landscape—were developed for an upper-middle-class market, and each displays a wide range of impressive houses. The hilly terrain of Prospect Park, too, was used for better-than-average houses. But the highest spot in the entire city is near Deming Heights in Northeast Minneapolis, and the houses surrounding the park there are no different from those several blocks away, and none even begin to approach the grandeur of Lowry Hill or Washburn Park houses. So height alone is not enough to prompt expensive housing developments.

What about the boggy areas? Did these attract a poorer quality of housing development? The answer appears to be that they did not. Usually an area that sloped precipitously from its surroundings was simply

2766 West River Road.

ignored by developers the first time around. The only thing that distinguishes these places today, aside from their obvious low-lying quality, is that they have consistently newer houses than do surrounding blocks. There is no perceptible difference in whom they were intended for or in size.

THE STAMP OF INSTITUTIONS AND PARKS

Another kind of aberration in the residential landscape, though not an unexpected one, is the presence of institutional and cultural land of various kinds. Churches, schools, and cemeteries fall into this category. Parks, too, can be considered part of this grouping. For the most part, the institutional land in Minneapolis (churches and so on) is not an impressive element of the landscape. The large downtown churches that are visible from a distance – like St. Mary's Basilica and Hennepin Avenue Methodist Church – are an exception to this general pattern. These buildings were meant to have an impact on the city, and they still do to some degree, though they are being overwhelmed in height by commercial and residential structures. Certainly no church in Minneapolis has the visual impact that St. Paul's Cathedral does. Nevertheless, Minneapolis has many churches that are architecturally distinguished and that lend a bit of drama to the communities they inhabit. In a similar vein, the schools of the city are important to individuals and communities, but few exert a major impact on the city. The obvious exception here is the University of Minnesota, which overwhelms by its sheer size – and its size lessens the effect of the few good buildings it contains (for example, Pillsbury Hall, Nicholson Hall, Bell Museum). There is one outstanding Minneapolis public school building – the castlelike Bremer school in North Minneapolis (now closed for educational purposes). Many other schools were built in what might be considered the "Minneapolis public school style," that is, English Gothic symmetrical structures that are still rather graceful, though most are aging rapidly.

The park system has been touched on briefly already. To many, these are the crowning jewels of the city, lending air, light, and open space to every section of Minneapolis. Though intended to be a "system," the parks were added and improved incrementally, depending on available funds. A few spots still bear traces of the nineteenth-century landscape design ideas that led to the creation of the Minneapolis system. Loring Park and Washburn-Fair Oaks, the latter actually designed by Frederick Olmsted himself, are Minneapolis's best remnants of the nineteenth-century park tradition. The WPA also left a mark on the parks and parkways of the city during the Depression, most notably in the massive effort to shape the Minnehaha Falls area and in the River Road parkway. Most of the other parks combine elements of the "high art" approach to parks (the rose garden and Eloise Butler Wildflower Garden) with a more practical approach to recreational needs (ball parks, tennis courts, and swimming pools).

RUSTY OR FORGOTTEN RAILS

Still another kind of variety within the regions is found in the economically obsolete land uses that persist on the landscape. Examples might include such things as railroad yards and tracksides or streetcar strips. Each of these had an important function in late nineteenth- and early twentieth-century Minneapolis. Today these functions are largely obsolete or have been rendered uneconomical. When Minneapolis was a busy railroad center, the vast spaces given over to rail uses were lively places that employed thousands of people. Since the railroads' freight-hauling functions have been taken over by trucks and are now suburbanized, these vast spaces are little used. Consequently, there is a fair amount of "dead" railroad land scattered throughout the city, but concentrated to some degree in Northeast, in the Hiawatha corridor, and along the river in North Minneapolis. Landmarks of the active rail era remain (primarily grain elevators) but little new construction has occurred on many of these sites. To some degree, now that these lands are little used, they merely serve to interrupt the residential landscape in a negative fashion.

The streetcar strips present a somewhat different case. Though the streetcars are gone, today's bus routes largely replicate the old system. What is missing is the intensity that was generated when streetcars were the primary mode of transportation for most city residents. Many former streetcar strips have become high-volume traffic routes and are more oriented to automobiles than to pedestrians. There are numerous nineteenth-century commercial structures that still line the sidewalks of the streetcar strips, serving as reminders of the past. Among these remnants are many good buildings, such as the Andrews building (208 E. Hennepin) a large masonry structure at Lyndale and Lake, the 118 East 26th Building (in south Minneapolis), and several commercial structures on West Broadway. These buildings, and others of this type, date from the 1880s and 1890s; all have classical facades and are limited to three stories in height. Most were at one time surrounded by other buildings of a similar type and scale. Increasingly, though, buildings of this type are being lost to infill structures of the auto era – that is, fast-food restaurants and other auto-related commercial uses. As the streetcar-era structures are replaced, the streets lose their appeal to pedestrians, along with their identity as places for

Crowell Block (1888), 614 West
Lake Street.

West Broadway commercial
strip. Late 19th century
structures, now modified.

people to shop on their way to and from work.

The streetcar strips of the city perform one other function: They are a key to the prosperity of the surrounding residential areas. Whether or not the commercial structures (both old and new) are occupied, and by what sorts of businesses, tells one a great deal about the economic fortunes of nearby residents. Some former streetcar strips now serve very specialized markets—for example, the artist-oriented restaurants and shops on 26th Street near the art institute and the antique markets near 50th and Penn in prosperous southwest Minneapolis. On a larger scale, the stores around Hennepin and Lake (such as Schlampps and Thomas Designs) obviously serve a higher-income clientele than do the shops and stores on West Broadway or on Central Avenue.

Apart from these elements that add variety to the landscape of Minneapolis, much of the rest of the city exhibits markedly similar characteristics. This is not to say that every part of Minneapolis is a carbon copy of every other part, but that the similarities among the regions tend to override the small differences that do exist.

Inexorable Change

Much of what we have observed, as well as our ability to categorize regions of Minneapolis, would argue that the city has a consistency that is readily visible. We can certainly observe the original patterns of development and construct a framework for understanding the city in this way. But not all places within the city remain the same over time; changes occur quite naturally, and at varying rates in different parts of the city. These differences in the rate and nature of change among the many regions of Minneapolis account for the special qualities of each individual region. There are several important elements that together lead to the greatest amount of change in the city. These will now be examined briefly, along with their effects.

THE AGING, OBSOLESCENCE,
AND DURABILITY OF BUILDINGS
AND DISTRICTS

All buildings get older. Some age more gracefully than others, but all are subject to speculation about continued use due simply to their age. Not every conceivable human activity can be adapted to fit structures of advancing age, nor can every older building be saved. Some structures become obsolete because there is no longer any need for them, nor any use to which they can be put (for example, the lumber

mills along the Mississippi, some vacant schools, train depots). Other buildings are eminently adaptable even though their original purpose has disappeared or the buildings are no longer suited to that purpose (for example, the State and El Lago theaters, the fire stations on 4th Street South and 12th Street North).

As we have observed, economics and taste have played a major role in determining what will last. Buildings that were constructed with care and that have had even a minimum amount of maintenance will in all likelihood last quite a long time. Whether or not they will continue to be be preserved depends on how compatible the stylistic taste of their time is with the present. In general, buildings that were more expensive to construct originally tend to last longer; Minneapolis has a greater supply of late-nineteenth-century Queen Anne and Colonial Revival houses than it does workers' cottages of the same period. Economics alone does not account for this. Houses that were built for the middle class in the last century would still symbolize success to those moving upward socially in this century. It was not only the symbolic quality of the houses that was important. They genuinely offered a better housing option in the sense that the high quality of the original construction kept out the elements and offered more space. Houses built for workers generally had little appeal to anyone who could afford better.

Just being an expensive older house does not guarantee salvation, however. Much depends on where a structure is located and whether pressures exist on that site for nonresidential uses. For example, many important older buildings were torn down in the 1960s to facilitate freeway construction. In an area, like downtown, where economic pressures make high-rise towers the preferred mode of construction, it is very hard to preserve all of the older buildings that remain. It is not only individual buildings that go through the process of aging and obsolescence—entire neighborhoods experience similar pressures. As the wealthy who built up one neighborhood move on to another, the first area declines in status, power, and maintenance. This is a familiar cycle to city residents and to academic observers alike.

What has become clear in recent years is that these transitions can go upward as well as downward. Declining neighborhoods have been brought back to life as an appreciation for city living, antique architecture, or unusual spaces has drawn many into areas once disdained by the middle class. Some parts of Minneapolis have come almost full circle: built by the prosperous middle class of the nineteenth century, left to the working classes in the twentieth, and now being reinhabited by the middle class. The Wedge and

Whittier areas of south Minneapolis are the best examples of this process locally; having been overlooked for years, they are now full of renovation and rehabilitation activity. It is no surprise that formerly wealthy and middle-class areas are most susceptible to being upgraded. Minneapolis has one glowing example of a rehabilitated working class area (Milwaukee Avenue), but most places experiencing such activities were originally built for middle-class residents.

ADAPTATION TO NEW CONDITIONS

The process of adapting buildings and neighborhoods to new conditions is, in effect, a variation on the theme of aging and obsolescence. The new conditions requiring adaptation can be economic (a change in technology), social (new and different immigrant groups coming to the city), or demographic (one generation having many children, the next having fewer). Each type of change will have an impact on the business life of the city as well as on its residential character. Several examples will illustrate this process: (1) When the mills were no longer able to operate economically, some were turned into warehouse space and some were vacated; larger downtown warehouses that had no economic use were also vacated. Buildings of this sort may remain nearly empty for decades without being torn down if located sufficiently far away from the pressures of development. If, however, it becomes economically feasible to turn warehouses and mills into shops and condominiums and there is a market to support such adaptations, these buildings become viable once again. After decades of nonuse and years of discussion about their future, it now seems that the industrial buildings on the riverfront are going to be adapted to fit the new conditions of people wanting to live downtown and to live in nontraditional structures (for example, mills, grain elevators). (2) Some changes can lead to an alteration in the landscape rather than the preservation of existing buildings. For instance, when large numbers of young adults moved into Minneapolis during the 1960s and 1970s, it was clear that the existing housing stock would have to be modified to meet increasing demands for units. To some degree, the standard World War II method of subdividing single-family houses was simply continued. But to a much larger extent, the physical landscape began to be changed in response to the increased demand. The form that this change took was the large-scale construction of two-and-a-half-story apartment buildings, particularly in places like Dinkytown and Whittier, where larger homes had been the predominant housing type. This had the effect of substantially altering the population profile in these areas and also of dramatically changing streetscapes that

had been fairly uniform into eclectic jumbles.

One element of rather recent origin has dramatically affected the look of Minneapolis: the interstate freeway system. In fewer than twenty years, the freeways have become embedded in our consciousness, though we tend to overlook them (literally). Yet the freeways too have something to tell us about changing conditions in the city. The paths they travel speak of the power—or lack of it—of areas nearby. The great dip that I94 takes to skirt the edges of Prospect Park tells of a lobbying effort that local residents made to protect their homes from demolition. The cleared and still-empty land along Hiawatha Avenue in south Minneapolis tells a different version of the same story. Clearance for the freeway occurred here in the mid-to-late 1960s as local transportation officials used available resources to buy up land before prices escalated beyond control. As increasing energy and construction costs have made the completion of the Hiawatha freeway unlikely, this route is now being studied for a light-rail transit line to the airport.

Certain kinds of legislation embody other examples of adapting to new conditions. Some areas of higher income development like Park Avenue and Nicollet Island changed quickly into more mixed land uses, while similar developments of a slightly later date (Lake of the Isles, for example) retained their high-income profile. These situations are not entirely accidental. The pressure to change from one kind of land use to another is almost constant in areas close to downtown, and it requires some kind of artificial mechanism to resist this process. The mechanism that Lake of the Isles and other relatively unchanging areas used was that of deed restrictions—locally generated agreements that prevented any kind of land use other than single-family and duplex dwellings. These protective tools came into being at the time that many upper-middle-income areas were being developed (1913, 1917), and so these assumptions were built into the places from the very beginning.

Zoning itself can be a harbinger of change. Minneapolis implemented a major new zoning ordinance in 1963—the first zoning changes in forty years—largely to encourage commercial development in residential areas. This new legislation greatly relaxed the density requirements in many close-in areas, and its major impact was to spur the construction of higher-density dwellings in formerly single-family and duplex . neighborhoods (like Dinkytown and Whittier). Some areas felt these effects so strongly that by 1975 political pressure led to the revision of the earlier zoning ordinance. Large sections of Minneapolis were downzoned to prevent the continued construction of multifamily units. The results of this most recent adaptation to changing perceptions and desires of residents are not yet fully obvious, but their effects will be felt in years to come as redevelopment pressure extends farther away from downtown.

It is important to remember something about the process of adaptation to new conditions: Only some parts of the city are touched by events that might lead to some kind of adaptation. Most parts of Minneapolis are relatively stable and primarily residential, so there is little reason to expect major kinds of adaptation to occur. Places that are especially prone to the pressures of new population groups or that are located in the older parts of the city (and thus subject to historical association and discovery) are the most likely candidates for this process.

TRENDS AND PLANS FOR FUTURE CHANGE

Our expectations about the city have changed significantly in recent years. In 1970 no one seriously expected Minneapolis to be a city where people would want to live downtown in former warehouses (as in the Itasca), or where century-old houses would be reclaimed and restored (as on Milwaukee Avenue). In reality, these things have changed the face of the city during the past decade. City officials have changed their view of what is possible in response to the new set of realities. The revival of the riverfront sounded like a dream in 1970. Now plans abound for turning the riverfront into prime residential territory—St. Anthony Main and the Winslow House have pointed the way to turn dead land into a high-income asset, and most observers assume that more development of this kind will soon occur.

The merits of redevelopment are debated almost daily; the only point of agreement seems to be that any change should be guided, rather than simply allowed to occur. Now residents are working with city planners to shape the future of the city. In some places (like the low-income Phillips area), residents are taking the process of development into their own hands; through community development and such tools as a land trust, they are working to assure that low-income people continue to have a place in the redeveloped city of the 1980s. Many questions are raised by all this interest in the future of the city. The first is obvious: How long will it last? Is this just another fad, or are people making a commitment to life in the city over life in the suburbs? If interest in reviving and restoring houses and neighborhoods can be linked to the peculiar tastes of the baby-boom generation as it settles down and buys houses, what happens when this generation matures? Nowhere in Minneapolis are any of these processes far enough along to have any ready answers. Nor do we know how trends that might emerge in the coming years

could either supplant or support the changes that have recently occurred. The face of Minneapolis is constantly changing in small ways, and in some areas it changes dramatically again and again. But some parts also remaining essentially constant over long periods of time (though different population groups may move through them). We can only assume, from our vantage point of knowing what changes have already occurred, that Minneapolis in the future will offer a wide range of options, both residential and commercial, just as it does today.

The Record in the Landscape

A great many individuals and events have contributed to the creation of Minneapolis's current landscape. Some we know about, and some we can only guess at. We do know that over the last 130 years, Minneapolis has become a city that can be understood in the aggregate and broken down into component parts; for the purposes of this project, we identified about 125 different regions of the city that had some coherence and consistency and that shared a similar development pattern. We have found in the landscape of this city three themes that can describe much of what is currently visible.

1. The landscape of Minneapolis expresses the pervasive conditions of time and place that led to its creation.

Large sections of Minneapolis remain virtually unchanged from the time of their initial development. For the parts of the city developed since 1940, this is not a miraculous feat. But most of the residential sections of the city—even many dating from the turn of the century—have not been dramatically changed. It is still possible to traverse the residential landscape, look at the types and styles of the housing, and deduce for whom they were built and when. For example, Lowry Hill, built up between 1890 and 1920, still displays nearly uniform streetscapes of large, stylized homes that have been well cared for over the years, housing a population similar to those for whom they were built. In a different way, Northeast Minneapolis tells the story of the people who have lived there. Many houses date from the 1880s and 1890s, but few display the abundant detail that typified this period. The houses here have been modified, often so much that their original shape and style is all but obliterated. These houses betray their owners' ambitions to "improve" the older housing stock they inherited, as well as their abilities to do so, using their own skills.

2. The landscape of Minneapolis expresses elements of individuality and of community.

Octagonal house, 1120 29th Avenue Northeast. Modified after construction.

On a large scale, individuality in building type or neighborhood tends to be found in higher-income areas, where individual preferences can be catered to during construction and sufficient funds can accommodate any stylistic quirks. Indeed, in these areas architects may be sought out specially to produce a completely individualized structure. Persons with wealth undoubtedly have an impact on the building process, but one needn't be rich just to personalize an existing structure. There are examples throughout Minneapolis of buildings that have been extensively altered to produce an effect of great individuality: a rectangular house on 29th Avenue Northeast that has been made into an octagon; another house in Northeast that has a normal shape but that boasts inanimate life of various kinds in every exterior nook and cranny; a small house on North Girard whose

facade has become that of a single story castle; a commercial structure on South 1st Avenue that boasts an elaborate Moorish facade. The mere existence of such flights of fancy lends interest to their streetscapes and forces the observer to pause and wonder about the individuals who created these private worlds.

More commonly, community is expressed in the streets and structures of Minneapolis simply by their remaining much the way they always have been. This unforced adherence to common stylistic preferences fosters a sense of shared goals and values among neighbors, and perhaps across time. Houses that were built in the 1920s for middle-class occupants, that still house this spectrum of society and remain essentially unchanged, connote a sense of continuity over several generations. Streets all over Minneapolis exemplify this

*Despatch Laundry building
(Louis Boynton Bershack,
1929), 2611 1st Avenue South.*

process, but it is perhaps most notable on several blocks of south Minneapolis where the exact house is repeated again and again: Craftsman bungalows on Portland between 46th and 47th, standard bungalows of the 1930s on the west side of Oakland between 43rd and

44th, and a block of 1930s duplexes on Park Avenue between 44th and 45th.

3. The landscape of Minneapolis expresses the process of inexorable change and evolution.

Every part of the city changes, though some places

*Main Street Southeast.
Renovated commercial
structures, built from 1850s to
1890s.*

experience change as a very slow and extremely
incremental process. Naturally, the places that are
noticed and written about are those places experiencing
rapid change, whether the change itself is regarded as
an improvement or as deterioration. For example, the
abandonment of the Near Northside by its middle-class
Jewish population in the 1960s was widely known, as is
the recent resettlement of the downtown fringe areas by
mobile professionals. What is seldom noticed or written
about are all the parts of the city that don't experience
dramatic change—the places that don't generate a lot of
real estate business because people stay in their houses
for a long time, and that will probably never need to be
restored because they are well maintained by whoever
lives there. We don't yet know all that it takes to create
change in the city, but we do know that it is better for
most residents when change comes slowly and they have
a voice in the process. Both levels of maintenance and
an area's perceived status can help determine the rate of
change. Once begun, substantial changes are difficult to

*St. Anthony Main (formerly
Salisbury Mattress Factory), St.
Anthony Falls Historic District.*

slow down or stop. In order for an area to change slowly, the residents must be convinced that they would rather live there than anyplace else. If they are not, and if they have sufficient resources, their part of the city will quickly be left to others, and the process of rapid change will be underway.

PART 4

Legacy of Design

Buildings, Architecture, Memory, Continuity

IN 1849, SIX YEARS before the city of Minneapolis was platted, the English writer John Ruskin wrote that without architecture, "we cannot remember." In his *Seven Lamps of Architecture*, Ruskin assigned one lamp to "Memory," for one of the principal tasks of architecture was to provide an ongoing sense of continuity between the present and the past.[1] Ruskin went on to observe that while the idea of history can deeply and effectively be revealed through the written word, the fact of history can only become real through physical artifacts. And for him there existed no man-made object that more poignantly conveyed the past than architecture. A single building, a streetscape, or a fragment of man-made landscape comments not only on the complexity of life at the moment that it came into being, but equally on the events that have befallen it in its later years.

It is not a surprise that Ruskin, with his insistence on architecture as memory, became one of the leading nineteenth-century proponents of historic preservation. If architecture is indeed the key to the reality of history, he argued, then we must protect these artifacts with the greatest of care. Not only must we battle for their preservation; equally important, we must not tamper with them so as to compromise the purity of their "hallowed antiquity."[2]

Ruskin's strong puritanical notions of preservation encountered the same opposition in Victorian England as they have engendered throughout much of twentieth-century America. The nineteenth century, with its near-religious faith in progress, placed very little value on buildings as memories of the past. It seemed obvious to all that the present was far superior to the past. The byword of progress then and now is insistent change; and change in turn transforms itself into temporariness. As Ruskin observed, temporariness comments on change as movement, but it cannot say anything about what is changing.[3] To understand change, one must have the architecture of the past to provide an interchange with the present.

The rapidity and the magnitude of change present both in the nineteenth-century Victorian city and in cities of this century have made it very difficult to maintain the sense of memory that was so important to Ruskin. Temporariness has been the dominant theme embraced by most urban environments in this century. The continuous change in land use—not only in the substitution of different activities for what formerly existed, but in sheer density of activities—has all but erased whole episodes of the past for many communities.

The classic pattern of a landscape, creation, stability, decay, and then eventual replacement, never occurs consistently throughout any urban environment. In some areas of a city, remnants of the past exist side-by-side with the new, while other areas may appear as encapsulated moments of the past. Nor should we think that buildings constructed of particular materials need have set lifespans. Even a building of wood can continue for centuries if it is reasonably well maintained; on the other hand, the desire for new or intensified land use, or simply the urge to create a new image, can cut short the life of a structure of granite and steel. So too with a segment of a landscape—it can remain reasonably

*Evergreen and Guilford Place.
Early Italianate and French villa
styles in Minneapolis.*

unchanged over decades or can be transformed at a moment's notice.

The city of Minneapolis is both typical and not so typical of the varied processes of change—of the retention of artifacts of the past and of the close-to-complete elimination of them. If we concur with Ruskin that it is worthwhile to cultivate memory so we can understand moments in the past, then Minneapolis, like other American cities, presents a highly mixed series of results. Entire fragments of the city's early history have disappeared; the blocks of suburban Tuscan and neo-Baroque villas surrounded by their extensive gardens, which once were located just south of the commercial downtown, have all been replaced by other building types.[4]

LEGACY FROM COMMERCE
AND INDUSTRY

It was the river and above all the Falls of St. Anthony that prompted the settlement first of St. Anthony and later of Minneapolis on the west bank.

Although the falls were picturesque and "awesome," the nineteenth century's response to the river was essentially utilitarian—it provided a transportation corridor, and the falls provided a source of power.[5] While we can still sense the importance of the falls in nineteenth- and early twentieth-century Minneapolis through the remaining flour mills and warehouses, we are no longer in position to comprehend its dominant position.[6] Of Cheever's Landing (situated on the east riverbank above the Washington Avenue Bridge), the first steamboat landing for St. Anthony and Minneapolis, nothing remains; nor is there any strong visual evidence of the many sawmills that once stood on the west bank of the river between Hennepin Avenue and 36th Avenue North. Since the early 1900s, the river has increasingly assumed the guise of a meandering waterway amid a boulevard park or through weeds and saplings struggling to establish themselves on derelict land.[7]

THE LOST RECORD

If we turn our attention to the city's downtown and

Evergreen and Guilford Place.
Early Italianate and French villa
styles in Minneapolis.

compile a list of major public and private buildings that once graced its streets in the late nineteenth and early twentieth centuries, we find that few remain. In most cases those proud monuments have "bitten the dust," but not because they were on the verge of structural collapse nor because their interior spaces could not be adapted to new needs. They were torn down because their images were viewed as old-fashioned or because of the desire to use the land on which they were situated for new, more profitable purposes.

With the exception of the warehouse district northwest of Hennepin Avenue, the current streetscapes and the city's silhouette are meant to be read as insistently modern and up-to-date. Ruskin's sense of memory, conveyed by buildings, has until recently been consciously denied.

In its development, downtown Minneapolis followed a pattern characteristic of most of our cities.[8] At first the downtown hung close to the Mississippi River — its source of power and industry. The increased industrialization of the riverfront and the arrival of the railroad encouraged a gradual movement of the center of the downtown to the south. By the early 1900s, this direction of movement seemed preordained. The warehouse and manufacturing activities northwest of Hennepin Avenue precluded any movement of the retail and office center of the downtown in that direction, while the old-fashioned decayed buildings in and around Washington Avenue South decreed that the symbolic center of progress was to be as far from them as possible.

Year by year the core of town moved to the south. Specialization intensified, with each of the major north-

south streets assuming a set role: Hennepin Avenue South as the entertainment street, Nicollet Avenue South as the place to shop, and Marquette and 2nd Avenue South as the financial district.

The southward movement of the city's downtown only ceased when the symbol and fact of downtown as the center of the community came into question. When the dispersed horizontal city came into being after World War II, Minneapolis, as did other American cities, organized and stepped up its urban renewal. The "natural" process of creation and decay was to be replaced by the "artificial" process of governmental planning coupled with coordinated public and private financing. Thus downtown Minneapolis today reveals both the open laissez-faire city of pre-1940, and the post–World War II governmental-corporate city of the late 1940s to the present.

SURVIVING FRAGMENTS

How well do the artifacts of the past sum up 130 years of development in Minneapolis? Some of the fragments are still there, but one must frequently be a Nancy Drew to discover many of them; and having come upon them, we must then attempt to uncover what they mean. A helpful way to cultivate Ruskin's sense of memory is to take a single building type and see what has happened over the years.

In America the claim that a village was at long last a town, or that a town had finally "hit the big time" and become a city, has (at least since the mid-nineteenth century) centered on one single building type: the office building. A remembrance of what

Early retail store and residence (1883), 2110 24th Avenue South.

Minneapolis must have been like as a village, in the decades of the 1850s and 1860s, can be obtained by sampling small two-story commercial buildings that have survived outside of the central downtown core. Though most of them were built later, these modest wood structures match in scale and in material what one would have found in Minneapolis's downtown in the 1860s. Reminiscent of this period are the two-story false-fronted clapboard building (c. 1880) at the southwest corner of Broadway and Irving Avenue North and a similar building at 2110 24th Street South (1883).

When a three- or four-story masonry office building was erected on its main street, the village could at long last pose as a town. Examples of these combined retail and office blocks still exist in Minneapolis, though most of them are found away from the downtown. The atmosphere of a nineteenth-century downtown commercial block can be obtained today by walking along sections of West Broadway. Smiley's Point at 2200 Riverside (1889–90), with its contrasting bands of light-colored cast stone played off against dark red brick, illustrates

how assertive one of these small commercial buildings could be. By the end of the 1870s, the city possessed street on street of two- to four-story masonry business blocks in banded Ruskian Gothic or in the Italianate mode. These streets of small business blocks have all disappeared in the downtown, but a few are still to be seen along outlying commercial strips. The Gothic Chute building (c. 1870s) at 301 Hennepin Avenue has vanished. But a three-story brick block that has survived at 925 West Broadway (1912), with its high ground floor and rows of narrow arched windows above, can provide us with some sense of how the Chute building might have related to people on the street.

MONUMENTAL OFFICES, MILLS, AND WAREHOUSES

We generally associate the Queen Anne style with domestic architecture, but it was equally in vogue for two- to three-story buildings, a classic example being the commercial block building at 13–21 5th Street Northeast (1890). At the end of the 1880s, the fashionable rage

was the Richardson Romanesque, with its ponderous masonry skin of roughly hewn red sandstone.[9] These buildings could be small in size, such as the block still standing at 614 Lake Street West (1888), or high-rise blocks like the twelve-story Lumber Exchange (Long and Kees, 1885). The later of these buildings (the Masonic Temple Building, now Hennepin Center for the Arts, Long and Kees, 1888–89, or the unfortunately destroyed Metropolitan building, E. Townsend Mix, 1890) indicate the arrival of an entirely new type of office building and of a marked change in scale for the city. Though we may think that their height and their enclosed square footage was modest, they were nonetheless highly revolutionary for their time. By the late 1890s, their structure was entirely steel frame, with their floors supported by the frame, not by their

Chute building (c. 1870s), 301 Hennepin Avenue; now razed.

Melrose Flats (1890–92), 13-21 5th Street Northeast.

Masonic Temple (Long and Kees, 1888–89); now the Hennepin Center for the Arts.

First National/Soo Line building (Robert W. Gibson, 1914), 105 5th Street.

and others began to suggest the narrow canyons that we associate with so much of New York. The steel frames of these buildings were covered with elegantly detailed surfaces of polished granite, terra-cotta, cast stone, and brick. Correctly detailed pilasters, columns, pedimented entrances, and extensive entablatures and cornices implied that the city's economic base was both stable and cultured. During the twenties the romance of the skyscraper intensified, and the preference for a single image disappeared. In the early twenties, the Medical Arts buildings (Long and Kees, 1923; Long and Thorshov, 1926–29) at the northeast corner of Nicollet Avenue and 10th Street used the Gothic image to symbolize medical sciences. In the next decade, the suggestion of a medieval tower (with a hint at the Moderne Art Deco) was beautifully realized in miniature in the Ivy Tower (Thomas R. Kimball, 1930) at 1115 2nd Avenue South. The skyscraper of the twenties for Minneapolis was of course the Foshay Tower (Magney and Tusler; Hooper and Janusch, 1926–29) at 821 Marquette Avenue South, which by a seemingly magical act transformed the obelisk form of the Washington Monument into a skyscraper for business. The flamboyant exhibitionism of this act was never equalled in Minneapolis, and what followed was sophisticated and quiet. The 1928–29 Rand Tower (Holabird and Root), now the Dain Tower, at 527 Marquette Avenue South, brought the academically correct Art Deco (Zigzag Moderne) to Minneapolis, and that imagery was repeated later in the "blocky" form of the Northwestern Bell Telephone building (Hewitt and Brown, 1930–32) at 224 5th Street South. The telephone company building marked the end of the first phase of skyscraper construction, which had commenced in the late 1880s. For the next chapter of this building type, Minneapolis had to wait until the post–World War II years of the 1950s and later.

If it had achieved its ideal in the 1930s, downtown Minneapolis would indeed have been identical to a slice of midtown New York—rows of skyscrapers rising from the flat riverside terrace and defining the streets as deep canyons. With the exception of a few scattered blocks, this never happened, so the profile was an alternation between low buildings and high-rise units of ten or more floors. This remained the character of the downtown as late as the 1960s.

These downtown low-rise buildings encompass a wide variety of uses, ranging from retail stores to restaurants, theaters, and offices. The specific economic needs that these buildings fulfilled was limited in time—from the 1870s through the second decade of this century. As one would expect, warehouse buildings were at first associated with the river and its falls, and then

masonry walls. Mechanically, they were a wonder, with their banks of elevators and their elaborate systems for heating and ventilation. These skyscrapers, as they were romantically called, indicated that land in the urban core could now be used to create densities never before realized.

The skyscraper quickly became the building type that established the prestige of every American city, and Minneapolis was no exception. Classical Beaux Arts skyscrapers and some that hinted at the medieval began to line Marquette Avenue South, 2nd Avenue South, and the adjoining cross streets, with the implication that this district might someday match New York's 6th or Madison Avenue. The 1914 Soo Line building at 105 South 5th Street (Robert W. Gibson), the 1925 Baker building at 706 2nd Avenue South (Larson and McLaren),

Baker building (Larson and McLaren, 1925), 706 2nd Avenue South.

industry on both sides of the river adjacent to the waterpower of St. Anthony Falls constructed buildings not only for the milling of flour but also for its storage. Fragments of what was once a highly congested industrial area, composed of mills, warehouses, and railways, still remain. On the northeast bank of the river, the six-story limestone-sheathed Pillsbury A Mill (LeRoy S. Buffington, 1881) still stands, as do parts of the Washburn Crosby milling complex (especially the 1880 A Mill and the Crown Roller Mill (1880) on the west side of the river. Like many of the warehouses of the 1880s and later, these milling structures were masonry boxes. They established their presence at the edge of the downtown not by their ornamentation but by their sheer size and by their sensitive use of proportions, patterns of windows, suggestions of pilas-

Northwestern Bell Telephone Company building (Hewitt and Brown, 1930–32), 224 5th Street South.

Crown Roller Mill (W. F. Gunn, 1880), 105 5th Avenue South.

ters, and occasional blind arches and entablatures and cornices.

In the railroad era, corridors of warehouses with accompanying manufacturing activities pushed inland from the falls. One of the most extensive of these districts followed the railroad tracks northwest of downtown, between 3rd and 5th Avenues North. Here the tracks were partially depressed, and a number of the principal streets, Washington Avenue North, 3rd and 4th Streets North, were bridged over much of the tracks. Still remaining as of 1982 are one of the steel bridges (built in 1893 by the Edge Moore Bridge Works, Wilmington, Delaware) and the drawbridge on 3rd Street North that made it possible to descend to the loading platform below the bridges. The six-story limestone ashlar block F. C. Hayer building at the corner of 3rd Avenue North and 3rd Street North (Joseph Haley, 1886) is similar in feeling to many of the early riverside mill buildings. Owners of a number of the later warehouse structures engaged major architects to design their buildings and achieved a strong visual image. Richardson Romanesque was the style employed in a number of these buildings; an example is the Champion building (Long and Kees, 1896) at 428–432 1st Street North or the nearby Lindsay Brothers building (Harry W. Jones, 1895) at 400–408 1st Street North. Fortunately, the two most impressive of the warehouses in this area still survive: the Butler Brothers warehouse (Harry W. Jones, 1906) at 100 6th Street North and the Minneapolis Van and Warehouse building (Cass Gilbert, 1904) at 106 1st Avenue North.

The farm machinery factory-warehouses along 3rd

Metal bridges over railroad (Edge Moore Bridge Company, Wilmington, Delaware, 1893), 3rd and 4th Streets North; recently demolished.

Third Street bridge over Mississippi River.

F. C. Hayer building (Joseph Haley, 1886), 250 2nd Avenue North.

Street South match those located northwest of the downtown in size and quality of design. The Advance Thresher Company building at 700 3rd Street South (Kees and Colburn, 1900), the adjacent Emerson-Newton Plow Company building at 704 3rd Street South (Kees and Colburn, 1904), and the Northern Implement Company building at 616 3rd Street South (Kees and Colburn, 1910), though modest in height (six to seven stories), assert their presence on the streets by the quality of their designs. They were meant to contribute to the architectural character of the city, and they succeeded—not only then but right down to the present moment.

These later warehouse-industrial structures illustrate the high priority placed on up-to-date imagery, as opposed to any effort to openly express their use. Hence

their appearance is more closely related to other contemporaneous buildings than to the historical sequence of earlier or later warehouses. For a nineteenth-century viewer, the small 1886 Itasca warehouse at 702 1st Street North could easily have been mistaken for a small office block; in the late 1930s to the 1950s, the curved glass brick entrance of the Shasta Beverage Company building at 3530 28th Street East (Walter M. Covy, 1946) could have been a movie house or a restaurant.

THE STREET GRID
AND COMMERCIAL STRIPS

The system of streets helps to create the legible image of Minneapolis. The grid that runs parallel or perpendicular to the river announces the location of the original city, while the later section-line grid seems to

Champion building (Long and Kees, 1896), 428–32 1st Street North.

imply that it was the *prairie*, not the river, that was to be the dominant symbol of the new urban hub of the upper Midwest.

Though not planned, the public character of the city was most pointedly established by the interpretation of the grids; this is especially true of the areas south of the downtown. Grid systems work best for urban imagery when they are terminated from time to time, and this is what happened in many sections of Minneapolis. In most American grid cities, accentuation of one street or another suggested boundaries within the system. Even as late as 1914, it was noted in the *Minneapolis Journal* that Franklin Avenue would soon be enjoying a new boom with the completion of the "new crosstown car line [that is] expected to double real estate values in five years."[10] These boundary streets were frequently streetcar routes and commercial strips. Clusters of one- and two-story stores and neighborhood theaters occurred as nodules along the arterial streets. Apartments and many duplexes were concentrated along the streetcar

Minneapolis Van and Warehouse building (Cass Gilbert, 1904), 106 1st Avenue North.

Advance Thresher Company
building (Kees and Colburn,
1900), 700 3rd Street South.

Itasca warehouse (attributed to
Long and Kees, c. 1886),
702–708 1st Street North; now
a condominium complex.

Shasta Beverage Company building (Walter M. Covy, 1946), 3530 28th Street East.

lines. The close linear nature of this housing contrasted with the usual single-family neighborhoods behind them and reinforced the image of these as streetcar strips.

With the construction of the freeway system in the 1960s and 1970s, these strips have in most instances become fragmented memories and endangered artifacts of the Minneapolis past. They are the one building configuration that not only attests to the multiple fingers of the once extensive street railway system but also stirs important recollections of what neighborhoods

were like over a period of many decades.

Equally endangered are the once-numerous neighborhood service stations. Many were embedded in the old strips; and many have disappeared, are now being used for other purposes, or have simply been abandoned. These range from simple brick period stations (such as the one at the southwest corner of 28th Street and Pillsbury Avenue South; 1926) to a pretend–thatched roof "ye olde cottage" type (at 4224 41st Street East, 1926) to a station that is both medieval and

Pure Oil Gasoline service station (1926), 3403 38th Avenue South.

colonial (at the northwest corner of Portland Avenue South and 38th Street East; 1927).

Some of the neighborhood theaters have managed to survive to the present as still-functioning theaters, but most either have disappeared or now serve other purposes. The narrow tower of the Moderne Hollywood Theatre (Liebenberg and Kaplan, 1937) at 28th Avenue and Johnson Street Northeast still poses as a neighborhood landmark. Along Lake Street, the Moderne Fine Arts Theatre (Avalon Amusement Company, 1937)

at 1500 East Lake and the Georgian, almost Baroque facade of the El Lago Theatre (Eckman, Holm Company, 1924) are still standing; the latter is no longer a theater, while the former shows X-rated films.

CURVES AMONG THE RECTANGLES

Irregularity of terrain, and other natural features of the landscape, was another element that checked the seemingly endless grid. If such features were located outside an urban core, they immediately suggested an ideal housing site for the upper middle class or the wealthy. The pattern of streets was almost always the curvilinear "natural" forms we associate with the eighteenth-century picturesque English garden. Because of the basically flat terrain, this grid-disrupting device occurs infrequently in Minneapolis; yet there are enough examples to make its effect apparent. In north Minneapolis a small upland enclave, Elmwood, occurs north of Olson Memorial Highway between Humboldt and Logan Avenues North. In south Minneapolis the sharp rise of Loring and Kenwood hills encouraged irregular street patterns. Farther south, Washburn Hill (developed by Thorpe Brothers from 1910 on), situated west of Nicollet Avenue South near 50th Street West, provided the city with its largest picturesque pattern of streets.[11]

Each of these picturesque episodes comments on quite different aspects of the city's past. The curved pattern of streets in the Elmwood district north of Olson Memorial Highway, with its smaller-sized lots, served briefly as a middle-class suburban neighborhood in the late nineteenth century. Before the turn of the century, the Kenwood and Loring Hills district boasted many of the mansions of the rich; Washburn Hill was pure upper middle class and was basically a development of the 1920s. As memories of the past, Elmwood and Washburn are pretty well intact—we can read them with ease. Such is not the case with Kenwood and Loring, where changes since the late 1890s have eliminated any strong reinforcement to their history. Their irregular street patterns remain, but the scale of the newer buildings alongside them and the injection of the freeway to the north of Loring Hill prevent us from responding to this picturesque district as a readable artifact of the past.

Remembrance—Public Space

If we turn to the public aspect of Minneapolis, the outstanding features are the parks and lakes, not the pattern of streets or the public buildings. The only streets that stand out as major public spaces are those directly related to the city's extensive park system. And

Hollywood Theatre (Liebenberg and Kaplan, 1935), 28th Avenue and Johnson Street Northeast.

while some public buildings have been—and still are—striking monuments, they have not created dominant visual symbols within the community. The churches are the one and only building type that has assumed importance in the public realm of the city.

FRAGMENTS OF IMAGERY IN THE STREET LAYOUT

The moments in time when individual areas were laid out and incorporated into the city—from the initial platting of St. Anthony in 1849 to the city's major transformation by freeways in the 1960s—are difficult to read by examining what presently exists. Here Ruskin's memories of the past are best gained not by walking along the streets but by abstracting the reality of history with the help of overlays of old maps, historic photographs, and written texts. The river orientation of the original street grid patterns (St. Anthony, 1849, and Minneapolis, 1855) still exists, but it is not easily readable when one is transversing the city. And if we carefully follow the expansion of the city toward the

northeast, north, and west sides after St. Anthony and Minneapolis were first platted, the divisions between the earlier and later additions are anything but clear. Then, too, the dates of the city's expansion do not necessarily mirror the period in which each of these areas was developed. Thus, to the north the region between 36th Avenue and Victory Memorial Drive became a part of the city in 1887, but it was not fully developed until after 1945. To the south the segment of the city between 54th Street and 62nd Street was incorporated into the city in 1927, but its development too had to wait until the post–1945 years.

During the City Beautiful movement, extensive plans were prepared in 1906, and again between 1909 and 1917, for grand boulevards terminating in major public buildings and monuments.[12] Only two partial fragments of these schemes were ever built. One included the pavilion at Gateway Park (Hewitt and Brown, 1915) and the Great Northern passenger station (Charles S. Frost, 1912) on lower Hennepin. The other is the Thomas Lowry Memorial (Karl Bitter, sculptor,

Gateway Pavilion (built 1915, razed 1960s); on site of Towers condominiums.

Northern Pacific railroad station (Charles S. Frost, 1912).

1914). Now located at the west corner of Hennepin Avenue South and 24th Street West, it first stood on the southern triangle at the junction of Hennepin and Lyndale Avenue South. Thus almost nothing of these great City Beautiful monuments remains, nor is there any visible legacy from the post–World War II grand planning scheme to create an open public mall from Hennepin Avenue southward along Washington Avenue to Portland.[13] A suggestion of the effectiveness of Beaux Arts axial planning can be experienced where Hennepin Avenue is terminated at Lakewood Cemetery. The colonnaded white granite administration building (Frank E. Read, 1908), as seen when one looks south on Hennepin Avenue, provides just the type of conclusion that Burnham and Bennett and others were trying to create in the city.

The one and only Beaux Arts planning scheme realized in Minneapolis was that of Cass Gilbert's mall (1907-1910) at the University of Minnesota.[14] Gilbert's plan for the mall, lined with colonnaded buildings, with

Thomas Lowry Memorial (Karl Bitter, 1914); moved in 1967 to triangle, Hennepin Avenue, Emerson Avenue, and 24th Street.

The mall, University of Minnesota.

its southern end opening toward and cascading down to the Mississippi River, was never fully carried out. As in other similar Beaux Arts academic plans, the open end of this mall was finally enclosed in 1940, with the construction of Coffman Memorial Union (Clarence H. Johnston, Jr.). Even so, we can still stand in front of the Union and, looking north to Northrop Memorial Auditorium (Clarence H. Johnston, Jr., 1929), obtain a sense of what these Beaux Arts City Beautiful proponents were trying to achieve in the way of grand formal public spaces.

Another aspect of past public space that can still be partially experienced is that of the streetcar corridors that at one time crisscrossed the city and connected it to its suburbs and to neighboring St. Paul. Examples are the broad thoroughfares of Central Avenue Northeast or Nicollet Avenue South. In Southwest Minneapolis, the diligent detective can still find the remains of the classic suburban streetcar right-of-way that ran from 31st Street West, along the south shore of Lake Calhoun, Lakewood Cemetery, the northeastern shore of Lake Harriet, and thence west adjacent to 44th Street West.

THE PARKS

In the late nineteenth century, the larger American cities slowly began to acquire extensive lands that could be developed as public park lands. But as was the case with the planning projects of the later Beaux Arts City Beautiful movement, few of these schemes of acquisition were ever fully carried out. An exception was Minneapolis. By the end of the 1930s, this city had created a park system unequalled by any other in America.[15] By carefully taking advantage of the natural features of the landscape—lakes, streams, and the river—the city established a visual and recreational greenbelt that visually tied together almost the whole of the city. It was this connected system of parks that provided the principal termination and accent to the city's generally rigid grid system of streets. Supplementing the connected belt of parks were other visually important public open spaces. The Parade and Loring Park provided a southern terminus of the downtown. Powderhorn Lake Park served as a large open breathing space for the south central area. And there were numerous small, carefully sited recreational parks throughout the city.[16]

Recreation shelter (1906),
Loring Park.

All of the parks continue to exert such a strong effect that they symbolize the present city and its continuity as much as they preserve remembrances of the past. Some fine specific symbols of the past persist. The curved flowing forms of the shoreline and islands of man-made Lake of the Isles and of the pond in Loring Park beautifully reflect the nineteenth-century Picturesque tradition of landscape architecture. Perhaps designed objects, ranging from buildings to bridges, provide the easiest and most suggestive means for acquiring a feel of the past. In Loring Park the small Queen Anne park shelter (1889) and the later Mission Revival park pavilion (1906) provide us with two historic episodes in this park's history. The pair of bridges between Lake of the Isles and Lake Calhoun (1910–11) and the one on the waterway between Lake of

Bridge #2 (1910–11), between Lake Calhoun and Lake of the Isles.

Pavilion (1904), Beard's Plaisance, Lake Harriet.

Chalet (1930), Theodore Wirth Park.

the Isles and Cedar Lake (1910–11) comment on the primacy of the classical Beaux Arts in the first decades of this century. The bandstand at Lake Harriet (1927), the open pavilion in the Beard's Plaisance (1904), and the refectory at Minnehaha Park (Downs and Eds, 1905) do succeed in conveying the rural feeling of Minneapolis and its parks at the turn of the century. Equally helpful in conjuring up memories of the past within the parks are the stone, wood, and stucco chalet (Magney and Tusler, 1923) that rises out of the hillside in Theodore Wirth Park and the sensitively scaled Nicollet Avenue South Bridge, which enhances rather than compromises Minnehaha Creek and Parkway lying below.

CONVERGENCE AND CONGREGATION

A traditional public element of any nineteenth- or twentieth-century American city was that of the point of entry. In Minneapolis the oldest passenger railroad stations are gone; so too is the later Beaux Arts Great Northern passenger station. Remaining is the Milwaukee passenger station and train shed (Charles S. Frost, 1897–98) at 201 3rd Avenue South. The tower of this station proclaimed its public nature, but its siting along Washington Avenue South was anything but ceremoniously public. Equally uncivic in its location was the Streamline Moderne Greyhound bus terminal (Lang and Raugland, 1936) at 29 7th Street North.

If Minneapolis can be said to have once had something approaching a "civic center," it was situated at the western side of Loring Park where Hennepin and Lyndale Avenues briefly come together before ascending Lowry Hill. Dominating this once-upon-a-time public space are the three largest churches of the city: the Basilica of St. Mary (Emmanuel L. Masqueray, 1907–25), the Episcopal Church of St. Mark (Hewitt and Brown, 1908–11), and the Hennepin Avenue Methodist Church (Hewitt and Brown, 1914). These churches are supplemented by Walker Art Center (Long and Thorshov, 1925; remodeled, Magney, Tusler, and Setter, 1940; new building, Edward Larabee Barnes, 1969–71) and the Dunwoody Institute (Hewitt and Brown, 1914), and by the Beaux Arts design and public setting of 510 Groveland, now the Groveland Avenue Hotel (Larson and McLaren, 1927), together with the National Life Insurance Company building, now Loring Park Office Building (Hewitt and Brown, 1924), located across from Loring Park at 430 Oak Grove. The builders of the freeways in the 1960s came close to completely destroying this center, but if one walks through Loring Park or through sections of the remaining Parade Grounds to the west, the public aspect of this open landscaped space and its monumental churches is still apparent.

Nicollet Avenue Bridge (1923), over Minnehaha Creek.

As a building type, churches occur in profusion throughout the whole of the city. In the downtown, Westminster Presbyterian Church (Charles S. Sedgwick, 1896–98) and the First Baptist Church (Long and Kees, 1887–88) match in importance as public buildings the Minneapolis City Hall (Long and Kees, 1888–1905) or the former public library (Long and Kees, 1889), which stood on the south corner of Hennepin Avenue South at 10th Street. Although there have been numerous losses over the years, Minneapolis churches do provide one of the most complete pictures of any single public building type to be found in the city. They also project a strong public image into a variety of different environments, ranging from the downtown itself to outlying commercial strips and on into the suburbs. Our Lady of Lourdes Church (1857), at 21 Prince Street Southeast, is one of the few very early public buildings left that does portray the siting of the town of St. Anthony above the great falls of the river. The location of the historic Gethsemane Episcopal Church (1882–84), at the corner of 4th Avenue South and 9th Street, helps us to realize

Milwaukee railroad station and train shed (Charles Frost, 1897–98), Washington Avenue and 3rd Street South.

Greyhound bus terminal (Lang and Raugland, 1936), 29 7th Street North; now a nightclub.

Episcopal Church of St. Mark (Hewitt and Brown, 1908–11), 511 Oak Grove.

Dunwoody Institute (Hewitt and Brown, 1914), 818 Wayzata Boulevard.

National Life Insurance Company building (now Loring Park Office Building) (Hewitt and Brown, 1924), 430 Oak Grove.

that this section of the present downtown was once an upper-middle-class residential neighborhood. In southeast Minneapolis, Andrew-Riverside Presbyterian Church (Warren H. Hays, 1886), at 500 8th Avenue Southeast, indicates the residential tradition of this area. Equally powerful community symbols in North Minneapolis are the Forest Heights Congregational Church (1908), at 2054 James Avenue North, and the 1938 Victory Temple, at 2401 Aldrich Avenue North. In South Minneapolis the many residential suburban churches convey a variety of different images: rural Gothic in the Plymouth Congregational Church (Shepley, Rutan, Coolidge, 1907), at 1900 Nicollet Avenue; the numerous symbolisms attached to the staid respectability of the classical Beaux Arts in the Christian Science Church (Solon S. Beman, 1912–14) at 4–10 24th Street East and in Temple Israel (Liebenberg and Kaplan, 1928), at the corner of West 24th Street and Emerson Avenue South; avant-gardism of the Prairie School in the Stewart Memorial Church (Purcell and Feick, 1908–09), at 116 32nd Street East; and the

Craftsman movement of the bungalow church in St. Andrew's Lutheran Church (1907), at 3118 49th Street West.[17] The diversity of religious and cultural background of the people of the city is well reflected in these religious structures. The Near Eastern domes of St. Mary's Russian Orthodox Catholic Church (Boehme and Cordella, 1905), at the corner of 5th Street and 17th Avenue Northeast, indicates one ethnic center, as does the Mihro Kodesh Synagogue, now the Disciples Ministry Church (S. J. Bowler, 1926), at the northeast corner of Oliver Avenue North and Oak Park North.

In addition to its churches, Minneapolis did fashion another building type that contributed to the public aspect of the city—its water towers. For functional reasons, these were placed on the highest ground available and naturally formed strong accents that came to designate individual sections of the city. Of these, the most assertive are the medieval witch's hat Prospect Park Water Tower (E. W. Cappelen, 1913), at Seymour Avenue and Malcolm Street Southeast, which establishes the center of the Prospect Park district; and the

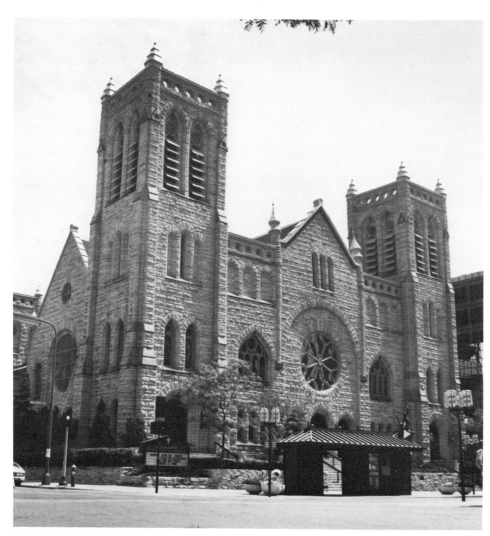

Westminster Presbyterian Church (Charles Sedgwick, 1896–98), 1201 Nicollet Avenue.

Minneapolis Public Library (Long and Kees, 1889), 10th Street South and Hennepin Avenue; razed in the 1960s.

Our Lady of Lourdes Church (built 1857, expanded 1881), Prince Street Southeast.

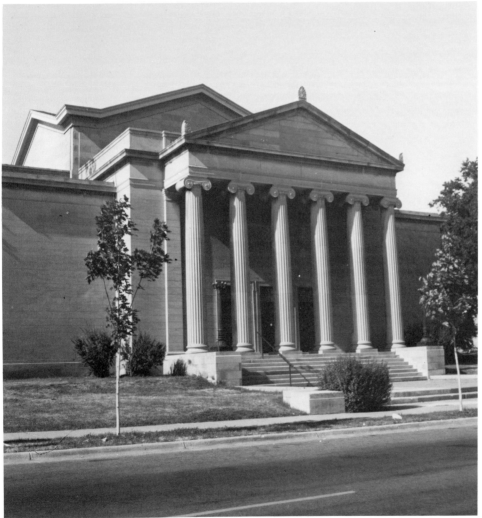

Victory Temple (1938), 2401 Aldrich Avenue North.

Plymouth Congregational Church (Shepley, Rutan, and Coolidge, 1907–08), 1900 Nicollet Avenue.

Christian Science Church (Solon S. Beman, 1912–14), 4–10 24th Street East.

St. Andrew's Lutheran Church (Downs and Eds, 1907), 3118 49th Street West.

Temple Israel (Liebenberg and Kaplan, 1928).

Stewart Memorial Church (Purcell and Feick, 1908–09), 116 32nd Street East.

Washburn Water Tower guarded by its medieval knights (Harry W. Jones; William S. Hewitt; J. K. Daniels, sculptor, 1931-32), on Prospect, which creates a similar symbolic center for the Washburn District Park.

In Minneapolis the buildings that one would normally think of as the principal public centers of the community do not in fact establish such preeminence. The handsome Romanesque Revival Minneapolis City Hall and Hennepin County Old Court House (Long and Kees, 1888-1905), at the northeast corner of 3rd Avenue South and 5th Street, is a distinguished example of this historic imagery, but its siting, just east of the center of the downtown, meant that it did not come to dominate all or even part of the scene. The same is true for the classical Beaux Arts Federal Office Building and Post Office (James Knox Taylor, 1912), at 200 Washington Avenue South; the PWA Moderne Post Office (Magney and Tusler, 1931-32), at 100 1st Street South; and the Minneapolis Armory (P. C. Bettenburg, 1935-36), at 500 6th Street South. And even though McKim, Mead, and White's Minneapolis Institute of Arts (1912-14) faces onto the open space of Washburn Fair Oaks Park, it is in fact sequestered away from the heart of the city.

Another telling clue to the value placed on the public aspect of life can be seen in the distribution of public school buildings (along with their playgrounds and landscaped grounds) and of many dispersed branch public libraries. The small branch public libraries, such as the one at 1314 Franklin Avenue East (Edward L. Tilton; Chapman and Magney, 1914) or the later Linden Hills Branch Library (J. V. Vanderbilt, 1930-31), at 2900 43rd Street West, are suburban in scale, but still they manage to suggest that they are official and public. The schools too managed to maintain the suburban image, primarily through their often extensive landscaped grounds, but also through their use of historic architectural images, whether it be medieval English as one finds in the Central High School building (W. B. Ittner, 1912-13), 4th Avenue South at 34th Street, or somewhat sparse classicism as in the Ramsey Junior High School building (Edward H. Engler, 1931-32), northwest corner of Nicollet Avenue South at 50th Street.

Perhaps these smaller public buildings, schools, branch libraries, and park recreation buildings, which were scattered throughout the residential districts, more perfectly sum up the middle-class view of government and community effort than do any of the various large public buildings situated in the downtown.

Remembrances — Flats to Apartments

Apartment buildings, flats above stores, connected town

Washburn water tower (J. K. Daniels, sculptor; William S. Hewitt; Harry Jones, 1931–32), Prospect Avenue near Minnehaha Creek.

Minneapolis Armory (P. C. Bettenberg, 1935–36), 500 6th Street South.

Franklin Avenue Branch Public
Library (Edward L. Tilton;
Chapman and Magney, 1914),
1314 Franklin Avenue.

Linden Hills Branch Library
(J. V. Vanderbilt, 1931), 2900
43rd Street West.

Ramsey Junior High School
(Edward H. Engler, 1931–32),
Nicollet Avenue South and 50th
Street.

houses, and duplexes did not assume the importance in
Minneapolis that they did in many Eastern and Midwestern cities. In part this was due to the general
feeling that the ideal in a middle-class society should be
the single-family detached house. But it was as well a
direct result of the city's size, its pattern of historic
growth, and above all the time period during which it
developed. Compared to other building types whose
history is highly fragmented, one can form a good idea
of the history of multiple housing from the 1880s on by
examining what still remains.

THE NINETEENTH CENTURY

In the late nineteenth century, apartment buildings
and row houses began to mushroom in the region south-
east of the downtown, in and around 7th to 15th Streets
South, with 9th Street South being the principal center.
But varied types of multiple housing were built
throughout the city, and some of it was quite early. On
Nicollet Island, for example, the French Second Empire
Grove Street Flats (Kenway and Wirth), at 2–16 Grove
Street, were built as early as 1877, and other three- and
four-story blocks were built throughout northeast
Minneapolis. In the city's early decades, the general
tendency was to build two-story flat buildings or two- to
four-unit row houses. If these were of any size, they
were usually constructed of masonry. The adjoining
town houses at 444–446 Madison Street Northeast
(pre-1884; altered to double house in 1888), with their
Eastlake false front, illustrate how even in the more
modest examples of multiple housing an effort was made
to establish some sense of urbanity.

Grove Street Flats (Kenway and Wirth, 1877), 2–16 Grove Street, before restoration.

Grove Street Flats after restoration.

The attached town house at 617–621 19th Avenue South (1886) is of brick, two stories high; the two connected houses at 2426–2428 14th Avenue South (1885) are of wood. In scale and detail, both suggest that they are simply enlarged single-family dwellings. By the mid-1880s the number and the size of multiple housing dramatically increased, and row houses were joined by an increased number of tenement flats. In North Minneapolis the Universal Stone Building Company erected in 1885 an L-shaped group of eleven two-story row houses built entirely of concrete blocks—a remarkable early use for this material.[18] More typical of the time was the row of seven units built by Hagen and Morse at 614–626 9th Street South (1886). This three-story brick building combined seventy-four rooms divided among seven units and was obviously meant to be occupied by the "better classes," that is, the upper reaches of the middle class.

One of the most intense building booms ever experienced in America took place at the end of the 1880s, and Minneapolis participated in it to the fullest. Two-to four-story tenements (most built for rental, others for sale) began to appear around the periphery of the downtown and along many of the streetcar commercial strips. The architect F. A. Clark designed a number of the larger and more pretentious of these tenement buildings, including the Potter and Thompson building (1888), at the corner of Chicago Avenue South at 10th Street South, and the La Fling twenty-four-flat building (1893), at the corner of 6th Avenue South and 9th Street South. From the beginning, single-family residential areas were interspersed with occasional row houses.

From the nineties on, there was an increased shift from town houses to duplexes. These duplexes generally posed as single-family houses—at least on their front elevations. From the mid-1890s on, the favored image was that of the white clapboard Colonial Revival box, generally exhibiting a one- or two-story porch facing toward the street. As with single-family housing, these duplexes were usually built for sale rather than for long-term investment on the part of the builder or investors. In their advertisements addressed to the middle class, the speculative builders urged that the purchase of one of these buildings would enable the owner-occupant to live as in a single-family detached house and at the same time to derive enough rent to meet the monthly payments.[19]

When the streetcar lines were electrified, beginning in 1889, and the extensive grid of street rails was established, there was an increased tendency to line these streets with duplexes and apartment buildings. At the principal nodes along the streetcar lines, tenement flats (rather than offices) generally occupied the second floor above the street-level retail stores. This spreading of multiple housing to the outlying districts was certainly one factor discouraging the growth of extensive districts of apartments in and around the downtown.

Only the area adjacent to and east and south of Loring Park began to take on the semblance of such a district. That was the only section of the city that eventually developed with blocks of three- to five-story apartment buildings. Most of these brick apartment buildings were constructed in the teens and twenties, and they replaced moderate to large single-family dwellings that had been erected in the eighties and nineties. The smaller of these apartment buildings contained six units, the larger as many as eighteen to twenty-five.

Fortunately, the openness of Loring Park, the irregularity of the street pattern around Lowry Hill, and the existence of tall boulevard trees kept the area from being overly urbanized. Because of the size and expense of these apartment buildings, they tended to be built by individuals or syndicates as long-term investments, and

Italianate duplex (1888), 444 and 446 Madison Avenue Northeast.

Eleven-unit concrete block apartment dwelling (W. D. Kimball, 1885), 3rd Street North and 26th Avenue North.

Three townhouses (1886), 614–626 9th Street.

they were almost always designed by architects. The three-story Richmond Apartments at 521 9th Street South (T. A. Clark, 1894) and the apartments at 614–626 9th Street South (1886) are characteristic of the larger units built before the turn of the century. The rapid shifts in architectural taste then taking place are apparent if one compares the Richardson Romanesque Oakland Apartments (1889), at 215 9th Street South, to the Lee Residence (1887), at 623–625 9th Street South, where the medieval quality of the Romanesque and classical Beaux Arts imagery nearly overlap in timing of development.

The investment interest in building four- to eight-unit apartments accelerated after 1910. And while a good number of these apartments were built along the streetcar lines, many others were scattered (along with duplexes) throughout the older residential sections. In the teens and at the beginning of the twenties, the predominant form was that of the Craftsman brick or stucco box, with its sense of shelter enhanced by its extended low-hipped roof. Other than their limited use of brick as decorative trim, these buildings tended to rely on their placement of windows and their general proportions to suggest their architectural character. Their exterior puritanical simplicity was repeated within, though the size of an average apartment was quite generous. In the larger apartment buildings

Colonial Revival duplex (c. 1905), 1767 Humboldt Avenue South.

Legacy of Design · 139

Two apartment buildings (N. J. Blenhof, 1927), 3947 and 3955 1st Avenue South.

Five apartment buildings (N. J. Blenhof, 1930), 4711, 4717, 4721, 4725, and 4731 Nicollet Avenue South.

sheathed in brick, occasional decorative effects were introduced through the use of different colored brick and by the projection or recession of single or multiple rows of brick, as occurred on two adjoining apartment buildings at 3947 and 3955 1st Avenue South (N. J. Blenoff, 1927).

In the twenties, an effort was made to transform the area northeast of Lake Calhoun into a new apartment district. This appeared to be an ideal location. The inhabitants of the apartments could enjoy not only the proximity of the lake but also a larger-than-normal commercial hub at the corner of Hennepin Avenue South and Lake Street West (eventually even boasting two motion picture theaters), together with numerous connections on the streetcar system. The characteristic apartment building constructed in the area contained six units, each of five rooms. The two lower units (or four if the building was a ten- to twelve-unit building) were placed in half-basements, so that the total height of the building was two and a half floors above ground. Reflecting the richer architectural imagery of the twenties, these buildings mirrored a variety of past modes, ranging from the medieval to the Colonial Revival, the Art Deco, the Spanish, and even the Islamic. Twisted columns and horseshoe arches of cast stone proudly announced that the apartment house at 3028 James Avenue South (C. J. Bard, 1929) was appropriately labeled "Moorish Mansion." Along Nicollet Avenue South, the historical reminiscence ranged from the medieval (apartment building, 4625 Nicollet Avenue South; Milton Goldstein, 1930) to exotic sunny Spain (apartment building, 4815 Nicollet Avenue South; Perry Crosier, 1931). Closer to the downtown, the apartment building at 2014 2nd Avenue South (Arthur Dahlstrom, 1928) represents one of the few buildings in the city of these years that clothed itself in a Colonial Revival image.

Apartment towers were a frequently encountered multiple-housing building type of the twenties in most American urban centers. In Minneapolis only two were built, though by the end of the decade a number were proposed. 510 Groveland (Larson and McLaren, 1927)

*Moorish Mansion apartments
(C. J. Bard, 1929), 3028 James
Avenue South.*

presented a reserved Beaux Arts Classic design, and its sensitive siting on Loring Hill successfully related it to the nearby towers of St. Mark's Episcopal Church and Hennepin Avenue Methodist Church. And if Chicago could have apartments on its lakefront, why not Minneapolis? The Lake Calhoun Club (Magney and Tusler, 1927–29; completed in 1946) is pure Chicago, plunked down on the north shore of Lake Calhoun. Cast stone cornices, entablatures, and pilasters suggested the classical derivation of its design. The Depression of the thirties delayed the completion of this building, and the weakness of the economy destroyed the dream of siting a number of these high-rise apartments around the northwest shore of the lake.

Such apartment towers were meant to provide luxurious housing for the upper middle classes, and 510 Groveland and the Lake Calhoun Club were directed toward this audience. The scarcity of such upper-middle-class housing in Minneapolis was just another indication of how firm the commitment was to the suburban (or Lake Minnetonka) single-family detached dwellings.

Apartment house (Milton Goldstein, 1930), 4625 Nicollet Avenue South.

Apartment house (Perry Crosier, 1931), 4815 Nicollet Avenue South.

Calhoun Beach Club (Magney and Tusler, 1927–29), Lake Street and Dean Boulevard.

THE DUPLEX CULTURE

On a walk or drive along the residential streets of Minneapolis, one is struck by the high percentage of duplex units that are interspersed among the single-family dwellings. For a city supposedly committed to the sanctity of the detached house, it is remarkable how many duplexes were built, not only before World War I but especially afterward, in the twenties and early thirties. As in the earlier years, the rationale presented to prospective buyers was both economic and geographic—one could make home ownership financially sensible and at the same time one could live in the "suburbs." The Minneapolis architect John W. Lindstrom produced several pattern books resplendent with Craftsman stucco duplexes.[20] The one at 1301 Lowry Avenue Northeast (1926) has all of the Craftsman ingredients, including a brick flower box, as does the typical duplex at 4556 Bryant Avenue South (1921). The later gabled half-timber and stone-trimmed facades of these stucco duplexes of the twenties and thirties were meant (at least symbolically) to lead one into believing that they were simply good-sized single-family houses. And in a sense they were, for each floor of the building contained just about the same amount of space, arranged in a plan identical to what builders were providing in their speculative ("spec") medieval bungalows.

Craftsman duplex (1921), 4656 Bryant Avenue South.

Like spec houses and bungalows of the time, the plans and facades of these duplexes, with their hint of the medieval, were perfect examples of pattern book architecture.[21] If two or more duplexes were built side by side, changes in fenestration and roof lines were introduced. One shift that was approved at the con-

Duplex plan from pattern book by John W. Lindstrom.

Duplex plan from pattern book by John W. Lindstrom.

clusion of the twenties was that a good number of these duplexes were built not by individual builders, but by construction/investor companies. Thus, along Hennepin Avenue South between 34th and 35th Streets West, seven duplexes were built by one company between 1929 and 1931, and it was noted that "the extension architecture will vary with Colonial, English and French types . . . giving individuality to each."[22] Another block of duplexes with similar varied images was constructed along the east side of Portland Avenue South between 44th and 45th Streets East (1928–31).

When building actively resumed after World War II, the construction of duplexes and apartments continued to infill older residential districts and to accompany new single-family housing in the last sections of undeveloped land. The mixing of these multiple units with single-family residences basically mirrored the pattern that had occurred in the 1920s and 1930s. But the character of those housing units had dramatically changed. The pre-1945 two-family two-story building now became a single-floor double bungalow, like those at 4625–27, 4629–31, and 4637–39 Cedar Avenue South (1945). These double bungalows were at least a third smaller than a twenties duplex. (A similar constriction of space occurred in the fourplex to eightplex apartment buildings.) The interior atmosphere of these typical double bungalows of the 1950s and early 1960s was that

Craftsman duplex (1926), 1301 Lowry Avenue Northeast.

Group of seven duplexes (1929–31), Hennepin Avenue between 34th and 35th Streets.

"Spec" duplexes (1928–31), 4400 block of Portland Avenue South.

of a motel rather than that of a single-family home. These single-floor double houses made only the slightest effort to conceal the fact that they were double units, though their low volume, covered by shelter-suggesting roofs, fitted them comfortably with the older adjoining residences. Occasionally in one- and two-story duplexes, like that at 5914–16 Nicollet Avenue South (c. 1955), shutters, paneled doors, and other lightly handled historical reminiscences suggested that the heritage of these double bungalows was supposedly Colonial.

The characteristic smaller apartment houses of these years were as utilitarian-looking as the double houses, and they made only a passing claim to exhibit "architecture." An exception would be the Hennepin Aristocrat Apartments (Liebenberg and Kaplan, 1961) at 3322 Hennepin Avenue South, where the popular Modern of the fifties was realized with vigor.

Group of double bungalows (1945), 4625–27 and 4629–31 Cedar Avenue South.

City of Lakes—and Homes

Since the early 1900s, Minneapolis has promoted the image of itself as the "City of Lakes"; but at the same time, like many other American cities, it has sought to project itself as the "city of homes." And "homes" meant not multiple housing but single-family dwellings, each situated on its own lot. Nor was the phrase "city of homes" meant to designate sharply divided districts based on class and wealth. The American ideal of a universal middle class, expressed in part by the symbol of the family ensconced in a suburban dwelling, was the ideal in Minneapolis; and to a considerable extent this

ideal was realized. "Owning a home," observed the *Minneapolis Journal* in 1916, is "a man's first duty as a good citizen."[23]

HOUSE AS HOME

From the 1870s on, the grid streets of the city, with their wide tree-planted boulevards, were lined with one- and two-story single-family houses—almost all of which were produced by small-scale builders. In a formal sense, this housing was not architect designed, although

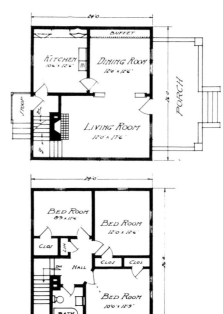

Plan for early 20th century
speculative house.

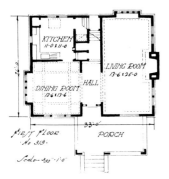

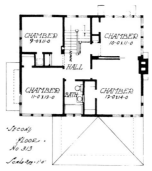

Plan for early 20th century
speculative house.

indirectly it was. The design source for these houses and cottages came in many cases from popular national and regional pattern books, later supplemented by popular home magazines and building trade journals. As speculative houses, those dwellings in most cases were built not for a specific family but for the "typical" middle-class family. The norm might be a modest story-and-a-half cottage for the artisan segment of the middle class or a spacious two-and-a-half-story barnlike structure for the upper middle class, but still it was a norm. As in all speculative housing of the nineteenth and twentieth centuries, a series of logical givens controlled their production. They must have an audience who could be prevailed on to purchase them; they must be economically feasible; they must provide for utilitarian needs; they must convey an acceptable image of fashion; and finally, of course, the product—in this case the house and its lot—must provide a reasonable return to the builder and those financing him.

In contrast to many other American cities, in Minneapolis the middle-class ideal of a single free-standing dwelling was basically maintained from the 1870s to the early 1970s. Attached row houses, such as one finds in many American cities, never became important in Minneapolis; and wood, in contrast to brick or other modes of masonry, remained as the dominant structural material for domestic architecture. The lot sizes in Minneapolis—while not large—were more than adequate for middle-class housing. The 50-by-120-plus-foot lot remained the norm. Since alleys were normally provided, most of the property, including the side yards, could be devoted to greenery of one type or another. The general effect then of a typical residential street in the city was that of a spacious green linear corridor—the paired boulevards with their trees and grass, supplemented by the greenery of front and side yards within which the dwelling stood. Even where, as was the case in sections of the Kenwood district, large houses were placed on modest-sized lots, the effect was still suburban, that is, with nature predominating.

The builders of Minneapolis's speculative houses produced dwellings that in plan and imagery could be found in just about any other American city. The Eastlake and Queen Anne cottages and houses built in the city in the 1870s through the 1890s were almost identical to what one would find being constructed in the outskirts of other midwestern or eastern cities. And the same was true of the Colonial and lightly Medieval Revival houses and bungalows of the 1920s and 1930s. Minneapolis's up-to-dateness in architectural fashions was reflected not only in the built houses, cottages, and bungalows, but equally in popular home builders' magazines that were produced in the city. *Keith's Home Magazine* (later named *Beautiful Home Magazine*) was published there between 1899 and 1931; and from 1922 to 1932 Robert T. Jones edited and published *The Small Home* magazine.[24] These popular home builders' magazines influenced speculative design in Minneapolis, and their illustrations and plans advertised houses that

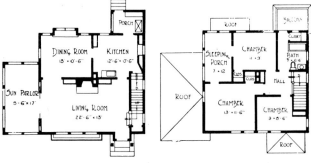

Plan for early 20th century speculative house.

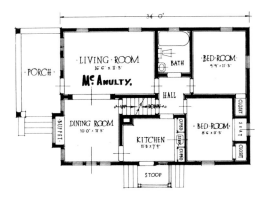

Plan for early 20th century speculative house.

had already been built in the city. Several of the architects of Minneapolis participated in the design of speculative houses and multiple housing. If one pages through pattern books (with plans for sale) issued during the teens and twenties by John W. Lindstrom, one will feel that this one architect was responsible for whole districts of the city.[25] Equally familiar are pattern book designs for houses, duplexes, and apartments by Arthur C. Clausen, Charles S. Sedgwick, McAnulty Minneapolis, Inc.—"The Largest Builder of Homes in the Northwest"—or by one of the city's various lumber yards.[26]

The ideal of Minneapolis as an extensive middle-class grid suburbia has essentially remained down to the present day. To a limited degree, this ideal was compromised in the 1960s and later by the freeway system, which destroyed the scale of the universal suburban grid, and by injections of high-rise housing for the elderly into traditional residential areas. On the other hand, there are few American cities with so many residential areas that have remained basically unchanged, in some instances for well over fifty years.

Since most of the housing in Minneapolis was built after 1900, one does have to search out historical fragments that will convey what the houses and streetscapes were like in the nineteenth century. The mystery in discovering pre-1900 historical reminiscences in housing is further heightened by the fact that very few dwellings remain today as they were originally built. If a house or a cottage has been around for a number of decades it has most likely been remodeled many times. If it is pre-1880, its Italianate or French Second Empire

Godfrey house (1848), near University and Central Avenues.

Cutter house (1856, 1887), 4th Street and 10th Avenue Southeast.

cornices and brackets have probably been removed; and if it once boasted sawed, molded, and turned woodwork of the later Eastlake and Queen Anne styles, this too has probably been eliminated. More than likely the porches have been replaced or enclosed; and exterior walls, which once were covered in shiplap or clapboard, have been covered with stucco or asbestos or asphalt shingles. Continual ongoing domestic remodeling does help to reinforce the visual homogeneity of a streetscape, but it does of course erase the strong sense of specific imagery that is needed to establish Ruskin's memories of the past.

NINETEENTH CENTURY LEGACY

There is no streetscape or even group of houses that can provide us with a glimpse of pre-1850 single-family housing in the city. The story-and-a-half Godfrey house (1848), now located in Chute Square, and the Stevens house (1849–50), which was moved from the downtown area to Minnehaha Falls Park in 1896, can provide us with an illustration of what a modest Greek Revival

Italianate cottage (1873), 2103 23rd Avenue South.

Italianate house (c. 1870), 2nd Street South and Cedar Avenue; now razed.

mansard-roofed dwellings scattered here and there, but not many are still standing today. The little story-and-a-half cottage (c. 1888) on Nicollet Island at 27 Maple Place represents a type that speculative builders did construct here and there around the city.

Nationwide, the standard artisan dwellings of the late nineteenth century were small (often not even twenty feet wide) end-gable story-and-a-half cottages. These were almost always speculative houses and were usually built two or more at a time. In Minneapolis, groups of these houses can still be found, although it is disturbing how many have been destroyed just in the past two or three years. Those that exhibit a mixture of Italianate and Eastlake details could be found until recently at 819, 821, and 823 Chicago Avenue South (c. 1880). In the 1900 block of 13th Avenue South (c. 1889) one can see another group of somewhat larger artisan's dwellings, and on Milwaukee Avenue both of the streets are lined with such cottages (c. 1885–1904). The Milwaukee cottages are of brick, which remained unusual for single-family housing in Minneapolis. Similar modest-scale workers' housing continued to be built through the early 1900s, as one can see in the 2600 block of Oliver Avenue North, where there are two groups of tiny gambrel-roofed Colonial Revival cottages (c. 1905) facing one another across the street.

The major market for nineteenth-century speculative

cottage was like.[27] Old drawings and prints show how this Greek Revival cottage type, accompanied by two-story end-gable units, occurred along many of the streets of St. Anthony, and after 1855 in Minneapolis itself. Equally difficult to establish as a strong remembrance are the few instances of the Gothic Revival. The Cutter House (1856, 1887) at the northeast corner of 4th Street Southeast and 10th Avenue Southeast remains; but the many modest Gothic cottages with their gable ends decorated with bargeboards have all but disappeared.

During the style's peak in the late 1860s through the late 1870s, there were never a great number of middle-class Italianate houses and cottages built in Minneapolis. A look at the small end-gable cottage (1873) at 2103 23rd Avenue South and the two-story center plan house (c. 1870) at 913 5th Avenue South illustrates how the artisan's cottage was simply a single-floor version of a conventional two-story Italianate house. Even less frequent than the Italianate were the mansarded French Second Empire cottages and houses. Engravings of the 1870s illustrate a few of these

Second Empire cottage (c. 1888), 27 Maple Place.

Two Colonial Revival "spec" cottages (c. 1905), 2625 and 2628 Oliver Avenue North.

houses was of course the middle middle class. These houses were built both singly and, as was the case with artisan cottages, in groups. These dwellings not only were larger than worker houses but exhibited a richer array of volumes, surfaces, and ornament, that is, in the popular mind, "architecture." Hidden today behind numerous remodelings and covered with stucco and asphalt shingles are a good number of middle-class speculative houses dating from as early as the 1870s. An example of an Italianate version, narrow in width, with a dominant bay window, is located at 1700 Washington Avenue Northeast (c. 1880); while at 2429 Aldrich Avenue North is a similar side-hall version (1885), in this case boasting Eastlake and early Queen Anne details rather than Italianate.

As with smaller cottages, wood as framing and sheathing predominated in these middle middle class "spec" houses in Minneapolis. On occasion brick was used, as one can see in two adjoining L-shaped houses at 1423 and 1427 4th Street Northeast (c. 1895). An unusual episode in Minneapolis was the construction of a group of housing units with walls of concrete block in and around the 2600 block of 3rd Street North. All of this housing was built by the Universal Stone Building Company in the mid-1880s. Included among these were three adjoining "spec" houses at 2611, 2617, and 2619 3rd Street North (1885).[28] In these houses the concrete

Two brick "spec" houses (1895), 1423 and 1427 4th Street Northeast.

One of three concrete block "spec" houses built by the Universal Stone Building Company (S. Littlefield, 1885), 2619 3rd Street North.

and Crafts movement. Four of these Colonial Revival houses exist side by side in the 100 block of West 29th Street (c. 1900) and in the 3100 and 3200 blocks of Portland Avenue South (1917), and similar groups are to be found in north and northeast Minneapolis.

The artisan and middle-class detached single-family houses that made up the bulk of dwellings in Minneapolis did not constitute what were referred to as the "showplaces of the city." As generally has occurred in the development of American cities, the houses of the upper middle class and, above all, of the wealthy, have suffered the most. As already mentioned in our discussion of the downtown and its expansion, the blocks of Italianate villas and French Second Empire houses that used to exist just south of the commercial downtown are all gone. A few modest examples of these modes can give us a vague sense of how these houses and their extensive ornamental grounds must have looked. The existing Frederick House at 2402 4th Avenue South (c. 1870) and the Fisk House at 424 5th Street Southeast (c. 1870) present an indication of what houses were like, but not of how they appeared within their spacious gardens.

blocks were treated as ashlar blocks, and they alternately protrude beyond the corners of the building, creating an effect of a concrete log cabin. Though their use of concrete was technologically experimental and advanced for the times, their architectural imagery fitted right into the fashions of the period, for in their proportions and in their details they are pure American Queen Anne.

By far the greatest number of late-nineteenth-century to early-twentieth-century middle-class speculative houses in Minneapolis were reasonably large square boxlike dwellings, normally sheathed in clapboard and sheltered by an end-gabled or hipped roof. The general image conveyed by these houses, with their columned front porches, occasional oval lunette, Palladian windows, and louvered shutters, was that of the Colonial tradition of American architecture. In the earliest of these houses, there was a mixture of the Queen Anne and the Colonial Revival. Later the Colonial element was joined by wood and stucco details that we associate with the turn-of-the-century American Arts

Four Colonial Revival "spec" houses (c. 1900), 117–125 29th Street West.

Though Minneapolis has lost all of its truly great Queen Anne houses, it has managed to retain a scattering of upper-middle-class examples. Fortunately, there are several neighborhoods where one can still experience at least a partial streetscape of these houses. One of these areas is the 1500 and 1600 blocks of Dupont Avenue North; the other is situated on 2nd and 3rd Avenues South between 31st and 32nd Streets. The primitive fortresslike quality of the Richardson Romanesque was a favored image of wealthy American families in the late 1880s and early 1890s. Minneapolis has lost most of these "castles," but there are still a few of these highly romantic knights-in-armor masonry piles around. The McKnight-Newell house (Charles S. Sedgwick, 1888) at 1818 LaSalle Avenue South and the Van Dusen house (Orff and Joralemon, 1892–93) up the

Frederick house (c. 1870), 2402 4th Avenue South.

House (Charles Sedgwick (?), 1888), 1501 Dupont Avenue North.

Van Dusen house (Orff and Joralemon, 1892–93), 1900 LaSalle Avenue South.

street at 1900 LaSalle Avenue were meant to be impressive when built, and they still are.

TWENTIETH CENTURY CONTINUITY

By 1900 the Colonial Revival image, with its suggestion of refinement coupled with nationalism, was extensively used by the middle and upper middle class. A delightful small-scale version of a Colonial bungalow with overscaled columns can be seen at 4539 Nicollet Avenue South (1906). The Carpenter house (William Channing Whitney, 1906) at 314 Clifton Avenue South looked to the period of the past characterized by American Federal style for its sources; the Gluek house at 2447 Bryant Avenue South (William M. Kenyon, 1902) and the one at 1833 Girard Avenue South (F. D. Orff, 1900) take us back even further into the mid-eighteenth century, with references to the Georgian. Enlarged versions of the square-box Colonial Revival were extensively built as speculative houses, particularly in south Minneapolis in the Kenwood district. Fremont Avenue South between 18th and 19th Streets and the

2400 block of Bryant Avenue South (1898–99) each display a row of these dwellings lining both sides of the street.

Though the Colonial Revival image continued to be employed in speculative as well as upper-middle-class houses well past 1910, by that date it was beginning to be pushed aside by the Arts and Crafts bungalows and the two-story boxy Craftsman stucco houses. In north Minneapolis the grid above Broadway was dominated by bungalows and Craftsman houses; and the same occurred in the southern area between Lake Street and 50th Street. As in the pre-1900 years, almost all of these houses were built for speculation, with only a marginal number of dwellings constructed by builders for specific clients or designed by architects.

The heyday in Minneapolis for the bungalow and the two-story Craftsman house was 1910 through 1925. As was noted in the *Minneapolis Journal* in 1922 in a discussion of the "Airplane Bungalow": "While this type of house has been popular for some time on the West Coast, it is gradually making its appearance in other

Colonial Revival cottage (1906),
2529 Nicollet Avenue South.

Carpenter house (William
Channing Whitney, 1906), 314
Clifton Avenue.

equally they are a poignant symbol of middle-class puritanical ideals of that moment in history. They convey a sense of informality and unpretentiousness, they are "rationalist" dwellings that centered around the family, and they were indeed affordable for the middle class. Two-bedroom stucco bungalows sold before World War I for less than $2,000 (including a forty- or fifty-foot lot) and the two-story, three-bedroom-plus-sleeping-porch houses could be obtained for $2,500 to $3,000. Down payments were modest, as was the interest on the mortgage.

Compared to pre-1900 "spec" houses, these bunga-low and Craftsman houses have generally been little remodeled (externally) over the years—an entrance porch perhaps enclosed, aluminum screens and storm windows attached, and that is usually about it. In many instances these bungalows were interspersed among older houses, but in some cases whole blocks of them were built. The east and west sides of Portland Avenue South between East 46th and 47th streets and the 4300 block of Park Avenue South and Oakland Avenue South are literally bungalow districts (1928–31).

As was the case in the nineteenth century, there was a wide economic ring of speculative houses built in the city during the first two decades of the century. Some of these were even designed by architects, such as the four, each different in design, built at 3404, 3408, 3412,

sections of the country."[29] As is true of the bungalow and Craftsman houses elsewhere in the Midwest, the examples in Minneapolis tend to be simple, severe, and functional. As a machine for living in the environment of the upper Midwest, they work admirably well, but

Gluek house (1902), 2447
Bryant Avenue South.

and 3416 Hennepin Avenue South. They were designed for the builders, Mapes and Ertsgaard, by the architect, Ora W. Williams.

The Arts and Crafts Craftsman image, with its commitment to suburbia and the rural, was taken up as well by a segment of the middle class who felt themselves economically prosperous enough to engage architects. The Minneapolis firm of Purcell and Elmslie (Purcell and Feick, 1907–09; Purcell, Feick, and Elmslie, 1909–13; Purcell and Elmslie, 1913–22) enriched the community with a scattering of Prairie houses, which over the years have brought national attention to the city. A few of these Purcell and Elmslie houses verge into the range of upper-middle-class dwellings, such as the Catherine Gray house (1907) at 2409 Lake of the Isles Boulevard East or Purcell's own house (1913) at 2328 Lake Place. Most of Purcell and Elmslie's dwellings in Minneapolis were quite modest in size and cost. The Bachus house at 212 36th Street West (1915) and the Hineline house at 4920 Dupont Avenue South (1910) were built for around $3,000, just

Block of Colonial Revival
houses (c. 1900), 1800 block of
Fremont Avenue South.

Craftsman "spec" houses 126 (1921), 116 (1923), and 106 (1921) 49th Street West.

a little more than an equivalent builder's dwelling of the time. Facing Mt. Curve Avenue, high atop the Kenwood Hill, are two of the largest of these Craftsman Prairie dwellings: the Lester Brooks (Thomas) house (Hewitt and Brown, 1905, 1915) at 1600 Mt. Curve Avenue, which was described in 1905 as "having an architecture of its own, approaching . . . the California Mission style," and the Winton house (George W. Maher, 1910) at 1314 Mt. Curve Avenue.[30]

But the increasing interest of the middle class and the upper middle class was in architectural images that suggested a much stronger connection with the past. The *Minneapolis Journal* remarked in the real estate section on May 16, 1926, "There is a wide variety of construction, from the brick Colonial to Spanish houses and bungalows."[31] Builders as well as prospective buyers became increasingly "ashamed of [the Craftsman bungalows'] awkward bulkiness."[32] By the end of the twenties, the single-story "spec" bungalow had taken on a medieval look: steep pitched roofs and gables, and half-timbering, accentuated by stone trim. The east side of the 4300 block of Portland Avenue South and the west side of the 4300 block of Oakland Avenue South (both groups built between 1929 and 1931) present entire blocks of these late twenties and thirties medieval cottages.

Almost identical roofs, gables, half-timbering, and stonework were employed by builders for their more expensive two-story houses. Medieval two-story speculative houses, such as the one at 4901 10th Avenue South (1927), constructed by McCaig and Jessup, "Designers and builders of good homes for 24 years," or that at

Three Craftsman "spec" houses (Ora W. Williams, 1920), 3404, 3408, and 3412 Hennepin Avenue South.

5405 3rd Avenue South (1930), were built by the hundreds throughout the city and out into the expanding suburbs.[33]

Though the resurgence in favor of the American Colonial did not come about until the 1930s, Colonial bungalows and houses continued to be a well-accepted image. The favored builders' mode was the gambrel-roofed Dutch Colonial (some of which were designed by the Architects' Small House Service Bureau).[34] At the same time the *Minneapolis Tribune*, through its home

*Bachus house (Purcell and
Elmslie, 1915), 212 36th Street
West.*

*Brooks/Thomas house (Hewitt
and Brown, 1905, 1915), 1600
Mt. Curve.*

Three Medieval Image "spec" bungalows (1928–31), 4300 block of Portland Avenue South.

Medieval Image "spec" cottages (1928–31), 4300 block of Oakland Avenue South.

Medieval Image house (1930), 5405 3rd Avenue South.

Minneapolis Journal demonstration house (Architects' Small House Service Bureau, 1922), 2919 Johnson Street Northeast.

building department, provided readers with numerous examples of the colonial in their "Plan Book for Home Building."[35] Wood clapboard and brick-sheathed Colonial houses were created to provide yet another choice for potential purchasers and to create visual variety along the streets. Impressive and "correct" rendition of the Colonial occurred in upper-middle-class dwellings, as is evidenced in the Johnson house at the northeast corner of Penn Avenue South and West 49th Street (Lang, Raugland, and Lewis, 1925), which was

built for the then-considerable sum of $30,000.[36]

But it was the medieval, with its hint at the romance of the fairy tale, that was the most popular architectural image for the upper middle class during the decade of the 1920s and early 1930s. In size these could range from the relatively small and cottagelike, such as the Cowle house at 5141 Luverne Avenue South (1926), to much larger houses like those found along the east and south shores of Lake Harriet. In their design, the Walling house (Magney and Tusler, 1930) at 4850

Lake Harriet Boulevard West and the house at 4866 Lake Harriet Boulevard West (1927) illustrate the originality and remarkable quality obtained by Minneapolis architects in their mirroring of this historic imagery. The full-scale image of a medieval English country house was generally reserved for the more distant countryside; in the case of Minneapolis, this usually meant Lake Minnetonka. An exception, well hidden behind its walls and extensive vegetation, is the Goodfellow house (Charles A. Gage, 1928), situated just off Lake Calhoun Boulevard West at 36th Street West.

The exotic and faraway image of the medieval (either English or French) was enriched by other historic images in the twenties. Highly popular nation-wide was the Spanish/Mediterranean. Some of Minneapolis's speculative bungalows and modest two-story houses are Hispanic, and here and there throughout the city one will encounter individually built examples, some produced by builders, other by architects. The Santa Barbara architect C. L. Carjola produced an elegant brick version for M. M. Madsen at 501

Johnson House (Lang, Raugland, and Lewis, 1925), Penn Avenue South and 49th Street.

Cowles house (1926), 5141 Luverne Avenue.

Walling house (1905), 4850
West Lake Harriet Boulevard.

Madsen house in Spanish
Colonial Revival (Chester
Carjola, 1929), 501 West
Minnehaha Parkway.

Minnehaha Parkway West (1928), and a much larger Hispanic dwelling was built for Frank M. Groves at 4885 E. Lake Harriet Parkway (C. W. Farnham, 1928).

Contrary to popular belief, the stock market crash of 1929 did not immediately affect the continued construction of housing in Minneapolis. More speculative housing was built in the city between 1929 and 1932 than had been built the previous three to four years, and many of the more important and memorable examples of single-family architect-designed houses were built during these years. But by 1932 most building activities had ceased, and it wasn't until 1937 to 1938 that there was even a partial resumption of building activities in residential architecture. In the few years just before the Second World War, some speculative housing was built, particularly in Minneapolis south of Minnehaha Parkway and 50th Street. In that housing, the 1920s preference for the medieval image was to a considerable extent replaced by the national Colonial. Much of the upper-middle-class housing built at the end of the thirties occurred outside of the city's corporate limits, notably in the country club district of Edina. When such housing was built in Minneapolis, it occurred on scattered lots around or near the lakes. The Slocum house at 1801 Logan Avenue South (McEnary and Kraft, 1941) showed how sophisticated and openly nostalgic these Colonial designs had become.

FILLING OUT THE CITY—
LATE 1930s AND POST–WORLD WAR II

The interest in rejuvenating the housing industry in the late 1930s was nationwide. To symbolize the future and the new age, a nonhistorical image—that of the Streamline Moderne—was often used. In Minneapolis several symbols of the new were built as demonstration speculative houses, an example being the house at 3748 Edmund Boulevard South, built by the Peoples Home Construction Company (1927). This $8,000 interpretation of the Moderne was equipped with the mandatory flat roof, corner and round windows, and of course the essential glass bricks.

When building activities resumed after the Second World War, there were only small sections of the incorporated city that had not already been built on. The region to the far north quickly filled up and spread out into adjoining Brooklyn Center, Crystal, and Robbinsdale, while to the south the undeveloped portions between 54th Street and the city limits experienced a similar development extending on into Richfield. Some single-family houses were built on the few remaining vacant lots, and as in the past, this infilling of existing neighborhoods was accomplished by small-scale builders. These post–World War II speculative bungalows and houses tended to be as spartan in their imagery as the bungalow and Craftsman dwellings of the teens. Clapboarded walls, pedimented entrances, and occasional shutters hinted that these bungalows and houses of the late 1940s and 1950s were supposedly to be read as Colonial. In other instances, stucco and brick walls, a gable or two, and an asymmetrical facade was, one suspects, to indicate that the medieval image had not been fully abandoned.

Architect-designed housing for the middle and upper middle classes occurred almost exclusively in the suburbs outside the city. The hilly, tree-shrouded

Moderne demonstration house (1937), 3748 Edmund Boulevard.

WCCO building (1983),
downtown Minneapolis.

landscape around Minnehaha Creek acted as a magnet to encourage some in-city architect-designed housing around Upton Avenue South and 54th Street West. From the mid-1950s on, the American middle-class dream of a single-family house (designed by either builders or architects) had to take place in the suburbs beyond the city's boundaries. This last episode of Minneapolis's housing expansion is now over a quarter of a century old. The vegetation has matured, and the dwellings are now subservient to nature as the suburban image always demands. These suburban-style streets are now old enough so that they too can take their place in our memories of the city's past.

Community and Continuity

Some could argue that the effort to preserve buildings or segments of the city is close to meaningless since such retentions are almost always compromised. Few buildings stand as they were originally built, and fewer still retain much of a sense of their environment at the time they were built. Ruskin's answer to this would be, "Imperfection is in some sense essential to all that we know of life. It is the sign . . . of a state of progress and change."[37] A balance between progress and change, on the one hand, and the need to preserve fragments of the past, on the other hand, will continually provide us with the richest of environments.

In Minneapolis the city's parks and the continual renewal of the city's downtown provide an excellent opportunity for the community to connect the present, the past, and the future. Preservation can work if we heeds Ruskin's admonition that these architectural fragments of the past "belong as much to those who are to come after us, and whose names are already written in the Book of Creation, as to us; and we have no right, by anything we do or neglect, to involve them in unnecessary penalties, or deprive them of benefits which it was in our power to bequeath."[38]

PART 5

Preservation amid Change

AS WE REFLECT on the development of Minneapolis up to this time, and address the task of preservation, we ponder some major questions. What is the process of evolution we are watching? What are the forces in it to which every city must adapt? And what local actions determine the different and distinctive performances of different cities as they try to preserve some of their legacy before the onslaught of change?

The City and Its Buildings

For a century Minneapolis has developed as the hub of a region. Today it is the center of a web of business and personal relationships, migration, and transportation and communication routes that reaches from Montana to the Great Lakes, from Canada to Iowa. It is an important node in the national and world systems of commerce and culture. Its crowds reflect the large population of the surrounding metropolis. Its markets reflect billions of dollars in annual exchange of an almost inconceivable array of goods and services. Financial institutions manage billions in accumulated savings and reflect the resulting power to build and rebuild—the power of individuals and organizations to generate, attract, and house still more activity.

The city is not only a center of action; it is also a store of wealth. It is a visible accumulation of knowledge and structures from the continuing effort to learn, save, and share. The city is a legacy from the contributions of individuals and communities who have lived here: rich, poor; laborers, professionals; business firms, governments, unions, churches. The city also symbolizes continuity. The contributions to the metropolis continue as new people and new institutions keep emerging. Generation follows generation. The action goes on.

Buildings are exciting symbols of the city. Homes, hotels, offices, hospitals, shops, factories, schools, roads, bridges—all speak of the city as a center of action and a store of wealth. The buildings have substance, durability, visibility, and sometimes monumental stature. And they are symbols of continuity and legacy. The mix of old and new structures reflects the continuity of both the place and the society. The mix of buildings displays reminders of the past. We have shown again and again how the city's architectural facade gives perspective on the process of evolution—not only of the city but also of the wider society, technology, and economy. We have shown how the mix of buildings gives perspective on long-term trends, catastrophic interruptions of those trends, and countless careening fluctuations in the course of events.

Catastrophe and Continuity

Thus the city changes, and buildings are caught in the process. The technologies and ideas they reflect are abandoned, distorted, or shredded as time passes.

Take a collection of houses a hundred years old. They have seen drastic changes in the generations of families they were supposed to shelter. The average number of children has fluctuated between four and one as European peasant immigrants, depression, "baby boom," "hippies," two-job couples, "empty nesters," and

The Change in Position of Minneapolis Within the Subdivided Area of the Seven-County Twin Cities Metropolis, 1900-1980.

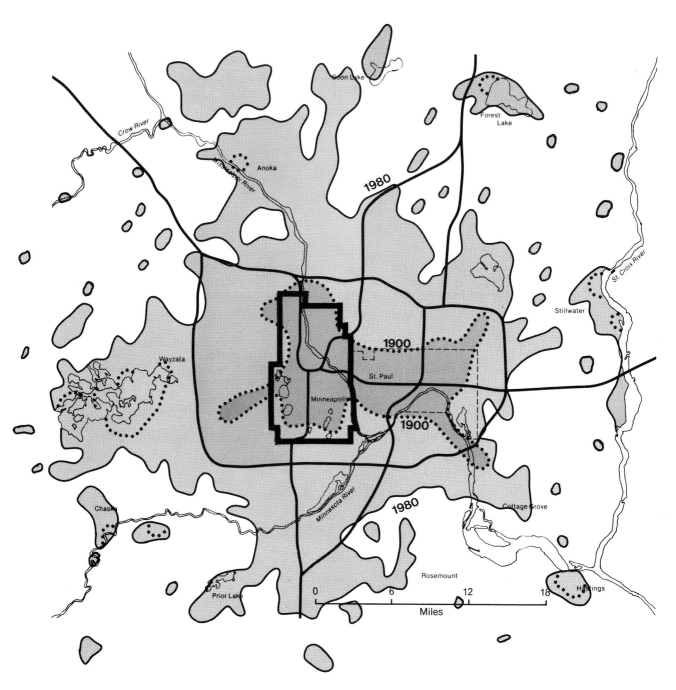

Figure 1.

Old warehouses and mills
district, with city hall clock tower
in foreground.

refugees from distant wars and tyrannies have come and gone. Kitchen equipment has changed from wood stoves to gas ranges to microwave ovens; kitchens have changed from centers of activity for big families to points of brief encounter for working professional couples. An upstairs bedroom once occupied by a thirty-square-foot iron bed, a chest, a dressing table, and a chair now houses a fifty-square-foot, one-ton water bed, an array of electronic and video equipment, and a library of hundreds of books, records, and tapes. One or two live-in servants have been replaced by two dozen electric motors in houses built with servants' quarters but only primitive wiring. Daily parking requirements, once zero for most houses, have ranged from one to four vehicles for a typical household in the past quarter century; and a big Saturday-night party might well require temporary parking for fifty cars, vans, and pickup trucks.

Or take a collection of warehouse buildings nearly a century old. While they have stood massively on their stone foundations, think how the image of a warehouse

has changed. Once it was an architectural monument to a proud entrepreneurial family. The family not only shared the summit of Minneapolis society but also occupied a pinnacle in the nation's hierarchical system of wholesale and retail distribution. Today a warehouse is a more plain, modular, functional symbol of a corporate organization trying to maintain itself in a highly competitive environment in which firms appear, expand, contract, divide, and multiply so much and so often that monthly magazines can fill their pages simply keeping track of the action. Meanwhile, the walls of those old warehouses were impregnated with soot and etched by sulfuric acid from the smoke of countless locomotives that switched boxcars from across the nation inside the warehouses' wrought iron gates. In later years, the same buildings have stood amid areas of derelict tracks, with volunteer cottonwood saplings growing between rusty rails and rotting crossties.

No class of buildings has been immune to such changes of activity. Not only homes and warehouses but also factories, offices, hospitals, schools, churches, and

Dayton's warehouse in Mid-city
Industrial Park, Industrial
Boulevard near East Broadway.

power plants have housed convulsive changes that have reflected the shifts in the basic economy and ways of living that have occurred during the short life span of Minneapolis. We have noted many such changes in our recounting of how the city expanded. Anyone who has watched can conjure up countless scenarios of change, adaptation, decay, and replacement of the stock of buildings.

Not only do activities change, but the store of wealth also changes. At the turn of this century the boundaries of Minneapolis virtually encompassed two-thirds of a Twin Cities metropolis where the annual personal income was perhaps $200 million. Today those boundaries enclose only the main core of a Twin Cities metropolis whose annual income is more than $10 billion (fig. 1). Metropolitan population has increased more than fivefold. Real income has grown fiftyfold. Where the combined banks held deposits in the tens of millions, deposits are now in the tens of billions. Two dozen large corporations headquartered in downtown Minneapolis control worldwide assets of about $40 billion.[1] That growing store of wealth has made it possible to transform the cultural life and the form of the city. Museums, enclosed malls, churches, research institutes, office towers, parks, and the sprawling university campus are monuments to the widening stream of income and savings. Meanwhile, the swelling stream of wealth has made the residue of poverty ever more conspicuous and troublesome. And somehow, like the greatest monuments to the growing store of wealth, the largest residue of poor people has concentrated in the city. The poorest one-tenth of the metropolitan

population today—mostly in the central cities—is a number greater than the total metropolitan population of a century ago. Hence a very noticeable share of the city's buildings have been adapted to shelter and service its concentration of the metropolitan poor.

If the activities and the store of wealth change, so do the legacies that the city's buildings represent. Reflect on the layers of history, geography, and architecture whose accumulation we have described. Each passing epoch has added to the city's inheritance of skills, beliefs, institutions, races, and ethnicity. The legacy grows increasingly deep and complex as the city's history is extended. It also becomes more cumbersome and incomprehensible, hence more in need of selection, generalization, and practiced interpretation.

Since these traits of the city—its activities, wealth, and legacies—are so dynamic, so is the collection of buildings. Again, one needs only look at the record written on the face of Minneapolis in its short history to see how the building facade has changed.

That change is hard to describe and therefore hard to think about. The changes run through time, and they play out on a complicated stage. They run along different dimensions of city life—the introduction of electricity, automobiles, elevators, union wages, birth control, subsidized home-mortgage loans. They coincide only partly in terms of the different buildings or districts a person encounters in the course of a day or a decade. To some extent the changes are *revolutionary*. They tend to come in distinct periods. An epoch is ushered in by one catastrophic change and abruptly ended by another. Yet the change is also *evolutionary*.

*Abandoned warehouse
(c. 1880), 5th Avenue North
and 2nd Street North.*

Each development adds to the accumulated legacy of buildings, and each new development is rooted in the lengthening past. Different kinds of change overlap one another in time and place. Thus, despite frequent catastrophes, there is always continuity.

As this avalanche of catastrophic yet continuous change tumbles through the years, embedded within it is a cycle of building and rebuilding. A generation of new buildings ages, decays, and is replaced with a newer generation. To some degree the construction cycle runs independently of changes in the activities, wealth, and legacies of the city.

The Cycle of Building and Rebuilding

The construction industry accounts for five dollars out of every one hundred in the national income. In recent years about forty-five percent of construction outlay has gone into residential building; about thirty percent to commercial, industrial, and public buildings; and the remaining twenty-five percent to nonbuildings, such as roads, airfields, utility lines, and dams.[2] In the Twin Cities and Minnesota, the proportion spent on public improvements has been a little larger than in the nation as a whole—a part of the "quality" often attributed to this place.

The volume of construction serves three essentially different purposes. Some new structures accommodate *new growth* of population, business, and public enterprise. Some construction represents *maintenance or rehabilitation* of old buildings. And some current construction *replaces* old buildings that are being abandoned. The mix of construction for new growth, replacement, and maintenance changes from year to year. Those changes are part of the city's continuous adaptation to the endlessly unfolding variety of demands and new technologies.

New construction, replacement, and maintenance also comprise parts of the continuing cycle of building and rebuilding (fig. 2). As the construction industry works through that cycle, it gradually creates and re-

The Cycle of Building and Rebuilding.

New Construction

For Growth

For Replacement

Maintenance

Abandonment

Deterioration

Preservation

Demolition

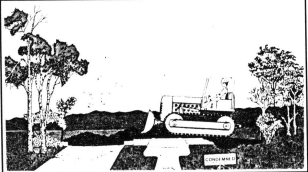

Figure 2.

creates the face of every settlement in the nation. As soon as a new building is completed, it begins to age. Then its owners and its occupants either maintain it or let it deteriorate. Deterioration, of course, is simply a result of less-than-complete maintenance. Deterioration can be rapid or gradual. On the other hand, if maintenance is complete, a building will endure indefinitely, although its appearance might change very much as new parts and materials are substituted for old. Historical preservation is a special case of maintenance. It represents not only perfect maintenance but also faithful retention of original appearance. The purpose is not only to keep the building efficiently usable but also to keep intact the design of the building and the way it symbolizes its bit of history.

For those buildings that are not fully maintained, the cycle leads finally to abandonment. Then the abandoned structures are demolished or they rot, rust, and crumble into the earth. In a growing or even a static economy, the need for floor space continues; therefore, before a building can be abandoned, no matter how decrepit it might be, it must be replaced. Seldom is a building replaced precisely where it stood, of course. To demolish and build at the same place at the same time usually costs more than we have been willing to pay. But more important, the replacement is likely to be needed in a different place than the old building. And the old place, if it is needed at all, is probably needed for a different purpose. Not only the old building but also its location have become obsolete for their original use. The relative location of any place keeps changing as a metropolis grows or shrinks around it, as the nation's population shifts, and as new transportation technologies evolve. Thus six old houses in central Minneapolis might be replaced by a new flat building on the same site, or they might be replaced by six new houses in the suburbs or six new houses in Arizona, California, or south Texas. The replacement cycle runs inexorably, and the choice of new location is open.

But the annual rate of new building, replacement, and abandonment is tightly limited. The engine that drives the construction industry is fueled by the stream of savings in the economy. Most of the nation's income stream pays for current consumption and production. The amount to be spent for expansion and replacement is limited by the amount that is saved after paying current bills. Average annual savings equal about fifteen percent of the gross national product. After replacement of equipment and construction for new growth, less than one-tenth of the savings is left for replacement of buildings and other structures.[3] Building may surge ahead for a time on the strength of a wave of borrowing, but it will stagnate later as credit is exhausted and debts must be reduced. Hence even a deliberate, systematic program to replace and abandon the city's stock of old buildings would take several generations.

A century of building in the Twin Cities has produced an enormous accumulation of structures that will eventually be either recycled or preserved. By the end of the 1970s, the market value of all the buildings in the seven-county metropolitan area was probably about $18 billion. The value of public works and utilities was perhaps $7 billion more. Thus the total value of all structures was on the order of $25 billion.[4] The share of that total in Minneapolis was about one-third, or $8 billion.

Of course, there is great variation in the value of structures from one part of the city to another, and there is a remarkable concentration in a small share of the buildings. For example, about one hundred fifty buildings in Minneapolis—a minuscule fraction of one percent of the total—account for about one-third of the total market value of all buildings in the city.[5] Most of those buildings are downtown or nearby (fig. 3). They represent a sizable share of the savings of people in the Twin Cities and the region. They range in age from those built in 1890s to those from the 1980s. The older ones are located in the central area because it was the focal point of the region's rail lines and the city's tram lines. The later highway network focused on central Minneapolis because the buildings were there, and many of them still had to be amortized. In turn, recent buildings have been added because the highways are there. Gradually a skyline and an image have been etched into the culture of the city, the region, and the nation's television watchers and magazine readers.

The age of buildings, like their value, varies greatly from one part of the city to another. We have already described the expansion of platting and development from the falls outward to the city limits and beyond. That was a fitful, leapfrogging process. Developers and builders pushed fastest and farthest toward the south. They slowed in the tangle of railroad tracks toward the east. They skipped to outlying lakeshores, hilltops, and industry sites. And they eventually returned to bypassed fields, marshes, and steep hillsides nearer the center. They built quickly and abundantly in the booms and sparingly in the panics and depressions. While the result is something of a jigsaw puzzle, the assembled places make the well-known age rings—younger on the farthest edges of the city, older toward the falls and downtown. In the landscapes of younger rings, maintenance dominates over deterioration. In the older rings, deterioration is much more common, interrupted by bursts of rehabilitation and redevelopment in downtown and many residential blocks.

Location of Buildings with Assessed Market Value More Than $2 Million in 1980

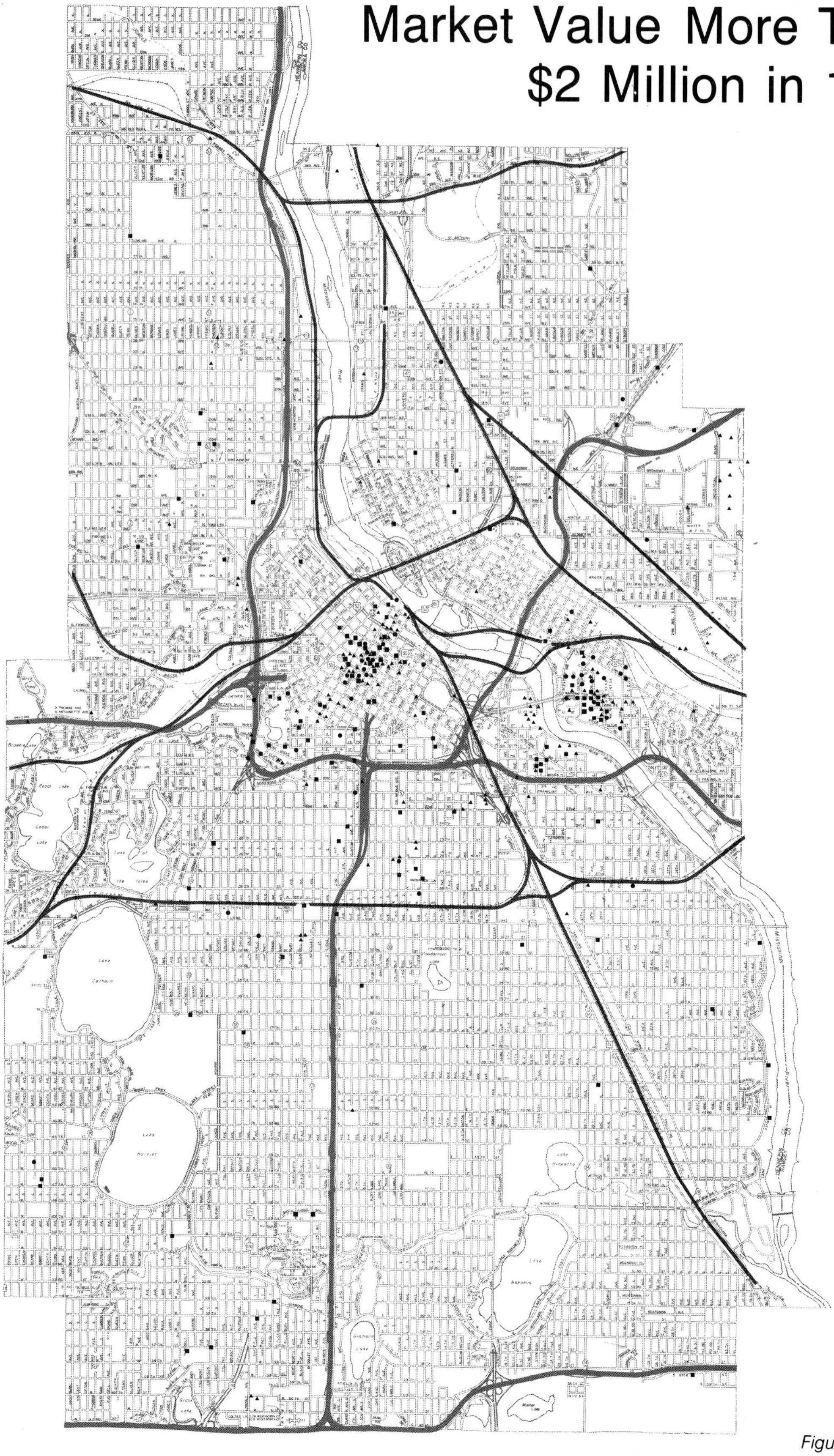

■ 1885-1918
● 1918-1948
▲ 1948-1980

Figure 3.

Age Rings and Development Zones at the Time of the 1920s Building Boom

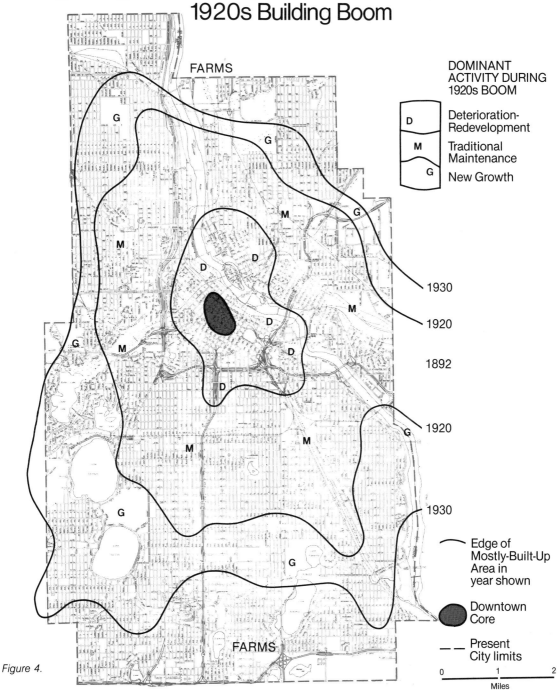

FARMS

DOMINANT
ACTIVITY DURING
1920s BOOM

D — Deterioration-Redevelopment

M — Traditional Maintenance

G — New Growth

1930

1920

1892

1920

1930

— Edge of
Mostly-Built-Up
Area in
year shown

Downtown
Core

- - - Present
City limits

0   1   2
Miles

FARMS

Figure 4.

The three geographical rings—*deterioration and redevelopment, maintenance,* and *new growth*—were in place by the time of the building boom of the 1920s (fig. 4). Inside the fringe of the pre-1892 area of the city were the remnants of the first pioneer settlement and the houses built for the first wave of poor European immigrants. Outside the pre-1892 ring was the area built up from the 1890s through the 1920s. Buildings in that ring were generally less than thirty years old when the 1920s boom began. Many of them housed the city's fast-growing middle class. Hence maintenance as well as newness dominated the landscape, although automobiles were rapidly increasing the crowding and the inadequacy of all pre–World War II neighborhoods. Beyond the 1892–1920 ring, new subdivisions were invading the woods and fields, pushing toward today's city limits.

By the end of the explosive post–World War II building boom, in the late 1950s, the inner zone of deterioration, redevelopment, and rehabilitation had

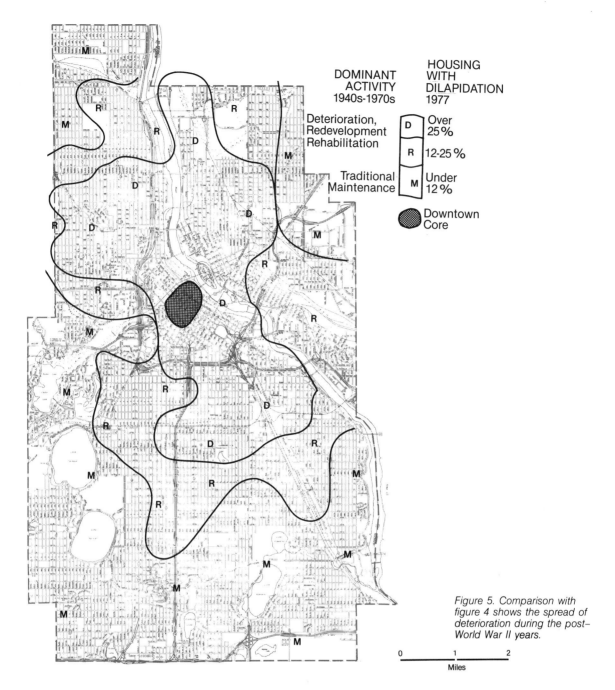

DOMINANT
ACTIVITY
1940s-1970s

HOUSING
WITH
DILAPIDATION
1977

Deterioration,
Redevelopment
Rehabilitation

D Over 25%

R 12-25%

Traditional
Maintenance

M Under 12%

Downtown Core

Figure 5. Comparison with figure 4 shows the spread of deterioration during the post–World War II years.

0   1   2
Miles

spread to all of the pre-1920, essentially pre-auto, city (fig. 5). In a 1978 survey, nearly one-fifth of all housing units in the city were in a significant or advanced state of dilapidation. Ninety-five percent of those units lay in the rings that were built up before 1920.[6] Meanwhile, in the auto age the vastly increased middle class had enlarged and shifted the zone of traditional maintenance, with its trim, landscaped yards and well-maintained houses (fig. 6). By 1956 the traditional maintenance zone had spread from the inner edge of the area of 1920s housing, in the city, across most of what we now call

the inner-ring suburbs. Beyond the 1956 frontier, the zone of new growth was sprawling across the rolling, open land of today's second- and third-ring suburbs. Thus, while the frontiers of new development and traditional maintenance advanced far beyond the city limits, the frontier of obsolescence and deterioration advanced from the edge of today's downtown across much of the area built before 1920. Unprecedented new building in the suburbs permitted record neglect or abandonment in the center.

In the 1970s, a different thrust developed. Costs of

The Metropolitan Setting of the Spreading Zone of Deterioration, 1956

DOMINANT ACTIVITY DURING POST-
WORLD WAR II BUILDING BOOM

D D Deterioration

M M Traditional
Maintenance

G G New Growth

● Downtown Cores

------ Minneapolis and St. Paul City Limits

Figure 6.

new residential building rose rapidly at the same time that the post–World War II baby-boom generation reached the age of household formation. Under the resulting pressure, many newcomers to the housing market looked inward to the older but still sound houses in the inner part of the ring of traditional maintenance–to neighborhoods built mostly between World War I and World War II. The years since 1970 have also seen unprecedented investments in downtown offices and high-rise housing. As a result the ring of deterioration, after a decade of unprecedented neglect, was invaded on its outer edge by the growing new, young middle class and on its inner edge by downtown rebuilding.

Thus the city today is a remarkable dynamic accumulation of structures with a great range of ages and enormous value. Within its shifting age rings, different buildings and districts that symbolize the city's history eventually either fall under the weight of obsolescence or stand as past and future monuments. The buildings and districts represent the current phase in the continuing cycle of building, aging, maintenance, preservation, deterioration, abandonment, demolition, decay, and replacement.

The Rate of Rebuilding

Recycling of the stock of buildings moves along at a gradual and very uneven rate. In the 1970s, for example, the nation had a net gain of about 16 million new households and built almost 18 million new dwelling units. Thus the number of new units built exceeded the new units needed for growth by almost 2 million. That meant that 2 million units could be used to replace an equal number of old units, and the old ones could then be abandoned. There were nearly 87 million housing units in 1980; hence the replacement units built in the decade accounted for 2.2 percent of all the housing stock. In other words, the replacement rate was 2.2 percent of the housing units at the end of the decade.[7] Obviously at that rate it could take centuries to completely recycle the residential areas of the nation's cities. The lower the replacement rate, the longer must be the life expectancy of buildings.

But the rate in the 1970s was sharply lower than it had been in the 1960s or the 1950s. In fact, it has fluctuated widely over the decades for which we have records (fig. 7). In the boom of the 1920s the housing replacement cycle ran at its highest recorded rate. But during the 1930s depression and World War II, construction fell behind the growth of household numbers. Families doubled up. There was little or no concern about saving old buildings from abandonment and demolition, though many were creaking under severe wear and tear. The post–World War II building boom restored the replacement cycle. As population growth slowed in the 1960s while new building continued at a high pace, the replacement rate went still higher. Once a building is replaced, it can be abandoned; so the abandonment rate in the 1960s escalated along with the rising replacement rate. More building in new areas meant more derelict land and vacant floor space in old areas. Then the pendulum swung once again in the 1970s. While the maturing baby-boom generation flooded the housing market, new housing production declined. It barely equaled, or fell short of, new household formation by the end of the decade. Once more we were scrounging in search of empty or underutilized floor space while discarding little or none regardless of its age or condition. Although expenditures for new replacement construction were double the outlay for upkeep of older structures in the 1960s, they fell to one-half the maintenance outlay in the 1970s.

The national pattern of home building and replacement has reflected not only these changes in overall conditions but also major migrations of people and capital. Thus the 1960s showed moderate or high rates of replacement and abandonment in all parts of the United States (fig. 8). Vacancy rates indicated that new housing was abundant in most of the South and Southwest, adequate elsewhere. In relatively slow-growing large metropolitan areas of the Northeast, abandonment was a highly visible part of the scene in the old core areas. Then in the 1970s, both new construction and vacancy rates declined (fig. 9). Replacement and abandonment rates dropped in almost all parts of the nation. Pressure grew to rehabilitate old housing— to catch up with previously neglected maintenance— wherever it was possible. Rehabilitation opportunities were greatest, of course, in the older northeastern cities where the largest amount of housing had been built in pre-automobile epochs. Only in Florida and parts of the Mountain West did new building keep substantially ahead of the growing number of households and thus maintain a high replacement rate. A sizable flow of capital from the Northeast to the South and West accompanied the shift from new building to slow growth and rehabilitation in the Northeast. By the late 1970s, per capita new construction was ten percent below the national average in the Northeast and ten percent above the nation in the South and West. Those differential rates of new construction in 1978 represented a transfer of about $16 billion in investment capital from the Northeast to the South and West—one-tenth of the total construction outlay in the nation.[8]

The Twin Cities lay in the neutral border zone between these contrasting regions of the country—a mixture of the old Northeast and the newer West. But the cycle of building and rebuilding—and the place of historic preservation within that cycle—in Minneapolis has strongly reflected the major national tides.

In the 1960s the housing replacement rate in the seven-county Twin Cities metropolitan area was a little more than nine percent. In the 1970s it had dropped to virtually zero; and if Metropolitan Council projections of building and population hold up, the housing replacement rate for the 1980s will be scarcely more than 2 percent.[9] At these current replacement rates and the current metropolitan household growth rate, it would take from 250 to 350 years to replace the existing housing stock. Thus even if preservation were not deliberate, it would—in some form—be unavoidable!

Meanwhile, what has happened in the core of the metropolis—the city of Minneapolis? More than 17,000 new houses and apartments were built during the 1950s boom. Twenty-six thousand more were added as the boom surged through the 1960s, another 11,000 in the slumping 1970s. Most of the new units were apartments. They replaced older houses in the ring of

New Housing Construction in Excess of New Households Formed - The Ability to Replace and Abandon Obsolete Housing - in Each Decade Since 1890 in the United States

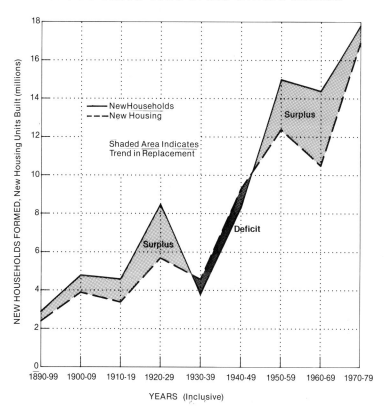

Figure 7.

deterioration and redevelopment. Consequently, demolition had to precede most of the new construction. Twenty-seven thousand units were demolished in the 1960s but fewer than 8,000 in the 1970s, in the face of increasing pressure to reuse old floor space rather than throw it away. Thus 37,000 new units were built in twenty years, while 35,000 were demolished. During the same two decades, the total number of housing units has fluctuated near 170,000.[10] Hence, about twenty-two percent of the stock has been replaced in twenty years:

two-thirds in the 1960s, one-third in the 1970s. At those rates, the city would rebuild itself in eighty to one hundred fifty years. Then a core city with an average age of fifty to seventy-five years would be surrounded by slowly rebuilding suburban rings with average ages of one hundred to one hundred twenty-five years. Newer core; older suburbs. Will that indeed be the picture as the Twin Cities approach the twenty-second century? And if it is, will the people who live here consider the newer buildings in the core to be

State of the Housing Building—
Abandonment Cycle in the 1960s

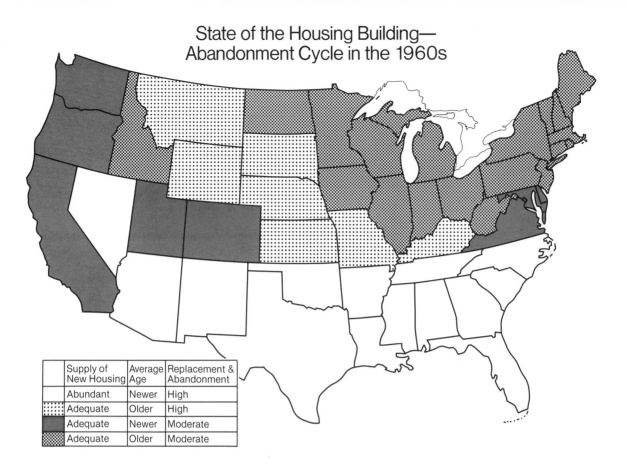

Supply of New Housing	Average Age	Replacement & Abandonment
Abundant	Newer	High
Adequate	Older	High
Adequate	Newer	Moderate
Adequate	Older	Moderate

State of the Housing Building—
Abandonment Cycle in the 1970s

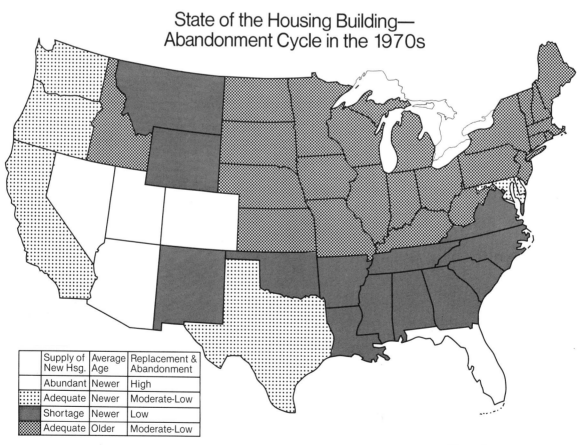

Supply of New Hsg.	Average Age	Replacement & Abandonment
Abundant	Newer	High
Adequate	Newer	Moderate-Low
Shortage	Newer	Low
Adequate	Older	Moderate-Low

Figure 9.

superior or inferior to the older ones in the suburbs?

Pending uncertain demolition and replacement by new structures for a new population, what is happening in the interim to the city's standing stock of buildings? The 1977 citywide housing condition survey found that about 28,000, or about eighteen percent, of the housing units were in some stage of structural dilapidation, mainly in the pre-1920 neighborhoods. Some were not worth any effort to restore. All were "probably beyond the present occupants' capability to restore . . . or even maintain."[11]

But there was some public money to help. For example, in Whittier neighborhood, about $0.5 million of public community development block grant funds were budgeted for housing rehabilitation and maintenance assistance over the three years, 1980–82. An additional grant from a private foundation committed another $1 million over two years. Spread over the six thousand homes in the neighborhood, those funds would provide about $250 per year per unit.[12] In Phillips neighborhood, the budgeted block grant funds could provide an average of $600 per year over a three-year period for about 3,000 owner-occupied homes, or an average of about $214 per year for each home over the same period if rental units were included in the program.[13] Citywide, about $47 million of public funds was programmed for rehabilitation and related projects over seven years. If that money were applied to the units that were dilapidated but salvageable, it would provide about $240 a year per unit, excluding administrative overhead.[14]

These average annual grants are probably below the normal upkeep requirements. Annual construction expenditure for upkeep averages at least one percent of building replacement value, nationwide. On a $30,000 dwelling, that means very conservatively at least $300 per year for maintenance and repairs. Furthermore, these public grants have an uncertain future, and they are being applied to structures that require not only current maintenance but rehabilitation after many years of neglect. Finally, even normal maintenance at current and past levels clearly is not enough to preserve the stock of buildings.[15]

The greater share of maintenance continues to depend on financing by private owners. In all of the Powderhorn North neighborhood, for example, in the five years 1973–77, nearly half of all structures had some repairs. Public funds were used in less than one-fifth of the cases.[16] Thus private outlays must far exceed public. The amount spent today must depend on the owner's income, the intrinsic value of the location, and the maintenance history of the building. The latter, of course, would depend in turn on the income of the

original builder and other past owners, and the long-term value of the location. Private investment has been high in the 1970s, also, because of the burgeoning number of new households investing in older neighborhoods for their first homes.

From readily available information, it is more difficult to evaluate maintenance and replacement of nonresidential structures. In the mid-1970s, the Twin Cities metropolitan community was spending about $740 per household per year for public capital improvements.[17] During the same period, for the same purpose, American cities with comparable populations averaged less than $250 per year per household.[18] At the same time, Twin Cities tax rates were comparatively high, and local government indebtedness per capita was among the highest in the nation. In its capital improvements plan for the first half of the 1980s, the city of Minneapolis projected capital outlays of $850 million, or about $170 million annually. A little more than half of those funds were projected to come from borrowing and the remainder from state, federal, and metropolitan grants. The plan would call for an average outlay of about $450 per city inhabitant per year, compared with less than $200 per capita for other American cities in Minneapolis's size class in the late 1970s (in 1981 dollars).[19] Obviously, Minneapolis, and the Twin Cities generally, has been spending at a rate substantially above the national average to replace, rehabilitate, and maintain its public improvements. Yet that level of outlay seems only to be keeping abreast of overall wear and tear and obsolescence. There is ample documentation of the fact that most American cities are doing worse. Choate and Walters summarize their book, *America in Ruins*, simply: "America's public facilities are wearing out faster than they are being replaced."[20] It appears that either Minneapolis will continue to spend at past levels to maintain the city's physical plant or the plant will gradually decay. And either America's decaying cities will move their budgets in the direction of that of Minneapolis or they will continue to decay. The course of action pursued here and elsewhere will be tortuous. The outcome is very uncertain. Where the framework of public improvements is not maintained, commercial and residential maintenance, replacement, and preservation will surely fail in the long run.

At the heart of the downtown, most of the largest financial organizations headquartered within the city have joined to lead a remarkable surge of new construction. The result will triple the mass of monumental buildings that help give that part of the city its excitement, durability, and historical significance. In the outlying commercial and industrial districts, on the other hand, buildings have been

*Downtown construction, 1980s:
City Center.*

maintained and replaced at about the same rate as their residential neighbors, or slower. Public grants for rehabilitation or redevelopment of neighborhood commercial areas have totalled perhaps one-sixth the amount of those for residential areas. There is proportionately heavier dependence on private investment. Overall the replacement and maintenance of commercial and industrial buildings is probably running at a rate comparable to that of housing.

In short, the city is recycling itself slowly and

fitfully. There seems to be an awakening to the fact that many structures must last longer and be maintained better or recycled faster than we had once thought. The present performance indicates that most buildings will continue to move through a life cycle of at least eighty to one hundred fifty years. A few will stand much longer than the average, a few not nearly so long. The *normal* process includes imperfect maintenance, gradual decay, and replacement. Little survives today from a century ago. Little might survive a century or two hence. The city's massive accumulation of structures is in reality a churning physical process. People are continually converting raw materials into new buildings and new buildings into solid waste. It is also a turbulent social process. People are continually converting dreams into actions and actions into memories. Historic preservation attempts to break into the cycle at a few selected places.

As a part of the city's physical assets, its buildings tend to become worn and obsolete, to lose their value with age. Their attrition and replacement are part of the evolution of the place. Yet the same buildings also represent the people and institutions who have built the city over the years. As symbols of legacy and continuity, they tend to gain value with age. Their preservation is part of the city's sense of coherence. Thus every building contains the arguments for both its demolition and its preservation. Somehow the fate of each structure is judged. How are the arguments weighed? Who makes the decision?

Priorities for Preservation

Amidst the turbulent process of urban evolution and the fitful process of recycling, there has emerged a pecking order of building survival. To be sure, all buildings are symbols of the converging forces of history at the places where they stand. But some simply have been physically more durable than others. Or they have better symbolized more important events to more powerful institutions, more people, or more powerful people. Some have endured by mere historical and geographical accident; for the sweeping, inexorable tides of change mask a large number of random local details. Thus not all structures have had the same chance of preservation, maintenance, or even mere survival. Today's survivors are only a sample of what might have survived. Future survivors will also be only a sample.

The market has certainly favored selected buildings, or ensembles of buildings, for survival to this time. After all, old buildings that we now want to preserve have already been preserved in some fashion for a long time. Especially valuable locations have been important.

They have attracted high-value initial investments and basked in the wealth and power of the investors.

Take the fine old homes of Lowry Hill or the lake district, the older monumental office buildings of downtown, the massive industrial buildings of the milling district, or the equally massive old warehouses. A high proportion were architect designed and built to last. And a high proportion have lasted until now simply because they were built so sturdily. Many of the homes have been well maintained continuously because the bluffs and lakes have continued to attract owners with the money to maintain them.

Some well-built structures in the central area suffered from neglected maintenance because of the declining value of their outmoded rail, waterpower, or streetcar locations. Yet others were maintained consistently as symbols of enduring institutions—for example, the First National Bank, the Soo Line Railroad, or the city and county governments.

The major hospitals, the university, and some of the churches have stood as Gibraltars of maintenance, or even preservation, amid seas of deteriorating surroundings. They have reflected continuity of ownership and the persistent wealth and prestige of their founding institutions in the economic and social marketplace. Other monumental buildings stand despite years of neglect and locational obsolescence in many neighborhoods, because their founders built with pride and resources that have become only scattered memories.

Beyond the influence of market forces, the work of professionals has helped to decide the question of survival. The story of the city's development has pointed up many examples where the designs of celebrated architects or engineers have further strengthened the chance of survival of a commercial or public building. Influential professional organizations, by honoring selected designs and designers, have further enhanced the chances of certain structures to endure. Emotions, too, have influenced the selection process. The city's built landscapes evoke memories and legends of individuals, organizations, events, places, styles. Many buildings are landmarks in tens of thousands of personal images and mental maps of the city. And simply as landmarks they have become part of the emotions of tens of thousands of Twin Cities people, often over several generations.

But perhaps the most important basis for selecting structures to be maintained or preserved has been the sheer course of events—overriding forces, essentially uncontrollable, basically unpredictable, outside the framework of "policy," unique to the place and its times. When we stand in Minneapolis in the 1980s and look back and ahead along the corridor of time, so much we see is the result of unique combinations of events here.

Think over the broad outlines of our Minneapolis development story. The crashing wave of initial settlement came in the particular context of this piece of the American frontier in the mid-nineteenth century. There were urgent needs, disorder, hasty building, little time for niceties or monuments. The wave of maturation came a generation later. From 1880 to 1900 big fortunes, big organizations, and a large established middle class emerged. The pioneer boom town was eradicated. The drive for improvement was both powerful and practical. The first major wave of monumental buildings arose on the skyline, and the first large middle- and upper-class neighborhoods sprawled away from the downtown core. Given the average building replacement rate and the growth rate over the subsequent years, the average life expectancy of a building was about eight decades.[21]

Thus the 1960s and 1970s were a critical time. The hour had come to recycle the structures from the beginning of that late nineteenth century period of the city's first maturation—maintain them better or watch them disappear to abandonment and replacement. We realized that although virtually all of the pioneer city was gone, nearly everything from the 1890s or later still remained. For the first time the city faced the possible loss of a large number of monumental buildings—not only major buildings but also homes and districts. The threat was aggravated by other forces converging on American cities, really by sheer coincidence, at about that same time. The housing replacement rate rose to high, sometimes unprecedented, levels in the 1960s, to accelerate abandonment in the old city core. That certainly helped to stimulate the sharp increase in large-scale, conscious, selective preservation efforts. Then the explosive growth of new households and escalating construction costs came in the 1970s. Those events triggered an unprecedented wave of remodeling and rehabilitation.

Now the question is whether those events of the 1960s and 1970s represent a new long-term direction or another unique episode in the careening course of Minneapolis and Twin Cities evolution. The record of savings, new building, maintenance, and replacement still suggests that our dominant goal, individually and collectively, is to discard yesterday's goods and change things for the better. The history of the modal building has been deferred maintenance, gradual deterioration, replacement, eventual abandonment, demolition, or decay. Average people have lived and usually worked in average buildings. Hence ordinary buildings, individuals, and institutions have not stimulated strong pressure for historic preservation. Time and again we were troubled

to find in our block-by-block survey of the city that the *modal* buildings or blocks in most neighborhoods rated low on the scales of various criteria for preservation. They seldom symbolized notable individuals, organizations, designs, or styles. If they were more than the required fifty years of age, they were often in poor condition or severely modified to cope with the changing demands of the parade of occupants who had passed through them. Yet, they were *typical* of the massive growth sectors and rings and the mosaic of regions that reflect the mainstream of the city's history.

As one looks ahead, then, some questions loom through the mist. How important will particular preservation policies be in comparison with our ability to adapt to the succession of catastrophic events that affect the city's evolution? As more people grow more aware of the symbolic importance of truly typical buildings and districts, will we attempt to invent ways to select and perpetuate some of them, in the face of almost inexorable forces to eradicate and replace them? Or will we shift from preservation to replication, as we have had to do in the case of eighteenth- and early-nineteenth-century landscapes that were already lost before there was an historic preservation movement? The effort to preserve—that is, to fully maintain—a small number of selected structures and districts is still set in a vast sea of marginal and sporadic maintenance. Could the preservation movement produce a small collection of monuments shining against a large, dull background of neglect and decay? Or will there be a gradual merger of the historic preservation movement into a widening, deepening stream of improved maintenance and adaptive reuse?

It is clear that the answers to those questions are entwined with major questions of individual, institutional, and national priorities. In Minneapolis and the Twin Cities the record suggests an above-average chance that the course of action will be rational and that the community will commit the resources to carry it out.

We might imagine how these questions of preservation and maintenance might be addressed and what actions might be taken in a future Minneapolis. Think of a community of citizens who hope for a world that will continue to grow more humane, who want to make their community a living, working demonstration of what can be done practically in contemporary America to advance those hopes. Then think of the steps they are likely to take.

First, they will monitor the changing condition of the city's physical structures, its open spaces, and the people who use them. The goal: to know what's new, what's deteriorating, how much, and why. They will publicize the information quickly and widely so the greatest possible number of people can be knowl-

*Abandoned cottage (c. 1900),
1815 6th Street South.*

*Eastlake/Queen Anne house,
moved to 2410 Stevens
Avenue South; restored 1982.*

edgeable and thoughtful about the meaning of those changes. Who is affected? How and how much? Why?

Next individuals and all kinds of interested groups will explore the facts and discuss them. Out of that will come proposals for action. Some people will want to build, demolish, preserve, neglect, or abandon. Others will be affected by those actions and will support, oppose, or seek compromising changes.

From that open, vigorous process will issue the continuing stream of actions that build, rebuild, and preserve the community. The new city will continually evolve from the old. The changes will reflect the community's reserve of entrepreneurial talent and energy and its rich array of ideas among different concerned parties. The changes will also reflect practical priorities, yet a sense of both historical continuity and the larger geographical setting of the place. The Minneapolis community will have done its best.

Is that likely to happen? Indeed, the community is now trying to carry on that continuing, rational process. We have been able to write this book about what has been built or abandoned, what has endured, and what deserves to be preserved by using only a part of the data that has been marshaled by city, state, and national agencies, both public and private. Our own survey of the city's buildings is a part of that body of information. The survey was stimulated by the community's determination to think more broadly and deeply about preservation. The city council, with the Heritage Preservation Commission and the planning department, provides a public arena in which the community's wealth of information, hopes, and judgments are converted into decisions to act. Those actions guide the process of building, rebuilding, and preserving.

Of course, the question must continue to be asked: Is the community doing its best?

Appendix

Notes

Bibliography

APPENDIX

Minneapolis Historic Sites Project

Consultants' Recommended Nominations

Sites Recommended for the National Register of Historic Places

Building	Address	Date	Reason
Minneapolis Armory	500–530 6th Street So.	1935	Arch/Art
Old Federal Building	200 Washington Ave. So.	1911–12	Arch/Hist/Dev
Minneapolis Post Office	100 South 1st Street	1931–32	Arch/Dev
Rand (Dain) Tower	527 Marquette Ave.	1928–29	Arch/Dev
Farmers & Mechanics Bank	90 South 6th Street	1941	Arch/Dev
Soo Line Building	105 South 5th Street	1914	Arch/Hist/Dev
Young-Quinlan Store	901 Nicollet Mall	1926	Arch/Hist/Dev
Westminster Presbyterian Church	1201 Nicollet	1897	Arch/Type/Dev
Cathedral Church of St. Mark	511–41 Oak Grove	1908	Arch/Type/Dev
Hennepin Avenue Methodist Church	511 Groveland	1914	Arch/Type/Dev
Northwestern Bell Building	224 South 5th Street	1930–32	Arch/Dev
Lumber Exchange Building	423–25 Hennepin	1885	Hist/Arch/Dev
Historic Episcopal Church	901 4th Avenue South	1883–84	Hist/Arch
The Spot Cafe	615 South 10th Street	1932	Arch
Swinford Town House/Apartment	1213–21 Hawthorne	1886/1897	Hist/Arch/Dev
Lee Town House	623–25 South 9th Street	1886	Arch/Dev
Oakland Flats	213 South 9th Street	1889	Arch/Hist/Dev
Old Federal Reserve Bank (Schiek's Restaurant)	111–19 South 4th Street	1891–93	Arch/Hist/Dev
Pillsbury Library	100 University Avenue SE	1902–04	Arch/Hist
Fisk House	424 5th Street SE	c. 1870	Arch/Hist
Willey House	255 Bedford SE	1934	Arch/Dev
The Mall	University of Minnesota	1908	LA/Hist/Dev
Bell Museum	University of Minnesota	1939	Arch/Dev
Armory Building	University of Minnesota	1895	Arch/Dev
Pillsbury Hall	University of Minnesota	1889	Arch/Dev
Nicholson Hall	University of Minnesota	1890	Arch/Dev
Phi Gamma Delta House	1129 University SE	1911	Arch/Dev
Pease House	814 University SE	c. 1864	Hist/Dev
Ard Godfrey House	Chute Square	1858	Hist/Dev
White Castle	329 Central SE	1936	Arch/Dev

Reasons for Recommendation

Arch – Architecture/Design

Hist – Historic

Dev – Illustrates Development pattern

Art – Contains important Art or applied ornament

Type – Good example of building Type

Tech – Illustrates Technological development

LA – Illustrates outstanding Landscape Architecture/Design

Building	Address	Date	Reason
Florence Court	1022 University SE	1886	Dev/Hist
Hafstad House	159 Arthur SE	1894	Arch/Dev
Cattanach House	1031 13th Avenue SE	1893	Arch/Dev
St. Mary's Church	1629 5th Street NE	1905	Arch/Hist
Lein Duplex	444-46 Madison NE	1888	Arch/Dev
Margaret Barry House	759 Pierce NE	1915/1922	Hist
Melrose Flats	13-21 5th Street NE	1890-92	Dev/Arch
Grain Belt Complex (Brewery, Office, Warehouse, Bottling Plant)	1200-1228 Marshall NE	1890-1900	Hist/Arch/Dev
Broadway Bridge	Mississippi River at Broadway	1887	Arch/Tech/Dev
Concrete Block Row House and Houses	300-314½ 26th Avenue No. and 2605-07 3rd Street No.; 2611-17-19 3rd Street No.; 2705-07, 2729, 2831 3rd Street No.; 2826 & 2828 4th Street No.	1885-86	Arch/Dev
Wirth Park Chalet	3200 Glenwood (in Wirth Park)	1930	Arch/Hist/Dev
Murphy House	716 21st Avenue South	c. 1870	Hist/Arch
Perkins-Russell Cottage	2103 23rd Avenue South	1873	Hist/Arch
Plymouth Congregational Church	1 Groveland Avenue	1907	Arch/Type
Bardwell-Ferrant House	2500 Portland	1883/1890	Arch
Crowell Block	614 West Lake	1888	Arch/Dev
Minneapolis Institute of Arts	200-212 East 25th Street/ 201 East 24th Street	1913-15	Hist/Arch/Dev
Vedler Building (Smiley's Point)	2200 Riverside	1889	Dev/Hist
Augsburg Old Main	731 21st Avenue South	1901	Arch/Hist
Menage Cottage (to be moved to St. Paul)	715 East 14th Street	1878	Hist/Arch
Despatch Laundry Building	2611 1st Avenue South	1929	Arch/Dev
Romanesque Row House	106 East 24th Street	c. 1880	Arch/Dev
Widstrom Tenement	619-21 19th Avenue South	1886	Arch/Dev
Thompson House	2215 Pillsbury	1903	Arch
Coe House & Stable	1700 3rd Avenue South	1884	Arch/Dev
Donahue House	2536 Stevens Avenue	1883	Arch
West 15th St. Row House	115-129 West 15th Street	1886	Arch/Dev
Christ Lutheran Church	3244 34th Avenue South	1949/1966	Arch
Long House	25 Groveland Avenue	1894	Arch/Hist
Quinlan House	1711 Emerson South	1924	Arch/Hist/Dev
Owre House	2625 Newton South	1912	Arch/Dev
Niles House	2801 Burnham Blvd.	1950	Arch/Dev
Lakewood Cemetery Chapel	Lakewood Cemetery	1908-10	Arch/Hist
Moorish Mansion (Fourplex)	3028 James Avenue South	1929	Arch/Dev
Kaufman House	20 Park Lane	1935	Arch
Granada Theater (Suburban World)	3022 Hennepin Avenue	1927	Arch/Dev
Thomas House	1600 Mount Curve	1905	Arch/Dev
Bachus House	212 West 36th Street	1915	Arch
Parker House	4829 Colfax South	1913	Arch
Goodfellow House	3537 Zenith Avenue	1928	Arch
Walling House	4850 West Lake Harriet Pkwy.	1930	Arch/Dev
Tuscany House	4916 Oliver Avenue South	1932	Arch
Dorr House	2111 West 52nd Street	1917	Arch
Chadwick Cottages	2617 West 40th Street	1902	Dev/Arch
Cummer Cottage	2521 West 40th Street	1902	Dev/Arch
Mueller House & Studio	4845 Bryant/4844 Aldrich So.	1912-13/1910-11	Arch/LA
Washburn Water Tower	51st Street and Highview Ter.	1931-32	Arch/Art/Dev

Sites Recommended for State Designation

Building	Address	Date	Reason
Ivy Tower	1115 2nd Avenue South	1930	Arch
Dayton's Department Store	700–734 Nicollet Mall	1901	Hist/Type/Dev
Former Greyhound Bus Terminal	29 North 7th Street	1936	Arch/Hist/Dev
State Theater	805 Hennepin	1920	Arch/Type/Dev
Gluek Building	16 North 6th Street	1902	Hist/Arch
Orpheum Theater	910 Hennepin	1921	Arch/Type/Dev
Augustana Lutheran Church	1015 South 7th Street	c. 1880	Hist/Arch
Times Annex Building	57 South 4th Street	1899	Hist/Arch/Dev
Midwest Merchandise Mart	800 Washington Avenue North	1910	Dev/Type
Andrews House	527 5th Street SE	1869	Dev/Hist
Lawrence House	622 5th Street SE	1872–73	Dev/Hist
Stryker House	628–30 University SE	c. 1870	Dev/Hist
Cataract Lodge (Garden Court)	101–09 4th Street SE	1925	Dev/Type
Miller Bag Company	861 East Hennepin	c. 1890	Arch/Dev
Thorsov House	208 Cecil SE	1912	Arch/Type
Prospect Park Water Tower	Seymour & Malcolm SE	1913	Arch/Dev
Emmanuel Lutheran Church	697 13th Avenue NE	1893	Arch/Hist
Forest Heights Church	2054 James Avenue North	1908	Arch/Hist
Sumner-Field Housing Project	6th Street North & Bryant	1934	Hist/Dev
Sears Roebuck Store	900–930 East Lake	1927	Hist/Dev
Gluek House	2447 Bryant South	1902	Arch/Dev
Engine House	CMSP Southside Yards	c. 1885	Dev/Type
Flour City Ornamental Iron	2637 27th Avenue South	1901	Hist/Dev
Hutchins House	2119 3rd Avenue South	1884	Arch
Wakefield House	4700 Fremont South	1912	Arch

Sites Recommended for Local Designation

Building	Address	Date	Reason
Munsingwear Building	700–728 Glenwood	1910–14	Hist/Dev
Steel Bridge	3rd Street & 3rd Ave North	c. 1895	Tech/Dev/Type
Seven Town Houses	614–26 South 9th Street	1886	Hist/Dev
Linne Building	521 South 9th Street	1893	Dev/Hist
Apartment Building	812–826 South 10th Street	1888	Dev/Hist
Fawkes Building	1628–32 Harmon Place	1916	Hist/Type
Dahlen Printing	41–43 Glenwood	1907	Arch/Type
Row House (Adams Hotel)	500–512 10th St. South	1888	Dev/Type
Meader-Farnham House	913 5th Avenue South	c. 1872	Dev/Arch
Italianate Cottage	816 Park Avenue	c. 1880	Dev/Arch
Drexel Apartments	1001–1017 Park Avenue	1889	Dev/Type
Town House	918–20 Portland	1888	Dev/Type
Two Town Houses	912–14 Park Avenue	c. 1890	Dev/Arch
Andrews Building	208 East Hennepin	c. 1880	Hist/Dev
Tuttle House	204 5th Street SE	c. 1870	Dev/Hist
St. George's Church	320–24 4th Street SE	1890	Arch/Dev
Switchman's Tower	14th Avenue & Quincy NE	c. 1905	Dev/Type
Royal Sales and Leasing	100 5th Street NE	1937	Arch/Type
Hollywood Theatre	2809–15 Johnson Street NE	1935	Arch/Dev
Victory Temple	2401 North Aldrich	1938	Arch
Courty House	4743 North Girard	1924	Arch
Shaarei-Zedeck Synagogue	1117–19 North Morgan	1936	Arch/Dev
Booth House & Barn	2118 14th Avenue North	1885	Arch/Dev
Young House	1501 Dupont North	1888	Arch/Dev
Petersen Duplexes	314–328 25th Avenue North	1889	Dev/Type
Mihro Kodesh Synagogue	1000–1006 Oliver North	1927	Hist/Dev
Kost House/Carriage House	1625 Dupont North	1887	Arch/Dev
Stevens House	1425 Dupont North	1884	Arch
Erth House	1617 Dupont North	1889	Arch

Reasons for Recommendation

Arch – Architecture/Design

Hist – Historic

Dev – Illustrates Development pattern

Art – Contains important Art or applied ornament

Type – Good example of building Type

Tech – Illustrates Technological development

LA – Illustrates outstanding Landscape Architecture/Design

Building	Address	Date	Reason
Novak House	2724 4th Street North	1896	Arch
Granlund House	2127 Lyndale North	1891	Arch
Italianate House	4817 Lyndale North	c. 1880	Arch/Dev
Commercial Block (Cooper Bldg.)	1419 Washington Avenue No.	c. 1880	Dev/Type
Dworsky Barrel Company	260 12th Avenue North	c. 1885	Arch/Dev
Hildebrand Store & Flat	2627–29 2nd Street North	1885	Arch/Dev
Sawyer House	2429 Aldrich North	1885	Arch
Former Hay Press Mfg. Office	826 44th Avenue North	1902	Arch/Type
Holthus Grocery	2654 Emerson North	1910	Dev/Type
Commercial Block	921–25 West Broadway	1912	Arch/Dev
Hubbard Building	1101–05 West Broadway	1890	Arch/Dev
Gatzemeier Building	400–402 West Broadway	1894	Arch/Dev
Commercial Block	413–19 West Broadway	c. 1880	Arch/Dev
Commercial Building	1501 West Broadway	c. 1880	Arch/Dev
IOGT Hall (now razed)	1416 South 2nd Street	c. 1885	Hist/Type
Former Fire Station G (Mixed Blood)	1501 South 4th Street	1887	Hist/Type
Hallin Store/Former Garage	2407–2415 Riverside	1924	Arch/Dev
Former Fire House & Stable	3006–12 Minnehaha	1894	Hist/Dev
Storefront Building	1428 South 5th Street	c. 1885	Dev/Type
Spec Houses	117–125 West 29th Street	c. 1880	Dev/Type
Former Northwestern National Life Bldg. (Loring Park Office Bldg.)	430 Oak Grove	1923	Hist/Dev
Minneapolis Women's Club	407 West 15th Street	1927	Dev/Type
Zinman-Brochin Apartments	119–29 Oak Grove	1921	Dev/Type
The Flame Restaurant	1521 Nicollet	1938	Arch
Dayton Apartments	1536 LaSalle	1919	Dev/Type
Kunz Oil Gas Station	2600 Pillsbury	1926	Arch/Type
Haugan Building (118 East Bldg.)	118 East 26th Street	1890	Arch/Dev
Apartment Building	2014 2nd Avenue South	1928	Arch/Type
Two Duplexes	2700–04, 2718–20 Aldrich So.	1906	Dev/Type
Ladd House	131 Oak Grove	1889	Arch/Dev
Bovey House (Architectural Alliance)	400 Clifton	1916	Arch
Bayless House	308 Ridgewood	1887	Arch
Groveland Hotel	510 Groveland	1927	Dev/Type
Spec House	3748 Edmund Blvd.	1937	Arch
Former Gas Station	4224 East 41st Street	1926	Arch/Dev
Spec House	5454 Clinton/322 East Diamond Lake Road	1940	Arch
Bungalow Court	17–29 East 54th Street	1928	Arch/Type
Fire Station #13	4201 Cedar Avenue	1923	Arch
Texaco Gas Station	3403 38th Avenue South	1926	Arch/Type
Former El Lago Theatre	3500–06 East Lake	1924	Arch/Type
Avalon Theater (Fine Arts)	1500 East Lake	1937	Arch/Type
Winton House	1324 Mount Curve	1910	Arch/Dev
Slocum House	1900 Knox	1941	Arch
Boardman House	1833 Girard South	1900	Arch
Ford House	2350 West Lake of the Isles Blvd.	1928	Arch/Dev
Uptown Theater	2900 Hennepin	1915/1929	Arch/Dev
Covell House	2504 West 40th Street	1905	Arch/Dev
Bruchholz/Craddock Houses	5000/5006 1st Avenue South	1924/1922	Arch
Magney House	5329 South Washburn	1922	Arch/Dev
Canning House	5140 Aldrich South/ 800 West Minnehaha Pkwy.	1924	Arch
Former Farmhouse	2708 West 60th Street	c. 1880	Dev/Type
Nicollet Bridge	Nicollet & Minnehaha Creek	c. 1920	Arch/Dev
Pierce House	4700 West Lake Harriet Blvd.	1910	Arch
St. Andrew's Church	3118 West 49th Street	1907	Arch/Dev

Reasons for Recommendation

Arch – Architecture/Design

Hist – Historic

Dev – Illustrates Development pattern

Art – Contains important Art or applied ornament

Type – Good example of building Type

Tech – Illustrates Technological development

LA – Illustrates outstanding Landscape Architecture/Design

Notes

Notes — Chapter 2, Legacy of the Working City

1. For a detailed account of the beginning of commercial enterprises and settlement in Minneapolis, see Isaac Atwater, *History of the City of Minneapolis*, 2 vols. (New York: Munsell & Co., 1893), pp. 29–49.

2. For biographies of scores of the first generation of civic leadership in Minneapolis, see Atwater.

3. Atwater, p. 672.

4. *Ibid.*, pp. 329–348

5. Lucile M. Kane, *The Waterfall That Built a City* (St. Paul: Minnesota Historical Society, 1966), pp. 62–80.

6. *Ibid.*, p. 102.

7. Atwater, p. 853.

8. *Ibid.*, p. 857.

9. *Ibid.*, pp. 854–856.

10. Charles Walker, *American City, A Rank and File History* (New York: Farrar & Rinehard, 1937), p. 9.

11. For a detailed history of the development of the Falls of St. Anthony, see Kane.

12. Kane, pp. 114–133.

13. *Ibid.*, p. 129.

14. *Ibid.*, pp. 134–165.

15. Calvin Schmid, *Social Saga of Two Cities* (Minneapolis: Minneapolis Council of Social Agencies, 1937), pp. 37–55.

16. Atwater, p. 307.

17. Edward Bennett, *Plan of Minneapolis* (Minneapolis: The Civic Commission, 1917), p. 1.

18. *Ibid.*, p. xii.

19. *Ibid.*, p. 3.

20. *Ibid.*, pp. 25–26.

21. *Ibid.*, p. 83.

22. *Ibid.*, pp. 119–120.

23. *Ibid.*, p. 156.

24. Schmid, pp. 15–16.

25. Kane, p. 176.

Notes — Chapter 3, Legacy of the Neighborhoods

1. Isaac Atwater, *History of the City of Minneapolis*, 2 vols. (New York: Munsell & Co., 1893).

2. Horace B. Hudson, *A Half Century of Minneapolis*, 2 vols. (Minneapolis: Hudson Publishing Co., 1908), p. 36.

3. E. Dudley Parsons, *The Story of Minneapolis* (Minneapolis: By the author, 1913), p. 34.

4. Elizabeth Gale, ed., *Minneapolis 1857–59* (published privately, 1922), pp. 13–49.

5. Parsons, p. 33.

6. *Ibid.*, p. 49.

7. Hudson, p. 36.

8. Parsons, p. 55.

9. Hudson, p. 38.

10. Marion D. Shutter, *History of Minneapolis*, 3 vols. (Minneapolis: S. J. Clarke Publishing Co., 1923), p. 91.

11. Atwater, pp. 150–240.

12. Shutter, p. 174.

13. *Ibid.*, p. 163.

14. Gustav Rolf Svendsen, *Hennepin County History* (Minneapolis: Hennepin County Bicentennial Commission, 1976), pp. 14–16.

15. Hudson, p. 67.

16. Atwater, p. 189.

17. Carl O. G. Hansen, *My Minneapolis* (Minneapolis: By the author, 1941).

18. Atwater, p. 419.

19. Parsons, p. 101.

20. Atwater, p. 338.

21. *Ibid.*

22. Parsons, pp. 99–100.

23. Atwater, pp. 340–341.

24. H. W. S. Cleveland, *Washburn Park Plat Map*, 1886.

25. Shutter, p. 231.

26. *Ibid.*, p. 233.

27. Shutter, p. 234.

28. Parsons, p. 113.

29. Note that these plans were developed in 1883, more than thirty years before the 1917 plan discussed in chapter 2.

30. Parsons, pp. 104–105.

31. *Ibid.*, pp. 115–116.

32. *Ibid.*, p. 116.

33. Atwater, pp. 693–694.

34. Parsons, pp. 97–98.

35. Hudson, p. 262.

36. *Ibid.*

37. Atwater, pp. 504–505.

38. Hudson, p. 544.

39. Hudson, pp. 544–545.

40. Lynn Weiner, "Our Sister's Keepers," *Minnesota History* (Spring 1978): 194–195.

41. Shutter, p. 648.

Notes—Chapter 4, Legacy of Design

1. John Ruskin, *The Seven Lamps of Architecture* (Sunnyside, Kent: George Allen, 1883), pp. 176–198.

2. *Ibid.*, p. 194.

3. *Ibid.*, p. 187.

4. Many of these villas and their gardens were illustrated in Alfred Theodore Andreas, *Illustrated Historical Atlas of Minnesota* (Chicago: By the author, 1874).

5. Isaac Atwater, *History of the City of Minneapolis*, 2 vols. (New York: Munsell & Co., 1895).

6. Minneapolis Riverfront Development Coordination Board, *Saint Anthony Falls Rediscovered*, ed. James Berman (Minneapolis: Minneapolis Riverfront Development Coordination Board, 1980).

7. Theodore Wirth, *Minneapolis Park System, 1883–1944* (Minneapolis: Board of Park Commissioners of Minneapolis, 1945).

8. John R. Borchert, "The Twin Cities Urbanized Areas: Past, Present and Future," *Geographical Review* 51, no. 1 (1961): 47–70.

9. Montgomery Schuyler, "Glimpses of Western Architecture: St. Paul and Minneapolis," *Harpers Magazine* 83 (October 1891): 736–755.

10. *Minneapolis Journal*, June 28, 1914, p. 6.

11. *Minneapolis Tribune*, May 8, 1910, p. 2.

12. Edward E. Bennett, "Preliminary Report of the Minneapolis Civic Commission," *The Western Architect* 17 (February 1911): 17–19; George B. Ford, "The Civic Improvement of Minneapolis," *Journal of the American Institute of Architects* 4 (October 1916): 427–429.

13. "The Architect and His Community: A Case Study: Long and Thorshov, Inc., Architects, Minneapolis," *Progressive Architecture* 29 (March 1948): 48.

14. Francis Meisch, "The Minnesota Campus: Past, Present and Future," *Minnesota Techno-log* 19, no. 5 (February 1939): 11–14.

15. "Progress in Park Making in Minneapolis," *Park and Cemetery* 21 (June 1911): 557–561; Charles M. Loring, "History of Parks and Public Ground of Minneapolis," *Minnesota Historical Society Collection* 15 (1915): 599–608.

16. K. B. Raymond, "Landscape Playgrounds More Popular," *Parks and Recreation* 11 (July–August 1928): 398–402.

17. St. Andrew's Lutheran Church was originally built as the Linden Hills Methodist Episcopal Church, and it was located at the southeast corner of Upton Avenue South and 44th Street West. It was designed by Downs and Eads in 1907, and it was moved to its present site in 1916.

18. This eleven-unit "tenement," each unit of which was two stories high with eight rooms, is located at the northwest corner of 3rd Street North and 26th Avenue North. It was designed by W. D. Kimball, who also was the architect for a number of spec concrete houses located nearby.

19. See ad by the Thorpe Brothers, *Minneapolis Journal*, April 6, 1930, p. 9. It was noted that these duplexes would present "every appearance of a large individual dwelling."

20. John W. Lindstrom, *Duplexes and Apartment Houses* (Minneapolis: By the author, c. 1916 and 1921). This architect and his earlier partner, Joseph Almar, published a pattern book, *Mansion and Bungalow* (Minneapolis, c. 1910), which also contained designs for multiple housing. Lindstrom and Almar advertised frequently in the pages of the *Minneapolis Journal*; see the issues of May 8, 1910, p. 7, and June 18, 1916, p. 6.

21. Lindstrom.

22. "$100,000 Seven Duplex Project Starts on Upper Hennepin," *Minneapolis Journal*, June 12, 1927, Real Estate Section, p. 1.

23. *Minneapolis Tribune*, June 11, 1916, Editorial Section, p. 6.

24. Both the Keith Corporation and the Architects' Small House Service Bureau of the United States, Inc. also published pattern books. Among those published by the Keith Corporation were *Keith's Attractive Bungalows* (Minneapolis, c. 1921) and *Ideal Homes* (Chicago ?, 1930). The Architects' Small House Service Bureau published *Small Homes of Architectural Distinction* (Minneapolis, 1927); as late as 1937 and again in 1941 the Architects'

Small House Service Bureau published volumes entitled *Bungalows* (Minneapolis, 1937 and 1941).

25. As with many publishers of pattern books, it is difficult to know just how many different or revised volumes were published by an architect such as John W. Lindstrom. Ads in the *Minneapolis Journal* mention *Mansion and Bungalow* in 1910; and by 1916 Lindstrom and Almar had written two more volumes: *Bungalows* (1915) and *Attractive Homes* (1915). In the 1920s, Lindstrom published *Duplexes and Apartment Houses* (c. 1921 and c. 1927) and *Two Story Houses* (c. 1922).

26. Arthur C. Clausen, *The Art, Science and Sentiment of Home Building* (Minneapolis: Brooks Press, 1909); Charles S. Sedgwick, *Sedgwick's Best Homes*, 12th edition (Minneapolis: By the author, 1921); McAnulty Minneapolis, Inc., *Your Home, and Your Home Plan Inside* (Minneapolis: McAnulty, c. 1919). Other examples of Twin Cities pattern books are Carr-Cullen Company, *Homes of Comfort* (Minneapolis: Carr-Cullen, c. 1923); Minneapolis Tribune, *Plan Book for Home Builders*, vol. 1 (March 1922) (Minneapolis: Minneapolis Tribune, 1922); Jay Axelrod, *Artistic and Practical Homes for the Average Man* (St. Paul: By the author, 1921); Russell F. Whitehead, *Good Houses* (St. Paul: Weyerhaeuser Forest Products, 1922); C. O. Larson and Martin H. Reitz, *The Manual of Homes* (St. Paul: Home Plan Book Company, 1947). Pattern books published elsewhere were often used in the Twin Cities. Those written by the Chicago architect Fred T. Hodgson (see his *Practical Bungalows and Cottages for Town and Country* (Chicago: Frederick J. Drake & Co., 1912) must have been used, for houses identical to his designs are found in both cities.

27. See the houses illustrated in the photograph "Panoramic Saint Anthony and Minneapolis in 1857" in Minneapolis Riverfront Development Coordination Board, *Saint Anthony Falls Rediscovered* (Minneapolis: Minneapolis Riverfront Development Coordination Board, 1980) (insert).

28. Other nearby single-family Queen Anne dwellings constructed of concrete block by the Universal Stone Building Company are the Kortgaard House (1885) at 2831 Third Street North and two houses built for Holway and Taylor at 2826 and 2828 Fourth Street North (1885).

29. *Minneapolis Journal*, April 23, 1922, Editorial Section, p. 8.

30. *Minneapolis Journal*, June 5, 1910, Second News Section, p. 12

31. *Minneapolis Journal*, May 16, 1926, Real Estate Section, p. 1.

32. "Typical Trends in Low-Cost Housing," *Architectural Record* 71 (January 1932): 44.

33. *Minneapolis Journal*, May 29, 1927, Real Estate, Building & Industrial Section, p. 7.

34. The *Minneapolis Journal* sponsored a Dutch Colonial demonstration house in 1922. This house is located at 2919 Johnston Street Northeast, and it was designed by the Architects' Small House Service Bureau, Inc. See *Minneapolis Journal*, April 16, 1922, Editorial Section, p. 6. Also see Thomas Harvey, "Mail-Order Architecture in the Twenties," *Landscape* 25, no. 3 (1981): 1–9.

35. Small perspective drawings accompanied by plans were often published during the 1920s and 1930s in the pages of both the *Minneapolis Tribune* and the *Minneapolis Journal*.

36. *Minneapolis Journal*, May 24, 1925, Real Estate & Business Section, p. 3.

37. John Ruskin, *The Stones of Venice* (London: The Library Edition, 1903–1910), vol. 10, p. 184.

38. Ruskin, *The Seven Lamps*, pp. 185–186.

Notes—Chapter 5, Preservation amid Change

1. From data in *Corporate Fact Book* (Minneapolis: Dorn Publications, 1981).

2. *Id.*

3. *Statistical Abstract of the United States 1981* (Washington: U.S. Bureau of the Census, 1982), table 1354, "Value of New Construction Put in Place, 1970 to 1980," p. 751. These rates are estimated in the following

way for any given year or decade: (a) number of replacement housing units was estimated by subtracting the number of new households formed from the number of new housing units built; (b) replacement units were expressed as a percentage of all new housing units built; (c) the percentage of housing units replaced was multiplied by the total outlay for all new construction to obtain an estimated outlay for replacement construction only. Data on households, construction outlays, gross national product, and savings were taken from *Historical Statistics of the United States* (Washington: U.S. Bureau of the Census, 1972) and *Statistical Abstract of the United States* (annual) (Washington: U.S. Bureau of the Census, 1971 through 1981).

4. Estimates based on total metropolitan personal income, national ratio of value of all structures to personal income, and national ratio of nonbuilding to construction outlays. Data from *Statistical Abstract of the United States 1980* (Washington: U.S. Bureau of the Census, 1981) and income estimates from Twin Cities Metropolitan Council.

5. Data tabulated from Hennepin County Assessor's Office by David Rivall, 1981.

6. *Housing Profile: Trends and Issues* (Minneapolis: City Planning Department, 1978), pp. 14–16; explanation of condition classes and percentages, pp. 14–15; map showing distribution of units in two worst classes, p. 16.

7. Sources of data: *Statistical Abstract 1980*, table 1397, p. 787, and table 69, p. 49.

8. Calculated from data in *Statistical Abstract of the United States 1979*, (Washington: U.S. Bureau of the Census, 1980), table 1367, p. 777, and table 10, p. 12.

9. Replacement rate for 1960–70 calculated from data in *U.S. Census of Population*, vol. 1, part 25, and *U.S. Census of Housing*, vol. 1, part 25, for 1960 and 1970 (Washington: U.S. Bureau of the Census, 1961–62 and 1972–73). Estimates for 1970 and 1980 calculated from data in *Housing Market Studies* (St. Paul: Twin Cities Metropolitan Council, 1981).

10. Data for 1950–1960 from *U.S. Census of Housing 1960* vol. 1, part 25 (Washington: U.S. Bureau of the Census, 1962); data for 1960–70 from *Population and Housing Summary of Minneapolis 1970* (Minneapolis: City Planning and Development Department, 1973), p. 3; data for 1971–79 from *State of the City 1980* (Minneapolis: City Planning Department, 1981), p. 36.

11. *Housing Profile*, p. 15

12. Block grant data from *Minneapolis Community Development Block Grant Program: Semi-Annual Activity Report* (Minneapolis: Office of the City Coordinator, 1981), p. 32; information on number of homes and private grant from Rebecca Smith, research assistant, Center for Urban and Regional Affairs (CURA), University of Minnesota, in personal communication, May 1981.

13. Block grant data from *Minneapolis Community Development Block Grant Program*, p. 32; information on number of homes from Rob Warwick, Phillips neighborhood planner, in personal communication, May 1981.

14. Total of community development block grant allocations listed over seven fiscal years, June 1, 1976, through May 31, 1982, with administrative costs deducted, for projects whose primary purpose is housing rehabilitation and related activities, from *Minneapolis Community Development Block Grant Program*, pp. 2–61.

15. The Minneapolis City Planning Department estimated that $190.3 million was spent on maintenance of structures, excluding new replacement construction, in 1979. Assuming that forty-five percent of that amount went into residential maintenance, the average outlay per dwelling unit would have been about $530, or one percent of an average dwelling unit value of $53,000, for all units in the city.

16. *Housing Rehabilitation in Minneapolis 1973–1977* (Minneapolis City Planning Department, 1978), pp. 27, 29.

17. *Regional Fiscal Profile* (St. Paul: Twin Cities Metropolitan Council, 1979), table 1, p. 24.

18. Calculated from data in *Statistical Abstract of the United States 1977* (Washington: U.S. Bureau of the Census, 1978), tables 483 and 484, pp. 300–301. The 1975 per capita total general expenditures for cities in the size classes of Minneapolis and St. Paul were about $400, hence about $1200 per household. Capital outlays accounted for about twenty percent of total expenditures in American cities. Twenty percent of $1200 is $240 per household.

19. Minneapolis projections from *Plan for the 1980s: Proposed Capital Improvement Program Framework and 1981–1985 Capital Improvement Program* (Minneapolis: City Planning Department, 1979), pp. 5–30. National comparison from *Statistical Abstract 1977*, tables cited in footnote 18.

20. Pat Choate and Susan Walter, *America in Ruins: Beyond the Public Works Pork Barrel* (Washington: Council of State Planning Agencies, 1981), p. 1.

21. Michael E. Gleeson, "Estimating Housing Mortality", *Journal of the American Planning Association*, 47:2 (April 1981): pp. 190–191 (tables).

Bibliography

Andreas, Alfred T., *Illustrated Atlas of Minnesota*, Chicago, 1884.

Architects' Small House Service Bureau, Inc. *The Small House* (published monthly in Minneapolis, 1922-1932).

Atwater, Isaac, *History of the City of Minneapolis* (2 Vols.), New York, 1895.

Abler, Adams, and Borchert, *The Twin Cities: St. Paul and Minneapolis*, Cambridge, 1976.

Bennett, Edward H., "Preliminary Report of the Minneapolis Civic Commission," *The Western Architect*, Vol. 17, February 1911, pp. 47-70.

——, *Preliminary Plan of Minneapolis*, Chicago, 1911.

Borchert, John R., "The Twin Cities Urbanized Area: Past, Present, and Future," *Geographical Review*, Vol. 51, No. 1, 1961, pp. 47-70.

Bromley, Edward A., *A Minneapolis Album — A Photographic History of the Early Days in Minneapolis*, Minneapolis, 1890; republished in 1973 by Voyageur Press as *Minneapolis Portrait of the Past*.

Flanagan, Barbara, *Minneapolis*, New York, 1973.

Ford, George B., "The Civic Improvement of Minneapolis", *Journal of the American Institute of Architects*, Vol. 4, October 1916, pp. 427-429.

Gebhard, David and Thomas Martinson, *A Guide to Architecture in Minnesota*, Minneapolis, 1977.

Goldfield, David R., "Historic Planning and Redevelopment in Minneapolis," *Journal of the American Institute of Architects*, Vol. 42, January 1976, pp. 76-86.

Heritage Preservation Commission, *Washburn-Fair Oaks: A Study for Preservation*, Minneapolis, 1975.

Hudson, Horace B., *A Half Century of Minneapolis*, Minneapolis, 1908.

——, *Hudson's Dictionary of Minneapolis*, Minneapolis, 1916.

Kane, Lucile, *The Waterfall That Built a City*, St. Paul, 1966.

Keith, M. L. (Editor and Publisher) *Keith's Home Magazine (Beautiful Homes Magazine)* (published monthly in Minneapolis, 1899-1931).

Lanegran, David, "Neighborhood Conservation in the Twin Cities," *Architecture Minnesota*, Vol. 4, 1978, pp. 14-20.

Lanegran, David and Ernest R. Sandeen, *The Lake District of Minneapolis*, St. Paul, 1979.

Martin, Judith A., *Recycling the Central City*, Minneapolis, 1978.

Martin, Judith A., and David Lanegran, *Where We Live — The Residential Districts of Minneapolis and St. Paul*, Minneapolis, 1983.

Minneapolis Riverfront Development Coordination Board, *St. Anthony Falls Rediscovered*, Minneapolis, 1980.

Nichols, F. D. "Homes of Minneapolis," *American Homes*, Vol. 7, September 1910, pp. 338-344.

Olsen, Russell, Edwin Nelson, and Fred Howarth, "Twin Cities Lines," *Interurban Special*, Vol. 14, No. 2, December 1953.

Robinson, Charles M., "Ambition of Three Cities," *Architectural Record*, Vol. 21, May 1907, pp. 337-346.

Schmidt, Calvin, *Social Saga of Two Cities*, Minneapolis, 1937.

Schuyler, Montgomery, "Glimpses of Western Architecture: St. Paul and Minneapolis," *Harpers Magazine*, Vol. 83, October 1891, pp. 736-755.

Shutter, Marion D., *History of Minneapolis* (3 Vols.), Minneapolis, 1923.

Svendsen, Rolf, *Hennepin County History*, Minneapolis, 1976.

Torbert, Donald R., *Significant Architecture in the History of Minneapolis*, Minneapolis, 1969.

——, *Minneapolis Architecture and Architects 1848-1908*, University of Minnesota thesis (unpublished), 1951.

Warner, George F., and Charles M. Foote, *History of Hennepin County and the City of Minneapolis*, Minneapolis, 1881.

Wirth, Theodore, *Minneapolis Park System 1883-1944*, Minneapolis, 1945.

Works Progress Administration, *Minnesota: A State Guide*, New York, 1938.